Mastering Amiga
Programming Secrets

Paul Overaa

Mastering Amiga Programming Secrets

© Paul Overaa 1995
ISBN: 1-873308-36-1   First Edition: January 1995

Editor: Mark Webb
Typesetting: Bruce Smith Books Ltd

Workbench, Amiga and AmigaDOS are trademarks of Commodore-Amiga, Inc. UNIX is a trademark of AT&T. MS-DOS is a trademark of Microsoft Corporation. All other Trademarks and Registered Trademarks used are hereby acknowledged.

All rights reserved. No part of this publication may be reproduced or translated in any form, by any means, mechanical, electronic or otherwise, without the prior written consent of the copyright holder(s).

Disclaimer: While every effort has been made to ensure that the information in this publication (and any programs and software) is correct and accurate, the Publisher can accept no liability for any consequential loss or damage, however caused, arising as a result of using the information printed in this book.
E. & O.E.

The rights of Paul Overaa to be identified as the Author of the Work has been asserted by him in accordance with the *Copyright, Designs and Patents Act 1988*.

Bruce Smith Books is an imprint of Bruce Smith Books Limited.
Published by:
Bruce Smith Books Limited. PO Box 382, St. Albans, Herts, AL2 3JD.
Telephone: (01923) 894355, Fax: (01923) 894366
Registered in England No. 2695164.
Registered Office: Worplesdon Chase, Worplesdon, Guildford, Surrey, GU1 3UA.

Printed and bound in the UK by Ashford Colour Press, Gosport.

The Author

PAUL OVERAA initially qualified as an analytical chemist and spent two decades working in a field of physical chemistry known as gas-liquid chromatography. It was during this time that he became heavily involved with compputerised data reduction techniques and computer programming. Nowadays he considers himself a programmer first and an analytical chemist second.

Paul has previously written books on low-level 6502 and Z80 assembly language programming, on Amiga programming in C and ARexx, and on both Commodore Amiga and Atari ST program design. He is a proficient C and 68000 assembly language coder, and an experienced Amiga programmer. As a technical author he also writes for a great many computer programming magazines and periodicals including Amiga Pro, Amiga Shopper, Amiga User International, Amiga Computing, and Computing. In the past he has worked for Amiga Format, Program Now, Computing, ST World, Atari ST User and the one time highly influential Transactor Amiga magazine.

In addition to computing columns he also provides expertise on MIDI programming for a variety of magazines and in the past he has written for Sound on Sound, International Musician, and many other publications. His main passion nowadays is computer programming with his research interests having a strong bias towards language-independent program design techniques. Other interests include Badminton, Yoga, mathematics and, when he has time and the weather on his side, windsurfing.

Contents

Preface 5

1 A Coder's Introduction 11
   Other Important Rules 13

2 Coding those All-important Abstract Data Types 17
   The Stack ADT 19
   The Routines In Use 29
   A Taste Of Things To Come 29

3 Using an ADT for Dynamic Amiga Resource Handling 31
   Making The Most Of Reusable Code 36
   Controlling The Resource Allocation Process 42
   The Intuition Angle 44
   Project Management 47

4 A Flash Interrupt Trick 51
   Putting The Pieces Together 54
   The High-Level C Approach 55
   Flashing Colours 58
   The Equivalent Assembler Example 60
   An Alternative Amiga-Oriented Solution 63

5 Using Exec Signals in Your Own Programs 65
   Signal Bits and Masks 68
   Some Task Signal Communication Mechanics 69
   Putting It All Together 69
   ADT Stack Based Signal Allocation 71
   Aiming For A More General Colour Flashing Solution 74

6 Getting Your Programs to Talk to Each Other . . . 77
   Adding Data To A Message Structure 78
   The Use Of Multiple Message Ports 82
   Setting Up A Message Port 83
   Sending A Message 83
   Some Main Program Coding Issues 85
   The Colour Flashing Program Itself 87
   Using A Flash Utility 90

7 Copper Lists: What They Are and How They Work .91
- The Copper Instruction Set 92
- Terminating A Copper List 94
- Getting Things Into Perspective 95
- Using Run-Time Libraries From Assembler Code 95
- Failed Open Library Calls 97
- Prefixes 97
- Library Vector Offset (LVO) Values 98
- First Coding Stages 98
- Preventing Multitasking 100
- Creating An Example Copper List 101
- Allocating Display Memory 104
- Setting The Bitplane Pointers 104
- Using The Copper List 105
- The High-Level Alternative 114
- Intuition 116

8 Copper List Shading Effects 119
- Making Up As You Go Along 130

9 How Viruses Get at the Amiga Library Functions 137
- How Library Access Really Works 138
- Vanishing Vectors 140

10 Music, Midi, and the MPX File Connection 143
- Standard Midi and MPX Format Files 145
- MidiWriteX 146
- Devices – An Introduction 147
- Devices Commands 150
- Opening And Closing A Device 152
- Device Use Summary 155
- The DoIO() Standard Interface Function ...156
- Timer Device 156
- MidiPlayX 157

11 The Workbench MidiPlayer Program 167
- The AmigaDOS Style MidiPlayer Command 168
- Overview Of The Standard Midi File Structure 169
- A Matter Of Design 172

Contents

    Chunk Analysis 176
    Adopting A Modular Approach 181
    The Intuition Angle 182

12 Colour Cycling **187**
    The Intuition Connection 188
    CycleMessages and Their Use 191
    Setting Up A Message Port .193
    Sending A Message 193
    Some Main Program Coding Issues 195
    The Colour Cycling Program Itself 197
    Using The Cycle Utility 201

13 Mixed Code Programming **203**
    XDEF and XREF 205
    Specific SAS/Lattice C Conventions 205
    Aztec C Conventions 206
    A Couple Of Examples 207

14 Creating Static Tile Effects – Part One **213**
    The Low-level Approach 217
    Drawing A Row Of Images .219
    The Complete Routine 220
    Building A Test Framework .223
    The Bottom Line 232

15 Creating Static Tile Effect – Part Two **233**
    A Crafty Twist Adds Another Dimension 238
    The DrawTiles() Routine – Advanced Approach 240
    Some Important Ideas 248

16 Creating Mosaic Effects **251**
    Making A Start 253
    The Co-ordinate Generation Scheme 254
    A Complete Mosaic Copy Routine 258
    The Blitter Minterm Byte 260
    Mosaic Disintegration 260

17 Scrolling and Intuition **263**
    Searching The Copper List .265

    The Scroll Routine 266
    Some Example Code 268
    The Downward Scroll 270

18 Boot Code and the TrackDisk Device 273
    The Boot Sectors 274
    Opening The Trackdisk Device 276
    Reading From The Trackdisk Device 280
    Writing To The Trackdisk Device 280
    Getting The Drive Geometry Data 280
    Custom Boot Code 281
    Producing The Code 282
    Putting It All Together 289

19 Some Extra Programming Tips and Tricks 295
    When It All Goes Wrong 299
    Helping Yourself 300

20 Parting Advice 303

Appendix A: The Warnier Diagram 307

Appendix B: More Program Design Notes 315
    Describing The Output Set 316
    The Input Set 325
    Diagram To Code Conversion 328
    A More Sophisticated Translation 336
    Byte Conversion Code – An Example 340
    Keeping It In Perspective 344

Glossary 345

Mastering Amiga Guides 359

Preface

This is an Amiga programming book with a difference. It is directed at Amiga users who already have some experience with the Amiga and who want to take things a little further. The aim is to explain a number of programming tricks and methods that will not only stand you in good stead as you progress down the road to Amiga programming literacy but additionally to provide food for thought along the way. You, the reader, are expected to be C literate and to have some knowledge of how Amiga programs are written. That includes things such as opening and using run-time libraries, setting up screens and windows, reading gadgets and so on, all of which are amply dealt with in most introductory Amiga C books. Most of the code is written for the C programmer and I've used ANSI style C throughout. All the code has been written and tested using the brilliant SAS C development system. Re-working the code for other compilers will not, in most cases, be a major problem providing you understand the ideas behind the code. I've concentrated on explaining the underlying ideas in detail – code reworking (to suit compiler X, Y or Z as the case may be) is something which, if deemed necessary, I leave to you. In the main the code is compatible with Release 2 onwards although some of the programs will run under AmigaDOS 1.3.

Needless to say as an Amiga C programmer you are expected to have access to the official include files and to be generally aware of how they are used. The best way to learn how to get the maximum benefit from the Amiga include files is to look at them, use them, and think about them – slowly but surely you will learn to find your way around them and, with practice, learn to use them in the way Commodore intended. If you are new to C you have a golden opportunity to study them in detail – make the most of this opportunity. The effort which has gone into them is considerable and, along with examples from the world of UNIX and the mainframe, these Amiga system include files are amongst the best header files ever written!

Some sections of the book, such as the chapter on mixed coding, include 680x0 assembler code. If you absolutely hate low-level coding then feel free to ignore the relevant parts of the text. If you don't – don't! Either way – use the book as a way of gaining insight into the Amiga's O/S, as an advanced C book, or just to latch onto all manner of hopefully interesting Amiga coding tricks. Along the way I've dealt with things like passing Exec messages between your own programs, getting one program to control another, flashing colours, colour cycling and colour shading tricks. I've also provided some MIDI related programs to keep the musicians amongst you happy.

On a very few occasions I've used diagrams called Warnier diagrams to illustrate the logic behind a piece of code. Because these diagrams may not be familiar to you I have included a couple of appendices that illustrate both the conventions and use of this powerful program design tool. What I've not attempted to do is force my own ideas about program design techniques on you, so in the main you'll find that text and code examples will be the primary vehicle of explanation. Do remember though that program design is an important first step in all non-trivial programs – Amiga and otherwise!

Although most of the topics are relatively self-contained it is probably best to work through the book chapter by chapter because later chapters usually assume that the material previously presented is understood. All that remains now is for me to thank you for buying the book, and to wish you a pleasant journey through its contents.

PAO January 95

1: A Coder's Introduction

All programmers have their own idiosyncrasies when it comes to coding style and I am certainly no exception to this. My ideas on what is right and what is wrong codewise, whilst doubtless being in broad agreement with the ideas of many other coders, will probably contain a variety of elements which will seem strange when first encountered. Having said that one of the *idiosyncrasies* that I have is that I like code to be as well structured and as *readable* as possible, so in this respect my style will hopefully make the examples easier to read rather than harder.

You will pick up a variety of style points as you work through the book but it will help initially to have some understanding of the conventions I tend to use. To start, here are some notes about my approach to C coding. C of course is a free format language which neither forces you to write intelligible code or prevents you writing unintelligible code. This means that it's largely up to the programmer to adopt style conventions which lead to the creation of programs that are understandable.

In the main I do try to stick to my own guidelines but not to the point where adherence becomes counter-productive. You'll find me using i, j, k etc, for loop variables just like most other programmers. Similarly there are times where fully explicit variable names end up too long to be practical – so shortened names have to be used. In short the guidelines I adopt are just that – guidelines, not rigid restrictions!

For the most part all that is needed is a common-sense understanding of the usefulness of such consistency.

Whilst on the subject of style and conventions, I firmly believe that the adoption of reasonably methodical in-line documentation pays handsome dividends. Occasionally you will however find pieces of example code which are devoid of any significant comments - the reason is usually that I have already explained the underlying ideas in the accompanying text.

One area where it is usually necessary to deviate from any self-imposed conventions is when dealing with system defined functions and variables. System definitions should always be used as defined and never altered – that way other Amiga programmers reading the code will understand what's going on. Anyway enough of these general lectures, here are the conventions which I both recommend and use:

1. Use understandable names for variables and functions – eg

   `CreateTimerRequestBlock().`

2. When creating #define macros, always use uppercase labels – eg

   `#define QUIT 18`

3. Capitalise the first words of function calls– eg

   `OpenSerialDevice(), DoNothing().`

4. Prefix global variable names with g_ as in

   `g_exit_flag!`

5. Add a _p suffix to variables which represent pointers.

6. Use uncapitalised lowercase for variables and separate the individual words of variable names using underscores – eg

   `g_serial_request_p.`

7. Partition individual routines using

   `/* —— */`

lines so that the various sections of code can be clearly identified.

Adopting conventions such as prefixing global variables with the character g_ and suffixing pointer variables using _p, enables the type of variable to be implied from its name. So, code which reads:

```
g_exit_flag=FALSE;   /* clear exit flag - user has decided
                        not to quit */
```

is to my mind a much preferred alternative to code which reads like this:

```
xit=0;        /* clear global exit flag - user has
                 decided not to quit */
```

Such conventions do of course have but one purpose – to make life

A Coder's Introduction

much easier for both myself and anyone else who may need to examine my code. For instance, a variable with the name g_window_p implies that the variable being dealt with is a pointer variable which has been declared as a global. In other words it's a pointer which exists during the whole lifetime of the program, and can be accessed from anywhere in the program without needing to be passed as a parameter.

Other Important Rules

My conventions have nothing to do with any official guidelines but plenty of other rules and suggestions exist for coders in that area and one of the main ones concerns the checking of system calls. The Amiga is a multi-tasking machine and because of this there is never any guarantee that a system call will be successful - a memory allocation call could fail if some other application has previously grabbed all available RAM. Similarly a request for use of the serial device could fail (if some other program has previously been granted exclusive access). Because of these eventualities there are three rules which Amiga programmers must always obey:

1. Always make sure you get what you ask for!
2. Always give back to the system any memory, device, or other facility which you explicitly acquire!
3. Always provide a robust error path so that if the system cannot provide the required facilities your program closes down in a proper fashion.

I have, incidentally, got some interesting approaches to error path handling that we'll be dealing with in the next two chapters. For the moment though, since there are a number of other generally accepted rules and guidelines which Amiga programmers should follow, I thought it would be useful to gather the most important of them together for easy reference:

1. If you need to access a system structure that may be shared between other tasks remember to lock out other tasks (eg by forbidding multi-tasking). This will prevent other tasks attempting to change the structure whilst you are in the middle of looking at it.
2. Never make assumptions about memory, system configurations (eg the presence of particular drives or device names), or the contents of system structures which are designated as private. Do not for instance assume that particular library bases or system structures will always exist at a particular location. Above all *never* call ROM routines directly.
3. The Amiga's operating system does not monitor the size of a programs stack. Many compilers however allow you to add

stack checking code to the compiled application code – although such checks slow the program down they are useful particularly during development of recursive routines which may become deeply nested.

• Remember that any data which is to be accessed by the Amiga's custom chips (bitplanes, image data, sound samples and so on) *must* be placed in chip memory.

• Do not use poll based loops to wait for external events. The system has methods for allowing a task to sleep by Wait()ing on particular signal bits - use them. Similarly you should not use software delay loops for creating timing delays.

• Do not disable either interrupts or multi-tasking for long periods of time.

• Do not access the hardware directly.

• Do not tie up system resources unnecessarily. For example, if your program does not need constant use of a printer then only open the printer device when the program actually needs it and close it as soon as possible. That way other programs will also be able to use the printer device.

• Get into the habit of checking for memory loss during program development. Programs should not continually eat away at the available free memory although there are times when an apparent free memory loss may occur the first time a program runs – but – start to panic if a similar loss occurs when the program is then run for the second time!

• All non-byte fields must be word aligned.

• All address pointers must be 32 bits. Do NOT use the upper 8 bits for data.

• Do not use self-modifying code.

• Custom chips registers are read only or write only. Do not write to read only registers and do not read from write-only registers.

There are also a few guidelines aimed at the assembly language programmer:

• System library functions must be called with register A6 holding the library or device base. Libraries and devices will assume A6 is valid at the time of such a function call.

• Registers D0, D1, A0 and A1 are scratch registers and their contents must be considered lost after a system library call. The contents of all other registers can be assumed to be preserved.

• System functions that return a value may not necessarily affect the processor's condition codes.

- Do not use a CLR instruction on hardware registers which are triggered by access because it can cause the hardware register to be triggered twice. Instead use MOVE(.size)#0, location instead.

- Do not use the 'MOVE SR' instruction. If you wish to get a copy of the processor condition codes use the Exec library's GetCC() function.

- Do not use the TAS instruction on the Amiga. Direct Memory Access (DMA) can conflict with this specialised instruction.

OK that's enough of conventions and ground rules – it's now time to start looking at some coding tricks.

2: Coding those All – Important Abstract Data Types

You're going to be hearing a lot about the Abstract Data Type (ADT) in this book and for a very good reason – ADTs provide some very real benefits to the programmer because they allow programming to be done at a conceptually much higher level. Codewise you may find this stuff a bit of a headache at first, but I suspect that when you see how these techniques are used in later chapters you'll come back to this topic with a renewed interest that will then last forever.

So what is an ADT? Well the term abstraction refers to the process whereby details at some particular level are discarded and only the main features of interest are considered. This in itself is no big deal and even in everyday conversation we continually abstract. Peter may well be a blue eyed six foot tall insurance agent, married with two children, who drives a grey Y registered 3 litre car which has four wheels, three of which are currently inflated to the correct pressure of 26 psi. *but* if you are just trying to convey the notion that Peter's car has a flat tyre then most of the above information is irrelevant - we all know that the simple phrase "Peter has a flat tyre" will do the job perfectly adequately.

In everyday conversation excessive detail tends to obscure any points being made and abstraction here serves a useful purpose – it protects us from having to deal with too much information. The same philosophy applies to technical discussions and, notwithstanding the fairly manageable obstacle of having to come to terms with *specialist jargon*, the result of using well defined terms for common complex operations is usually an overall simplification of the communications process.

Procedures, functions and subroutines are, in the computing world, abstractions of a different sense. Here potentially complex sets of operations can be described and used using just a name, a few parameters, and some details about the effect produced. Again such abstractions have many advantages. By defining functions which reflect the structure of a problem being solved a C programmer can not only minimize the cluttering of their thought processes with excessive detail but, by using what are effectively functional building blocks, can tackle the problem-solving situation at a significantly higher level.

The same principles apply to data items as well. Floating point numbers, strings etc., are all data types which provide us with similar *abstraction orientated* benefits. At the assembler/machine-code level all data items consist of bits, bytes, or groups of bytes but most high-level languages allow the programmer to use a number of more useful *data types*. These are objects of some specified unit type which will have a number of associated, and well defined, operations available. C's integers, for example, can be added, subtracted, multiplied and so on. As well as a selection of basic data types most high-level languages usually provide additional data item facilities. Namely they allow sets of data items to be grouped together in some useful way. In C, arrays and structures come to mind. The declaration:

```
int my_array[100];
```

for instance, allows us to store one hundred integers and refer to them using an index which identifies the relative position in the array. Again there are a number of operations, +, -, *, \, / etc, which can be performed on the array elements. We can, and frequently do, add additional 'facilities' to such definitions – we might for instance write our own InitialiseArray() function which would set the elements of some array to a user defined initial value.

To solve most problems we need, unfortunately, rather more data structure facilities than general languages such as C can offer. It is often useful to work with lists, stacks, trees, graphs and so on. Some languages incidentally do indeed provide support for these more complex structures – Lisp, for instance, has strong list processing capabilities. Ideally it would be nice if general high-level languages, such as C, also had such facilities built in but, for a number of implementation reasons, this 'in-built complex data structure path' has not been followed. One difficulty is that there is usually no single efficient method for doing this – complex data type implementations often need to be tuned to a particular problem. One thing is certain though – the definition of the characteristics of such complex data structures can be made without worrying about the implementation issues at all and it is this pathway that leads us into the world of the Abstract Data Type or ADT.

The ADT philosophy is essentially simple: by defining the important characteristics, ie the properties, of an abstract data structure, and identifying the allowable operations, we arrive at an ADT definition which, together with its associated set of allowable operations set (the *ADT interface* definition), becomes a 'data structure' building block which can be used to solve problems. The benefit of the ADT oriented approach then is that it allows the programmer to use lists, stacks, trees etc, almost as easily as they would use integers, floating point numbers and strings.

I'm not going to talk about the theoretical ADT issues. Instead I want to look at the practical side of things. Why? Because ADTs, or rather the real-life implementations of ADTs, are extremely useful and I happen to be a firm believer in the view that the time for understanding the theoretical arguments is after you have developed a gut feeling for the benefits of ADTs, not before.

In most cases where a programmer chooses to use an ADT approach it will be up to them to provide a suitably efficient implementation in terms of the real data structures that a chosen language supports. Pascal programmers are at an advantage here because almost all existing ADT texts have opted for Pascal or Pascal-like descriptions of ADT routines. Translation of textbook descriptions of common ADT forms to real code is, for the Pascal programmer at least, a relatively straighforward job. In the main there's less direct help available for the C programmer but once the basic properties of a given ADT are understood, writing the corresponding C code, at least for the simpler ADTs, should not prove unduly difficult.

The Stack ADT

I'm going to kick off with a fairly simple ADT type, the stack, and examine some implementation-orientated ideas (a stack, in case you need reminding, is just a set of objects logically arranged in a Last-In-First-Out order). The type of operations which can be usefully associated with a stack structure is well known. There has to be some way of defining and initialising a stack, of placing (pushing) items onto the stack, and of retrieving (popping or pulling) them from the stack. It might, for some purposes, be felt that other facilities should be included. Perhaps it would be advisable to test a stack to see if it is empty, or look at the top item of a stack without removing it. Here things get very implementation/use dependent. Looking at the top of a stack, for example, is not really a fundamental operation because it could be done using a combination of pop and push commands. If however an application was going to need to frequently look at the top of a stack without removing it the pop/push method, though clean in an abstract sense, is unlikely to be favoured from a point of view of efficiency.

As far as implementation itself goes there are several options. One way of implementing a stack is to use an array in conjunction with a *stack pointer* variable as in figure 2.1.:

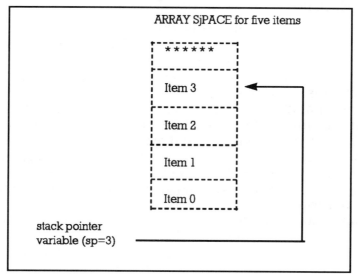

Figure 2.1.

This is quite efficient, very easy to implement, and perfectly adequate for many applications. An array and its related stack pointer variable can be linked together using a C structure:

```
#define SIZE 5
struct stack {
        int stack_pointer;
        int items[SIZE];
};
```

which then allows the use of declarations of the type:

```
struct stack s;
```

Slightly more flexible arrangements, using unions, can allow dissimilar objects to be stored on the same stack but this is not a practice to be encouraged unless there is an over-riding reason for creating mixed object stacks. Similarly the use of pre-processor modifiable, unit types such as:

```
struct stack {
        int    stack_pointer;
        STACKTYPE items[SIZE];
};
```

coupled with #define based modifiable STACKTYPE definitions, are frequently suggested as C solutions for generic ADT stack building. These type of schemes are fine as far as they go, but they are essentially all 'define at compile time' static solutions which can produce a number of problems in practice. As far as array based implentations are concerned stack overflow is of course another danger which needs to be considered.

To see the benefits of more flexible paths it is best to consider some potential uses of the stack ADT. Within a single program we may want several stacks handling several different types of objects. We may also want to have different types of stacks in existence at different times. There are two other general issues to consider. Firstly, we should be aiming to create a stack module that can be used in any number of programs without being re-compiled. Secondly, we should be aiming to create a module which hides any implementation details from the programs which will use it – it should in fact be sufficiently transparent to allow the possible rearrangement of any of the internal underlying data structures without it affecting the ADT/applications-program interface at all. If for instance we opted for routines based on an static array stack implementation, and then at a later stage wanted to swap to a linked list dynamic memory allocation form, then we should be able to achieve this change without it affecting any of the programs using the ADT (other than the fact that the new stack ADT module would have to be linked in place of the earlier one).

In the following example I've actually opted for a list based approach using calloc()/free() calls to provide dynamic memory allocation for the items being stored on the ADT stack. The only limitation on stack size with this approach will be the amount of available system memory.

Within the stack module the routines are based on two types of structures. A stack descriptor structure contains a pointer to the first item on a linked list of stack items (NULL if stack is empty), and a value representing the size of the objects being placed on the stack:

```
struct StackDescriptor {
    struct StackItem *FirstItem;
    UBYTE ItemSize;
};
```

Also defined is a stack item structure which contains a next item in the stack list pointer, and a reference to the first byte of some unspecified data item:

```
struct StackItem {
    struct StackItem *NextItem;
```

```
        UBYTE   Data[1]; /* actually user defined amount of data
*/
};
```

The code for the stack routines use these structures internally but the definitions are not required to be either known nor used by applications program using the module. In fact, as far as the stack ADT user-interface is concerned, only five access routines are available.

s=CreateStack(t)	This initializes a stack suitable for storing items of type t specified by the applications program and returns a pointer s to the stack's descriptor.
e=PushStack(s,x)	This stores item x on stack s and returns an error flag e that is TRUE if an error has occured.
e=PopStack(s,x)	This retrieves an item from stack s and places it in variable x. Errors are signified by the returned error flag e being TRUE.
KillStack(s)	This unloads and then removes the stack s from the list of currently defined stacks. No return value.
f=StackEmpty(s)	This tests stack s to see if it is empty and returns a flag f as TRUE if there are no items on the stack.

Table 2.1. Stack access routines.

These calls are macros designed to create a slightly more friendly interface to the user. You can get further details from the header and source code listings which follow:

```
/*========================================================*/
/*Listing 2.1: The stack ADT header file.
/* Source:           Stack ADT header                    */
/* ---------------------------------------------------- */
typedef void STACK;

/* These macros are used to create a slightly more friend
ly interface to the user. They just remove the need for
explicit sizeof(), casting    and address taking opera-
tions in the applications code. */

#define CreateStack(t)     CreateStk(sizeof(t))

#define PushStack(s,x)     PushStk(s,(UBYTE *)&(x))

#define PopStack(s,x)      PopStk(s,(UBYTE *)&(x))

#define KillStack(s)       KillStk(s)

#define StackEmpty(s)      StkEmpty(s)

/* These are the prototypes for the underlying stack
access routines which do the real work. */

STACK    *CreateStk(ULONG unit_size);
```

```c
void    KillStk(STACK *descriptor_p);
BOOL    PushStk(STACK *descriptor_p, UBYTE *data_item);
BOOL    PopStk(STACK *descriptor_p, UBYTE *data_item);
BOOL    StackEmpty(STACK *descriptor_p);
/* ------------------------------------------------- */


/*Listing 2.2: The underlying stack ADT routines.


/* ========================================================= */
/* SourceCode:       Stack ADT routines                  */
/* ------------------------------------------------- */
/* Notes: These routines allow a program to use a true
dynamic stack data structure without the knowing anything
about how it's done.       */
/* ------------------------------------------------- */
#include <types.h>
#include <stack_adt.h>
struct StackItem {
    struct StackItem *NextItem;
    UBYTE  Data[1]; /* actually user defined amount of
    data */
};
struct StackDescriptor {
    struct StackItem *FirstItem;
    UBYTE  ItemSize;};
/* ------------------------------------------------- */
STACK *CreateStk(ULONG unit_size)
{
struct StackDescriptor *stack_descriptor_p;
if (stack_descriptor_p=(struct StackDescriptor *)
            calloc(1,sizeof(struct StackDescriptor)))
    {
    stack_descriptor_p->ItemSize=unit_size;
    }
return((STACK *)stack_descriptor_p);
}
/* ------------------------------------------------- */
void KillStk(STACK *descriptor_p)
```

```c
    {
    UBYTE *dead_block_p; struct StackDescriptor
        *stack_descriptor_p;
    stack_descriptor_p=(struct StackDescriptor *)descriptor_p;
    while (stack_descriptor_p->FirstItem)
        {
        dead_block_p=(UBYTE *)stack_descriptor_p->FirstItem;
        stack_descriptor_p->FirstItem=stack_descriptor_p-
        >FirstItem->NextItem;
        free(dead_block_p);
        }
    free(stack_descriptor_p);
    }
    /* -------------------------------------------------- */
    BOOL PushStk(STACK *descriptor_p, UBYTE *data_item)
    {
    BOOL error_flag=TRUE; COUNT i; struct StackItem
        *new_item_p;
    struct StackDescriptor *stack_descriptor_p;
    stack_descriptor_p=(struct StackDescriptor *)descriptor_p;
    if (new_item_p=(struct StackItem *)
        calloc(1, sizeof(struct StackItem
        *)+stack_descriptor_p->ItemSize))
        {
        new_item_p->NextItem=stack_descriptor_p->FirstItem;
        stack_descriptor_p->FirstItem=new_item_p;
        for (i=0;i<stack_descriptor_p->ItemSize;i++)
            {
            new_item_p->Data[i]=*data_item++;
            }
        error_flag=FALSE;
        }
    return(error_flag);}
    /* -------------------------------------------------- */
    BOOL PopStk(STACK *descriptor_p, UBYTE *data_item)
    {
    BOOL error_flag=TRUE; COUNT i; UBYTE *dead_block_p;
    struct StackDescriptor *stack_descriptor_p;
```

```
    stack_descriptor_p=(struct StackDescriptor *)descriptor_p;
    if (stack_descriptor_p->FirstItem)
        {
        for (i=0; i<stack_descriptor_p->ItemSize; i++)
            {
            *data_item++=stack_descriptor_p->FirstItem-
            >Data[i];
            }
        dead_block_p=(UBYTE *)stack_descriptor_p->FirstItem;
        stack_descriptor_p->FirstItem=stack_descriptor_p-
        >FirstItem->NextItem;
        free(dead_block_p); error_flag=FALSE;
        }
    return(error_flag);
    }
    /* -------------------------------------------------- */
    BOOL StkEmpty(STACK *descriptor_p)
    {
    BOOL empty_flag=TRUE; struct StackDescriptor
    *stack_descriptor_p;
    stack_descriptor_p=(struct StackDescriptor *)descriptor_p;
    if (stack_descriptor_p->FirstItem) {empty_flag=FALSE;}
    return(empty_flag);}
    /* -------------------------------------------------- */
```

The above routines have been written according to the basic jobs they have to perform and no particular trouble has been taken to maximize their efficiency. You will also see that in most routines I have used a local variable to copy and re-cast the (void *) descriptor pointer parameter as a StackDescriptor pointer. Here I just felt that, because it avoided continual re-casting in order to use the structure definitions this inefficiency just made the code that much easier to read.

It is fair comment to ask why I did not opt for creating routines which worked directly with StackDescriptor pointers instead of opting for a generic form (void *). Here are the header and routines again using just that approach.

```
/*Listing 2.3: A less satisfactory header file ADT
approach
/* ==================================================== */
/* -------------------------------------------------- */
/* Source:     Stack ADT header for alternative routines */
```

```
/* Notes: This header contains structure tags that would
          change if the underlying stack implementation
          method changed. */
struct StackItem {
    struct StackItem *NextItem;
    UBYTE  Data[1]; /* actually user defined amount of
    data */
};
struct StackDescriptor {
    struct StackItem *FirstItem;
    UBYTE  ItemSize;
};
typedef struct StackDescriptor STACK;
/* These macros are used to create a slightly more friend
   ly interface to the user. They just remove the need for
   explicit sizeof(), casting and address taking opera
   tions in the applications code. */
#define CreateStack(t)  CreateStk(sizeof(t))
#define PushStack(s,x)  PushStk(s,(UBYTE *)&(x))
#define PopStack(s,x)   PopStk(s,(UBYTE *)&(x))
#define KillStack(s)    KillStk(s)
#define StackEmpty(s)   StkEmpty(s)


/* These are the prototypes for the underlying stack
   access routines which  do the real work. */
STACK   *CreateStk(ULONG unit_size);
void    KillStk(STACK *descriptor_p);
BOOL    PushStk(STACK *descriptor_p, UBYTE *data_item);
BOOL    PopStk(STACK *descriptor_p, UBYTE *data_item);
BOOL    StackEmpty(STACK *descriptor_p);
/* -------------------------------------------------- */


/*Listing 2.4: Some less portable alternative ADT rou-
tines.
/* ==================================================== */
/* SourceCode:   Alternative Stack ADT routines         */
/* -------------------------------------------------- */
/* Notes: These alternative routines also allow use of a
          dynamic stack ADT. A change in the underlying
          implementation method would however, because of
          the visibility of the list oriented structure
```

```
            definitions in the header file, result in the
            applications programs having to be re-compiled
            rather than just re-linked.       */
/* -------------------------------------------------- */
#include <types.h>
#include <stack_adt.h>
/* -------------------------------------------------- */
STACK *CreateStk(ULONG unit_size)
{
STACK *stack_descriptor_p;
if (stack_descriptor_p=(STACK *)
            calloc(1,sizeof(STACK)))
         {
         stack_descriptor_p->ItemSize=unit_size;
         }
return(stack_descriptor_p);}
/* -------------------------------------------------- */
void KillStk(STACK *descriptor_p)
{
UBYTE *dead_block_p;
while (descriptor_p->FirstItem)
         {
         dead_block_p=(UBYTE *)descriptor_p->FirstItem;
         descriptor_p->FirstItem=descriptor_p->FirstItem->NextItem;
         free(dead_block_p);
         }
free(descriptor_p);
}
/* -------------------------------------------------- */
BOOL PushStk(STACK *descriptor_p, UBYTE *data_item)
{
BOOL error_flag=TRUE; COUNT i; struct StackItem *new_item_p;
if (new_item_p=(struct StackItem *)
         calloc(1, sizeof(struct StackItem *)+descrip
         tor_p->ItemSize))
         {
         new_item_p->NextItem=descriptor_p->FirstItem;
```

```c
                descriptor_p->FirstItem=new_item_p;
                for (i=0;i<descriptor_p->ItemSize;i++)
                    }
                    new_item_p->Data[i]=*data_item++;
                    }
                error_flag=FALSE;
                }
    return(error_flag);}
    /* -------------------------------------------------- */
    BOOL PopStk(STACK *descriptor_p, UBYTE *data_item)
    {
    BOOL error_flag=TRUE; COUNT i; UBYTE *dead_block_p;
    if (descriptor_p->FirstItem)
        {
        for (i=0; i<descriptor_p->ItemSize; i++)
            {
            *data_item++=descriptor_p->FirstItem->Data[i];
            }
        dead_block_p=(UBYTE *)descriptor_p->FirstItem;
        descriptor_p->FirstItem=descriptor_p->FirstItem->NextItem;
        free(dead_block_p); error_flag=FALSE;
        }
    return(error_flag);
    }
    /* -------------------------------------------------- */
    BOOL StkEmpty(STACK *descriptor_p)
    {
    BOOL empty_flag=TRUE;
    if (descriptor_p->FirstItem) {empty_flag=FALSE;}
    return(empty_flag);}
    /* -------------------------------------------------- */
```

The problem is this – in this latter arrangement we are dependent on the StackItem and StackDescriptor tags being visible in the header file and this header is used by the applications program. A change in the underlying stack implementation mechanism would, in all probability, affect these definitions and that would mean that the applications programs themselves would have to be recompiled if the stack ADT implementation mechanism was changed. In the arrangement used for the header/source provided initially such a change could be kept totally transparent. Incorporating some newly designed stack ADT would just involve linking the new ADT module to the existing, already compiled, main applications code section. [Note: When you are comparing the two sets of ADT header/sources remember that the typedef definitions of STACK are not the same.]

The Routines In Use

This short example should give the general idea of how these routines can be used. A stack is created for storing TEXT size objects (actually chars), and the LIFO characteristics of the stack ADT is then used to reverse a string:

```
/* ------------------------------------------------- */
/*Listing 2.5: A simple program to illustrate the use of
the stack operations.*/

/* EXAMPLE OF THE STACK ADT ROUTINES BEING USED TO REVERSE
   A STRING */
/* ------------------------------------------------- */
#include <types.h>

#include <stack_adt.h>

main()

{

UBYTE i=0; TEXT x[]="This Is Just A Test Line";

STACK *mystack_p;   /* declare stack identifier variable */

mystack_p=CreateStack(TEXT); /* ask for a stack storing
TEXT sized items */

while(x[i]) PushStack(mystack_p, x[i++]); /* store charac-
ters */

i=0; while(!(PopStack(mystack_p, x[i++]))) ;  /* remove in
LIFO order */

KillStack(mystack_p); /* cancel the stack facility
(release memory) */

printf("%s\n",x); /* display reversed string */

}
/* ------------------------------------------------- */
```

A Taste Of Things To Come

If you've not come across ADTs before you probably wondering what the point is of all this apparent complexity. After all, with the above example most C programmers could write a routine to reverse the characters of a string using just a few lines of loop code. The important things to note are that firstly my example dealt with high-level stack operations (pushing and popping characters), and secondly that even though the ADT code was using list operations which were dynamically allocating all necessary memory – my example code didn't need to worry about any of that type of detail. In short by linking my stack ADT code to a program I'm able to make stack operations available to the program without having to code those operations from scratch. What we need now is a larger, more Amiga-oriented example in order that the benefits of the ADT approach can be put into perspective. It just so happens that this topic is next on the agenda.

3: Using an ADT-Stack for Dynamic Amiga Resource Handling

Most Amiga programs, as you'll doubtless already know, need to obtain various types of system resources in order to run. It might be chip memory for graphics images, use of hardware such as the serial, or perhaps access to things like the timer device. No matter what facilities are involved there is always one snag as far as the Amiga programmer is concerned – the Amiga itself doesn't keep track of the resources being used and so programs themselves need to do this type of house-keeping. Why? It's because when a program terminates it is responsible for handing back the things it has acquired from the operating system (O/S). Obviously memory must be returned to the system, devices must be closed and so on because otherwise the poor old O/S is not going to know that the program has finished with them. Programs must not only ask for the resources they need but must check that such requests are successful. Worse than that, the order in which various closedown steps are carried out is often important – a program opening a window in a custom Intuition screen must; open the Intuition library, open a screen and then open the window. Many operations like these can fail – a program will not be able to open a custom screen if some other program had previously grabbed all available chip memory.

Coding in small programs rarely presents any difficulties but as programs get to more realistic sizes many more things need to be done. Screens, windows, device access etc – sometimes a program may need to perform dozens of jobs before it is even up and running and often resources will need to be allocated dynamically, ie during the time the program is running. Consider, for example, a program which uses a number of separate windows (each with different menus). A user might activate one window and, from the associated menu, select an option which causes the serial device to be opened. Having done that the user might then have second thoughts about what they were doing, switch back to the main window, and quit the program. When terminating, the program will need some way of knowing that the serial device was open in order to close it.

Needless to say these types of considerations can obviously make life for the Amiga programmer both messy and complicated. What we really need is a scheme which can handle not only those initial program setting-up operations, but one that is flexible enough to allow any additional resources required to be allocated whilst the program is running. In my early Amiga days I developed a static list based technique to do this but a few years ago I came up with another approach that provides more flexibility. It involves something which, for reasons that will soon become patently obvious, I call *dynamic resource allocation*.

Sounds tricky I know but the basic principles are easy enough to understand. In fact the idea, as far as the logic itself goes, is almost trivial because it replies on a stack data structure. Stacks of course store things on a last in first out basis and what my scheme does is ensure that *any* routine which successfully allocates or opens some returnable or closeable system resource pushes the address of a corresponding deallocation/closedown routine onto a stack.

To allow for allocation failures as the program runs I adopt the convention of having all allocation routines return error numbers that indicate whether they've succeeded or not. Providing these conventions are followed the program can perform its closedown operations by pulling those deallocation routine pointers from the stack and executing the corresponding routines. By the time the stack is empty all acquired system resources will have been handed back. The beauty of this approach is that the stack automatically deallocates things in the reverse order to the original allocation – things which are allocated last get deallocated first (this is a good, safe, general rule to adopt for all Amiga programs).

I use this type of approach in almost every Amiga program that I write – in fact the code arrangements (which by now are well tried and tested) allow me to create separate, and often re-usable, *allocator* modules. This *isolation*, or *modularisation*, is an important part of creating larger programs and I'll be using it in many of the examples in this book. Because of this it's obviously necessary to spend some time outlining the approach so that you can understand the framework being used in subsequent examples.

The first question that needs to be answered is this: How do we set up the allocation/de-allocation code and get the right pieces of code executed at the appropriate times? Let's start by looking at some examples that show some typical operations. Listing 3.1 shows two routines which open and close the Intuition library, listing 3.2 provides another example pair that create and remove a window. Don't worry unduly about the specific details here – it is the overall theme that is important here, not the actual purpose of the code:

```
/* ------------------------------------------------- */
/*Listing 3.1 - Intuition library opening and closing with
stack based resource tracking!*/

UBYTE OpenInt(void)
{
UBYTE error_number=NO_ERROR;
if(!(IntuitionBase=(struct IntuitionBase *)
     OpenLibrary("intuition.library",INTUITION_VERSION)))
        error_number=ALLOCATION_ERROR;
else {
        g_function=CloseInt;
        PushStack(g_resource_stack_p,g_function);
        }
return(error_number);
}
/* ------------------------------------------------- */
void CloseInt(void)
{
CloseLibrary((struct Library *)IntuitionBase);
}
/* ------------------------------------------------- */
Listing 3.2 – Another set of allocation/deallocation rou-
tines which push a deallocation pointer onto the stack.*/


/* ------------------------------------------------- */
UBYTE CreateWindow(void)
{
UBYTE error_number=ALLOCATION_ERROR;
```

```
        g_window_p=OpenWindowTags(NULL,
            WA_Left,20, WA_Top,20,
            WA_Width,WINDOW_WIDTH, WA_Height, WINDOW_HEIGHT,
            WA_DragBar, TRUE,
            WA_DepthGadget, TRUE,
            WA_CloseGadget, TRUE,
            WA_SmartRefresh, TRUE,
            WA_IDCMP, IDCMP_CLOSEWINDOW | IDCMP_MENUPICK | IDCMP_GADGETUP,
            WA_Title, "General Testing Framework",
            WA_PubScreen, g_public_screen_p,
            TAG_END);
    if (g_window_p)
        {
        GT_RefreshWindow(g_window_p,NULL);
        error_number=NO_ERROR;
        g_rastport_p=g_window_p->RPort;
        g_function=KillWindow;
        PushStack(g_resource_stack_p,g_function);
        }
    return(error_number);
    }
/* -------------------------------------------------------- */
void KillWindow(void)
{
CloseWindow(g_window_p);
}
/* -------------------------------------------------------- */
```

Notice that the first of each of the two pairs of routines shown in listings 3.1 and 3.2 are using a PushStack() function and in each case the value being pushed, ie stored, is the address of the corresponding deallocation routine (the second routine in each listing). The net result is that, providing both of these allocation routines are successful, both deallocation routine pointers will have been placed on the stack. Further allocation routines will similarly add the addresses of their closedown routines and so the stack ends up holding pointers to all of the deallocation/closedown routines that will need to be performed when the program terminates. The good news now is that, irrespective of the number of routines present on the resource stack, the complete deallocation/closedown procedure can always be carried out with a single line of code:

```
while(!PopStack(g_resource_stack_p,g_function)) g_func-
tion();
```

This loop removes a pointer to a deallocation routine and then executes that function. It does this continually until the stack is empty (I'll recap on my stack conventions again in a moment).

Amiga programs usually have to do quite a lot of things when they first start up. Screens, windows, menus, gadgets etc, need to be set up. To handle the execution of the, possibly large number of, initial allocation routines used by a program I use a function pointer trick – C routines have addresses which can be accessed and used much the same as the address of a C variable. Because of this an array can be set up which contains pointers to the allocation routines to be executed. Here is an example controller array from a program that controls the operation of 18 (9 allocation and 9 deallocation) routines:

```
#define DISPLAY_COUNT 9

UBYTE (*display_list[])() = {
        OpenInt,
        OpenGraphics,
        OpenGadtools,
        LockScreen,
        GetVisInfo,
        CreateWindow,
        CreateMenu,
        CreateMenuLayout,
        InstallMenu
        };
```

The array identifies the set of routines that need to be executed at startup and of course similar types of arrays can be used at any point within a program where a number of successive allocations need to be made. All that is needed now is some loop code which will read through the pointer list and execute the corresponding routines. Listing 3.3 shows one of my standard functions which does the trick:

```
/* ------------------------------------------------ */
/*Listing 3.3: The auto-allocator function.*/

UBYTE AllocateResource(UBYTE count,UBYTE (*list[])())
{
```

```
        UBYTE i, error_number;
        for (i=0;i<count;i++)
                {
                if(error_number=list[i]())  i=count; /* force exit
                from loop */
                }
        return(error_number);
        }
        /* -------------------------------------------------- */
```

Making the Most Of Reusable Code

During these discussions you've probably noticed that I've taken it for granted that Push/Pull type stack operations are available to my allocation module. The bad news of course is that if you want such stack facilities in C then you must either create them yourself or borrow someone else's code. What did I do when developing this allocation technique? Well, I didn't borrow anyone else's code. Nor did I sit down to write new routines to provide stack operations. What I did of course was to link my existing, already compiled, abstract data type (ADT) stack module into the program and Bingo – instant stack handling facilities became available. As code gets re-used in this way it does of course, because it get thoroughly tested, tend to become very reliable.

What you should note in the allocation code fragments provided so far however is that I've only used those access functions PushStack(), PopStack() etc, that form part of the stack ADT interface definition. You should NEVER try to access the internal routines of an ADT module – that would defeat the whole purpose of developing an ADT in the first place. In fact when you examine the source code for the programs which use this technique (which you'll find on the disks which accompany the book) you will find no references to the stack ADT internal structures, the underlying list manipulation routines, or anything else. In short these internal characteristics are of no consequence to the applications programs wishing to use the ADT. All that a program needs to concern itself with is the set of allowable ADT operations that have been defined.

When I wrote my stack ADT code I had, as mentioned in the last chapter, a number of very specific requirements in mind: it was to be possible to use any number of different stacks handling any number of different object types, have different types of stacks in existence at different times, use the module in any number of programs without having to re-compile it and not be limited to working within a fixed memory space, save that of the limit of the system itself. Last but not least I wanted a module which could easily be ported to different machines and ANSI C was the obvious choice here.

ADT Stack

You'll notice incidentally that I chose to use *vanilla C*, ie ordinary common or garden C code, for implementing my stack ADT rather than the Amiga's Exec list functions. This again was for reasons of improved portability - if, for example I wanted to port my ADT code to say an Atari Falcon or ST machine, I can do it easily. If I'd implemented the ADT using Exec list facilities I'd have had to re-write all of the list handling code!

Are you beginning to see the benefit of the ADT yet? In the chapter 2 example I was using the stack routines to store characters of a string. In this latest use I'm using exactly the same code to store pointers to C functions and this flexibility is one of the main benefits of having ADT style code available. Equally important is the fact that I'm able to re-use existing code, rather than worry about writing stuff from scratch. To use the routines in my resource allocation module all I had to do was include the header file (stack_adt.h) into the program source, compile as normal, but link additionally with the ADT stack object code module (stack_adt.o).

As I've already mentioned, a lot of the routines and code fragments that I'll be discussing in this book will be provided on disk using examples that use this allocation technique. The allocators for each program will need to perform different functions but all will adopt the overall layout that this chapter has dealt with. Because these allocation modules are so fundamental it seemed a good idea to provide one complete listing for reference. The following code comes from a short Workbench oriented general program that I'll be using as a framework for many of my examples:

```
/* ================================================== */
/*Listing 3.4: A Typical Allocator Module*/

/*              Module name: allocator.c              */
/* -------------------------------------------------- */
#include "general.h"extern struct NewMenu menu1[]; /
* -------------------------------------------------- */
UBYTE AllocateResource(UBYTE count,UBYTE (*list[])())
{
UBYTE i, error_number;
for (i=0;i<count;i++)
    {
    if(error_number=list[i]())
    i=count; /* force exit from loop */
    }
return(error_number);
```

```c
}
/* ------------------------------------------------ */
UBYTE OpenInt(void)

{
UBYTE error_number=NO_ERROR;
UBYTE *s="intuition.library";
if(!(IntuitionBase=(struct IntuitionBase *)
      OpenLibrary(s,INTUITION_VERSION)))
        error_number=ALLOCATION_ERROR;
else    {
        g_function=CloseInt;
        PushStack(g_resource_stack_p,g_function);


return(error_number);
}
/* ------------------------------------------------ */
void CloseInt(void)

{
CloseLibrary((struct Library *)IntuitionBase);
}
/* ------------------------------------------------ */
UBYTE OpenGraphics(void)

{
UBYTE error_number=NO_ERROR;
if(!(GfxBase=(struct GfxBase *)
      OpenLibrary("graphics.library",GRAPHICS_VERSION)))
error_number=ALLOCATION_ERROR;
   else {
           g_function=CloseGraphics;
           PushStack(g_resource_stack_p,g_function);
           }
return(error_number);
}
/* ------------------------------------------------ */
void CloseGraphics(void)

{
CloseLibrary((struct Library *)GfxBase);
}
```

ADT Stack

```c
/* ------------------------------------------------- */
UBYTE LockScreen(void)
{
UBYTE error_number=ALLOCATION_ERROR;
if (g_public_screen_p=LockPubScreen(NULL))
     {
     g_viewport_p=&(*g_public_screen_p).ViewPort;
     error_number=NO_ERROR;
     g_function=UnlockScreen;
     PushStack(g_resource_stack_p,g_function);
     }
return(error_number);
}
/* ------------------------------------------------- */
void UnlockScreen(void)
{
UnlockPubScreen(NULL,g_public_screen_p);
}
/* ------------------------------------------------- */
UBYTE CreateWindow(void)
{
UBYTE error_number=ALLOCATION_ERROR;
g_window_p=OpenWindowTags(NULL,
     WA_Left,20, WA_Top,20,
     WA_Width,WINDOW_WIDTH, WA_Height, WINDOW_HEIGHT,
     WA_DragBar, TRUE,
     WA_DepthGadget, TRUE,
     WA_CloseGadget, TRUE,
     WA_SmartRefresh, TRUE,
     WA_IDCMP, IDCMP_CLOSEWINDOW | IDCMP_MENUPICK |
     IDCMP_GADGETUP,
     WA_Title, "General Testing Framework",
     WA_PubScreen, g_public_screen_p,
     TAG_END);
if (g_window_p)
     {
     GT_RefreshWindow(g_window_p,NULL);
```

```c
        error_number=NO_ERROR;
    g_rastport_p=g_window_p->RPort;
    g_function=KillWindow;
    PushStack(g_resource_stack_p,g_function);
    }
return(error_number);
}
/* ------------------------------------------------- */
void KillWindow(void)
{
CloseWindow(g_window_p);
}
/* ------------------------------------------------- */
UBYTE OpenGadtools(void)
{
UBYTE error_number=NO_ERROR;
if(!(GadToolsBase=OpenLibrary("gadtools.library",GAD-
TOOLS_VERSION)))
    error_number=NO_GADGTOOLS;
else {
    g_function=CloseGadtools;
    PushStack(g_resource_stack_p,g_function);
    }
return(error_number);
}
/* ------------------------------------------------- */
void CloseGadtools(void)
{
CloseLibrary((struct Library *)GadToolsBase);
}
/* ------------------------------------------------- */
UBYTE GetVisInfo(void)
{
UBYTE error_number=NO_ERROR;
if(!(g_visual_info_p=GetVisualInfo(g_public_screen_p,TAG_E
ND)))
    error_number=ALLOCATION_ERROR;
else {
```

```
        g_function=FreeVisInfo;
       PushStack(g_resource_stack_p,g_function);
       }
return(error_number);
}
/* -------------------------------------------------- */
void FreeVisInfo(void)
{
FreeVisualInfo(g_visual_info_p);
}
/* -------------------------------------------------- */
UBYTE CreateMenu(void)
{
UBYTE error_number=NO_ERROR;
if(!(g_menu_p=CreateMenus(menu1,TAG_END)))
        error_number=ALLOCATION_ERROR;
else {
       g_function=ReleaseMenu;
      PushStack(g_resource_stack_p,g_function);
       }
return(error_number);
}
/* -------------------------------------------------- */
void ReleaseMenu(void)
{
FreeMenus(g_menu_p);
}
/* -------------------------------------------------- */
UBYTE CreateMenuLayout(void)
{
UBYTE error_number=NO_ERROR;
if(!(LayoutMenus(g_menu_p,g_visual_info_p,TAG_END)))
        error_number=ALLOCATION_ERROR;
else {
      /* Function must be tested for success but
         no deallocation operations are needed! */
}
return(error_number);
```

```
}
/* ------------------------------------------------- */
UBYTE InstallMenu(void)
{
UBYTE error_number=NO_ERROR;
if(!(SetMenuStrip(g_window_p,g_menu_p)))
        error_number=ALLOCATION_ERROR;
else {
    g_function=RemoveMenu;
    PushStack(g_resource_stack_p,g_function);
    }
return(error_number);
}
/* ------------------------------------------------- */
void RemoveMenu(void){ClearMenuStrip(g_window_p);           }
/* ————————————————————- */
```

Controlling The Resource Allocation Process

So far I've explained about the way the pairs of resource handling routines are set up, and described the controller array (the list of function pointers) and controller routines used to define the initial setting up procedures. In order to cause the inital allocations to be performed we do of course have to explicitly call the allocator function and I usually do this using a small module that I call main.c (because it contains C's main() function). Here's a typical piece of example code:

```
/* ===================================================== */
/*Listing 3.5: Short modules like this are used to control
the allocation operations*/


/*              Module name: main.c              */
/* ------------------------------------------------- */
#define ALLOCATE_GLOBALS
#include "general.h"
extern struct NewMenu menu1[];
#define DISPLAY_COUNT 9
UBYTE (*display_list[])() = {
        OpenInt,
        OpenGraphics,
        OpenGadtools,
        LockScreen,
```

```
        GetVisInfo,
        CreateWindow,
        CreateMenu,
        CreateMenuLayout,
        InstallMenu
        };
UBYTE *alert_message_p =
"\x00\x4A\x14"
"*** RECOVERABLE ALERT - CANNOT RUN PROGRAM ***""\x00\x01"
"\x00\x4A\x24"
"Version 37 or upwards of the GadTools library is
required" "\x00\x01"   "\x0\x4A\x34"
"** PRESS LEFT OR RIGHT MOUSE BUTTON TO CONTINUE **" "\x00"
;main(int argc, char *argv[])
{
UBYTE error_number=NO_ERROR;
if(!(g_resource_stack_p=CreateStack(void *))) error_num-
ber=NO_STACK;
else {
     /* attempt to allocate resources: */
     error_number=AllocateResource (DISPLAY_COUNT,dis
     play_list);
     if (error_number)
        {
        if(error_number==NO_GADTOOLS)
           DisplayAlert(RECOVERY_ALERT,alert_message_p,80);
        }
         else error_number=AmigaProg();
     while(!PopStack(g_resource_stack_p,g_function))
     g_function();
     KillStack(g_resource_stack_p);
     }
return(0);
}
/* Logical end of program */
/* ===================================================== */
```

Basically this module tries to create a stack ADT and if it succeeds it then calls the function pointer list allocator function and if this returns with a 'no error' indicator control passes to the main part of the program – which in this example I've labelled as the AmigaProg(). function. This function only ever returns when the user has signalled that they want to quit and so at this point the function pointer stack is emptied as the deallocator routines are called, the stack is then deleted and the program terminates.

When you examine the source code on disk you'll see that the program uses some Release 2 (version 37) library functions so it is not going to run under Workbench 1.3 or earlier. Knowing that the only likely reason for the program failing on startup is going to be that someone is attempting to run the program on a 1.3 based machine I've include a DisplayAlert() function that is called if a gadtools allocation error occurs. This just informs the user that the GadTools version 37 library is required to run the program.

The Intuition Angle

The Intuition related aspects of this chapter's example code may also be of interest to those of you who are new to Amiga coding. The program uses a window that opens in the Workbench screen and under Release 2 this screen has to be locked during the time a window is set up and opened. Menus also have to be installed and this must obviously only be done if the window itself is successfully opened. Get use to the format of the allocator functions. I use them a lot. For example the moment it is known that the window has been sucessfully opened the address of the appropriate window closing routine, KillWindow(), gets pushed onto my resource handling stack. This ensures that it will be closed automatically when the program finishes. I have incidentally opted for using the GadTools Library rather than the older style Intuition approaches and this is primarily for simplicity – things like menus are far easier to set up using the GadTools arangements. You'll be able to see this from the menu definition shown in listing 3.6. The GadTools library is able to convert this description directly into the menu that appears on the screen!

```
        struct NewMenu menu1[] =
        Listing 3.6: A simple Gadtools menu definition*/


        {
                {NM_TITLE,"PROJECT    ",              0 ,0,0,0,},
                {NM_ITEM, "Quit to WorkBench",        "Q",0,0,0,},
                {NM_END, NULL,                        0, 0,0,0,},
        };
```

From Release 2 of the Amiga's operating system there have, amongst other things, been new methods for opening screens and windows which involve the use of tag lists. Many of these operations can be performed in a variety of seemingly different ways with much of the flexibility being provided primarily for those developers who, compatibility-wise, are in the unfortunate position of being stuck between a rock (the 1.3 O/S) and a hard place (Release 2 and later).

Not everyone will encounter such problems. Given that the 1.3 user base is likely to diminish fairly rapidly now as users upgrade and models like the brilliant A1200 and A4000/030 make their mark, many developers have wisely opted simply to provide (and maintain) separate versions of their products. This latter approach is also the one that most Amiga users will want to adopt with their own programs because experience shows that once they've working with the new environment their interest in 1.3 coding will dwindle rapidly! Nevertheless in order to appreciate some of the new system function options (available from Release 2 onwards) it is necessary to understand how Tag lists fit into the compatibility scenario.

As you'll doubtless know the Amiga header files contain templates for vast numbers of system structures and these define the various entities used by the system. If, for instance, you wished to open a window in 1.3 (and earlier) you would create a NewWindow structure, fill in the appropriate details, and then call the Intuition library's OpenWindow() function. In order to provide the Release 2 system enhancements however, some established operations, like window opening, required additional parameters to be specified and Commodore's problem was to find a way to do this that would minimise any compatibility upsets. In fact what they wanted to do was come up with a solution that would eliminate the need to extend existing system structures in future O/S releases altogether. The approach that has been adopted is based on the use of arrays, or lists of arrays, that contain self-identifying parameter values (each parameter item consists of an identifier and a corresponding 'real' value). Since these lists provide a way of tagging additional parameters onto existing O/S structures, they've been called Tag lists. Where appropriate, newly devised library function calls look for such items and use them (either in addition to, or as a replacement for, any existing structure data they might have used in the past). What does a TagItem structure look like? If you look in the Utility/tagitem.h header this is the sort of arrangement you'll find:

```
struct TagItem {
    Tag ti_Tag;        /* Typedef'd as just another ULONG */
    ULONG ti_Data;
};
```

It's just a pair of long word (four byte) values! The first provides a 32 bit TagItem identity, the second a corresponding 32 bit data value. Most tag identity values are context specific and in the intuition.h header file for instance you will find all manner of Intuition-related tag identities (eg WA_Left, WA_Top, WA_Width and WA_Height are used to specify window position and size information). A number of general tag item values have also been defined and can be found, along with the TagItem structure itself, in the utility/tagitem.h header file. Here are the most common general symbolic names you'll encounter:

TAG_IGNORE	Indicates that the associated data item should be ignored.
TAG_SKIP	Skip this and the next ti_Data TagItems.
TAG_MORE	Marks the end of one array and indicates that at least one other TagItem array exists. The ti_Data field points to the next TagItem array to be used.
TAG_END	Signals the end of an array (ti_Data is unused).

Table 3.1. Symbolic tag identity names.

It's important to realise that Tag lists have been adopted to, and hopefully, solve the problem of adding additional parameters to function calls once and for all. In short, from Release 2 onwards they are an integral part of the system and the bottom line is that if you're interested in getting into up-to-date Amiga programming you MUST understand how they work.

So far I've been trying to paint a general picture about how and why Tag lists came into existence. The bad news is that there are now actually five different ways to write window opening code. For a start, the programmer can set up an ExtNewScreen structure containing a pointer to a tag list, and in this case the OpenWindow() function call can be made in the usual fashion. Alternatively, the OpenWindowTagList() function can be used and this has the following prototype:

```
struct Window *OpenWindowTagList( struct NewWindow *,
struct TagItem *);
```

This latter routine can actually be used in two different ways: Firstly, the originally required parameters can be specified, à la 1.3, in a NewWindow structure with additional (Release 2 onward) arguments being provided in a separate tag list. Secondly, a NULL NewWindow pointer can be used coupled with a tag list that contains all window opening parameters (only the non-default value tags need be supplied).

That covers three of the approaches available for making a window opening call. Unfortunately (or fortunately depending on your viewpoint) two more variations exist based on the use of the amiga.lib OpenWindowTags() function. Rather than passing a single tag list pointer this function expects to get its tag parameters from the stack (along with a NewWindow pointer). Don't panic, the amiga.lib function stub does all this automatically and, from the C coders viewpoint, the only difference when using this routine is that the various values are specified as arguments of the function call using this type of scheme:

```
struct Window *OpenWindowTags( struct NewWindow *, tag id
and    value pairs...)
```

Again the NewWindow pointer can be NULL so, if you want to use tag based parameters exclusively, you can.

Another area of Intuition-related code which may be of interest to less experienced coders concerns the handling of gadget and menu events passed back to the program from Intuition. This type of code may look frightening when you first see it, but the basic principles are very easy to understand. The program executes a Wait() or WaitPort() which puts it to sleep (ie puts it on hold so that it stops requiring processor time) until the user hits a gadget or makes a menu selection. At this time it is Intuition that's doing all the *event recognition* work and having identified a particular user action it sends the program an *IntuiMessage*. The first thing that your program knows about all this is when Exec wakes it up and tells it that the signal that it is waiting on has been satisfied. The program then knows that a message has arrived and so it collects the message, looks in the message's Class field to identify its type, and *returns* the message using a reply function (which lets the sender know that the message has been dealt with and can be deallocated or re-used). Having done all that it must then perform whatever action is suitable for the particular message in question. My normal approach to event handling is to use a preliminary routine to identify the general type (gadget or menu) and then deliver each class of message to an appropriate handler routine.

Project Management

Once you start writing programs that involve many different modules and header files actually looking after the contents of those files becomes a headache in its own right. There are three quite important topics that ought to be mentioned here because they are *standard* approaches which almost all established C programmers use on all machines. Firstly, there is the problem of defining and declaring variables. One program module can use variables defined in other modules providing 'extern' references are included in the module wishing to use them (to let the compiler know that the variables are declared elsewhere). Variables must of course be declared normally in just one file (so that memory can be allocated for storage) but there is a sneaky #ifdef C pre-processor trick available that lets you use the same header file for both declaring and externally referencing a set of variables. The fragment shown in listing 3.7 (which comes from the example's general.h file) will only generate the extern reference if ALLOCATE_GLOBALS is *not* defined. By defining this value at the start of just one of the file modules all the necessary variables are declared and all other modules end up with the extern form statements as is needed. The benefit? A single file serves both declaration and external referencing purposes and this makes for substantially easier file maintenance.

```
/*Listing 3.7: A useful header file pre-processor trick in
action*/
/* part of general.h */
#ifdef ALLOCATE_GLOBALS
    #define PREFIX
  #else
    #define PREFIX extern
#endif
PREFIX void (*g_function)();
PREFIX STACK *g_resource_stack_p;
PREFIX struct   IntuitionBase    *IntuitionBase;
PREFIX struct   GfxBase          *GfxBase;
```

The second issue concerns the avoiding of masses of *magic numbers* embedded in the code. C's preprocessor facilities can be used to create header files that contain definitions of important constant items. This both aids source code readability and makes it easier to update values used across any number of files. Listing 3.8 gives a few examples but you'll find many more in the disk source files.

```
/*Listing 3.8 Preprocessor #define statements can also
improve source code readabilty.*/
#define   INTUITION_VERSION    33
#define   GRAPHICS_VERSION     33
#define   GADTOOLS_VERSION     37
```

The third area of program file management interest is related to how multiple module programs are physically put together. This chapter's program as already explained is formed from a collection of independently programed object code modules which handle the allocation and control of resources along with a variety of Intuition-oriented tasks. As you now know a stack ADT module also has to be linked to the program to support the abstract data type stack operations used by the allocator module.

If the source code related to any one of these modules is updated (due to enhancements or bug fixes) then not only does that particular module need to be recompiled but it must be re-linked with the already existing unchanged modules in order to produce the new version of the program. C Compilers provide 'Make' utilities which allow such file dependencies to be specified and the SAS C offering is called 'Smake'. In (most) simple cases a make file script line consists of a target file name followed by the names of any files upon whose contents it is dependent. Following this, on the next line, come the actions that should be carried out when one of those dependent files change.

In the example shown in listing 3.9 a change to the allocator.c file would cause allocator.c to be recompiled to produce a new allocator.o file that in turn triggers the re-linking of the example program. The benefit of the utilities which allow make files to be used is that once the required definitions are set up the programmer never has to think about what files have to be remade when things get changed. You, the programmer, make your desired changes: and the 'make' utility automatically compiles just those files that are needed and re-links all the files to provide a new version of the project. Your compiler manuals will contain details of the 'make' utilities provided with your compiler. Read them - needless to say 'make' files become important as projects get larger!

```
/*Listing 3.9: The SAS C makefile for this chapter's exam-
ple program.*/
# ===========================================================
# General Test Program smake file
# -----------------------------------------------------------
Test: main.o allocator.o amiga.o
sc:c/slink FROM LIB:c.o "main.o"            "allocator.o" \
"amiga.o" "stack_adt.o" \
TO Test LIB LIB:sc.lib+LIB:amiga.lib
main.o: main.c general.h prototypes.h          sc:c/sc
main.c
allocator.o:   allocator.c general.h prototypes.h
sc:c/sc allocator.c
amiga.o:   amiga.c amiga.h general.h prototypes.h
sc:c/sc amiga.c
# ===========================================================
```

4: A Flashy Interrupt Trick

The 680x0 microprocessors have sophisticated interrupt processing but, as far as the Amiga programmer is concerned, the processor interrupt facilities fade into the background. To be honest an in-depth knowledge of 68K interrupt handling doesn't actually help the Amiga coder that much.

This statement may seem a strange way to start a chapter on Amiga interrupt coding, but it is absolutely true. As an Amiga coder you are unlikely to ever get near to the real 600x0 interrupt system. Why? It's because the decoding/despatching of both system and task-related interrupts are handled at a much higher level – it's the multi-tasking Exec system that you deal with, NOT the 680x0 chip. Exec, as one of its many jobs, supports an interrupt management scheme which allows many different tasks to be requesting (and using) interrupt facilities at the same time. The processing itself involves a complicated series of actions involving the 4703 (Paula) chip and a number of Exec supervisor operations. The result, however, at the end of the day is simple: when the right interrupt signal comes along Exec makes sure that the appropriate piece of code gets executed as though it were a subroutine!

Interrupt processing on the Amiga is an area which has not received much exposure either in magazines or the Amiga's main-stay reference books. The Addison Wesley RKM *Libraries* volume, probably provides the best accounts but, although the ideas are well explained, little tutorial help is offered. More importantly than that though there is, from a practical viewpoint, a big chunk of the story missing. From the beginner's viewpoint what is needed is an explanation of the overall scheme of things backed up with some example code which can help put things into perspective. What I want to do first therefore is take a couple of examples that adopt a straightforward approach and explain what's going on. You might, if you aren't familiar with mixed code programming, find it useful to read Chapter 13 in conjunction with this chapter because it deals with the nitty gritty details of how such code is put together.

Before we start on our interrupt trail it's necessary to understand that interrupts are serviced on the Amiga through the use of two types of arrangements – interrupt handlers, and interrupt servers. A handler is essentially a single routine which carries out exclusively all processing related to a particular 4703 interrupt. A *server* on the other hand allows for an interrupt signal to be shared, ie it allows a number of routines to be tied to a particular 4703 interrupt.

I've opted for examples that use the Amiga's Vertical Blanking interrrupt. When the Amiga's operating system is kicked into life, Exec ties this interrupt to a server chain and out first job is to arrange to add our interrupt routine code into this chain. The Exec library offers a couple of system routines, called AddIntServer() and RemIntServer(), which allow a piece of interrupt code to be added or removed from the system in a properly organised manner. Here are some brief function details:

Function Name:	AddIntServer()
Description:	Add an interrupt server to the system chain
Call Format:	AddIntServer(interrupt_number, interrupt_p);
C Prototype:	void AddIntServer(ULONG, struct Interrupt *);
Registers:	AddIntServer(D0, A0)
Arguments:	interrupt_number interrupt bit numbe interrupt_p pointer to an initialized Interrupt structure
Return Value:	None
Notes:	See RKM manuals for additional details.

Function Name:	RemIntServer()
Description:	Remove an interrupt server from system chain
Call Format:	RemIntServer(interrupt_number, interrupt_p);
C Prototype:	void RemIntServer(ULONG, struct Interrupt *);
Registers:	RemIntServer(D0, A0)
Arguments:	interrupt_number - interrupt bit number interrupt_p - pointer to an initialized Interrupt structure
Return Value:	None
Notes:	See RKM manuals for additional details.

The interrupt numbers are defined in the hardware/intbits.h header file(or the equivalent assembly language include file hardware/intbits.i) and for our vertical blank interrupt we use the value INTB_VERTB (actually 5). The second parameter is a pointer not to a piece of code but to a system Interrupt structure, which in C looks like this:

```
struct Interrupt
{
struct Node      is_Node;
APTR             is_Data;
VOID             (* is_Code)();
};
```

It's this structure that Exec uses to provide a linked list of jobs which must be done when the interrupt occurs. Basically an Interrupt structure is an ordinary Exec Node with a couple of extra items tagged on. You do incidentally need to know about the contents of a Node structure because a number of its fields have to be filled in before you can use the Interrupt structure. Here are the necessary details:

```
struct Node
{
struct Node *ln_Succ;    /* pointer to successor   */
struct Node *ln_Pred;    /* pointer to predecessor */
UBYTE  ln_Type;          /* must set this to NT_INTERRUPT */
BYTE   ln_Pri;           /* can be set from +128 to -127 */
char   *ln_Name;         /* points to a NULL terminated string */
};
```

The Node structure's type, priority and name fields have to be set up with sensible values, and the is_Code pointer must contain the address of your interupt routine. The is_Data field is available simply for convenience – Exec will pass anything you place in this field directly to the interrupt routine using the 680x0's A1 register. With an interrupt server chain the priority value will determine where abouts in the server chain your routine will be placed (normally you should leave the priority field as zero). Exec carries out these interrupt jobs in order of their priority but it checks the 680x0's zero flag before deciding whether to execute the next server routine. The bad news here is that if the zero flag is NOT set then Exec doesn't bother executing any of the server routines further down the chain! Needless to say – if you give your routine to a high priority, and then forget to set the zero flag on exit, other routines in the chain will not be executed. Vertical Blank servers should therefore always return with the 680x0's zero flag deliberately set!

This is easy to do when your routine is coded in assembler but with high-level languages such as C the approach tends to vary depending on which compiler you are using. SAS C for instance provides a function called putreg() that allows a value to be forced into a 680x0 register and a putreg(REG_D0,0) call appears to set the 680x0's zero flag to a suitable (true) value. With other compilers other functions may be specified or you may have to terminate the interrupt routine using a return(0L) function.

Putting the Pieces Together

So far the basic ideas, given that a suitable piece of interrupt code is available, are relatively straightforward: set up the required Interrupt structure and use the AddIntServer() routine to get the code added to the jobs that are done every time a vertical blank interrupt occurs. Just before the program terminates use a RemIntServer() call to remove the job.

The interrupt code itself should be written as a subroutine and the general rule with all interrupt coding is that the code should be kept short and fast. This is especially important on the Amiga because a lot of *housekeeping* operations happen during the Amiga's interrupt times. One important thing to remember is that you cannot assume that it is always safe to read global system structures and so on because they may actually be in the middle of being updated at the time your interrupt occurs. There are ways around this although the most obvious, disabling the interrupts for a short period of time, is not always the wisest course of action. There are a few other *gotchas* to watch for as well – you cannot for example use system calls which, either directly or indirectly, call Exec's own AllocMem() and FreeMem() memory allocation and deallocation routines.

Everything I've talked about so far has involved the relatively mechanical aspects of interrupt use, ie the adding and removing of pieces of code from an interrupt server chain. What we now need to do is look at some example interrupt code and here there are both high-level and low-level ways of approaching the coding.

The High-Level C Approach

I'm going to start by sketching out the overall framework of some interrupt code that just decreases the value of a global variable, called g_delay, by one every time a vertical blanking interrupt occurs. After doing this the routine will check to see if the value of this variable has become zero and, if it has, it will reset it to an arbitrary original value again. Here's the code in question:

```
void __saveds InterruptCode(void)
{
if (!(-g_delay))
   {
   g_delay=DELAY;    /* reset original value */
   }
putreg(REG_D0,0);
}
```

This example is Lattice/SAS C compiler oriented in that I've used the __saveds keyword (needed because the interrupt code will be entered directly) and the putreg() function to set the 680x0's zero flag. Other compilers will require different approaches and you'll need to check your own compiler documentation for these details. To install the interrupt code is easy - you just initialise an Interrupt structure and use the Exec AddIntServer() routine like this:

```
void PatchOn(void)
{
/* initialise interrupt structure fields and link into
server chain... */
g_interrupt.is_Node.ln_Type=NT_INTERRUPT;
g_interrupt.is_Node.ln_Succ=NULL;
g_interrupt.is_Node.ln_Pred=NULL;
g_interrupt.is_Node.ln_Pri=0;
g_interrupt.is_Node.ln_Name=NULL;
g_interrupt.is_Code=InterruptCode;
g_interrupt.is_Data=NULL;
AddIntServer(INTB_VERTB,&g_interrupt);
}
```

Removing the code from the interrupt job list is even easier:

```
void PatchOff(void)
```

```
    {
    RemIntServer(INTB_VERTB,&g_interrupt);
    }
```

As you'll realise from the above code the basic arrangement for adding an additional piece of code to an interrupt server chain is, in principle at least, reasonably straightforward. What throws most people is getting the details right so it's important that the various steps are understood within the context of a runable example. The following example installs the interrupt routine described earlier and then executes a loop which just looks at the contents of the g_delay variable whilst the loop counts to 1000. No changes are made to the contents of g_delay from within the main program but as the contents are printed you'll see the value changing between 1 and 16. What's happening of course is that the interrupt routine is changing the value of the g_delay variable and this should be proof enough that the interrupt code has been installed into the vertical blanking server chain.

```
/* ======================================================= */
/*Listing 4.1: A runable interrupt code example*/

/* Program name: CH4-1.c */
/* ------------------------------------------------------- */
/* some includes... */
#include <stdio.h>
#include <exec/types.h>#include <dos.h>
#include <exec/interrupts.h>
#include <hardware/intbits.h>
#include <proto/all.h>/* some prototypes... */
void __saveds InterruptCode(void);
void PatchOn(void);
void PatchOff(void);
/* some defines...*/
#define DELAY 16
/* some globals... */
UBYTE g_delay=DELAY;
static struct Interrupt g_interrupt;
/* ------------------------------------------------------- */
main(int argc, char *argv[])
{
```

```
    ULONG i;
    PatchOn();
    for (i=0;i<1000;i++) printf("%d\n",g_delay);
    PatchOff();
    } /* Logical end of program */
    /* -------------------------------------------------- */
    void PatchOn(void)
    {
    /* initialise interrupt struct fields then link into
       server chain... */
    g_interrupt.is_Node.ln_Type=NT_INTERRUPT;
    g_interrupt.is_Node.ln_Succ=NULL;
    g_interrupt.is_Node.ln_Pred=NULL;
    g_interrupt.is_Node.ln_Pri=0;
    g_interrupt.is_Node.ln_Name=NULL;
    g_interrupt.is_Code=InterruptCode;
    g_interrupt.is_Data=NULL;
    AddIntServer(INTB_VERTB,&g_interrupt);
    }
    /* -------------------------------------------------- */
    void PatchOff(void)
    {
    RemIntServer(INTB_VERTB,&g_interrupt);
    }
    /* -------------------------------------------------- */
    void __saveds InterruptCode(void)
    {
    if (!(--g_delay))
       {
       g_delay=DELAY;    /* reset original value */
       }
    putreg(REG_D0,0);
    }
    /* -------------------------------------------------- */
```

Flashing Colours

The framework we've just developed is easily modified to produce a simple *flashing colour* routine and their are two areas where the code needs to be changed. Frstly we need to obtain the red, blue and green colour values of the appropriate colour register. This information can be obtained by using the graphics library GetRGB4() routine and then doing some bit masking and shifting to identify the individual values like this:

```
g_colour_value=GetRGB4(g_viewport_p->ColorMap,COLOUR_REG);

g_red   = (g_colour_value&0x0F00)>>8;

g_green = (g_colour_value&0x00F0)>>4;

g_blue= g_colour_value&0x000F;
```

Once these values are available all we need to do to make the colour *flash* is alternately switch the colour in the register between its original value and black. We set the colour to black by clearing the colour register's red, blue and green components to zero like this:

```
SetRGB4(g_viewport_p,COLOUR_REG,0,0,0); /* set to black */
```

then, when the next change is due, we reset the colour register using the original red, green and blue values:

```
SetRGB4(g_viewport_p,COLOUR_REG,g_red,g_green,g_blue);
```

The following listing is of an interrupt code module that does this and you'll see that a global toggle variable is being alternately set and cleared in order to allow the right SetRGB4() call to be made. On disk you'll find this module linked into a program whose general framework is based on the example outlined in Chapter 3.

```
/* ====================================================== */
/*Listing 4.2: A simple colour flashing program*/

/* Module name: interrupt.c for ExampleCH4-2 */
/* ------------------------------------------------------ */
#include <exec/types.h>
#include <dos.h>
#include <exec/interrupts.h>
#include <hardware/intbits.h>
#include <proto/all.h>
#include "general.h"
void __saveds InterruptCode(void);
#define COLOUR_REG  3
struct Interrupt g_interrupt;
UWORD   g_colour_value;
```

A Flashy Interrupt Trick

```c
UBYTE  g_red, g_green, g_blue, g_toggle=FALSE;
void PatchOn(void)
{
/* set delay value and read colour reg values: */
g_delay=DELAY;
g_colour_value=GetRGB4(g_viewport_p->ColorMap,COLOUR_REG);
g_red   = (g_colour_value&0x0F00)>>8;
g_green = (g_colour_value&0x00F0)>>4;
g_blue= g_colour_value&0x000F;
/* initialise interrupt struct fields: */
g_interrupt.is_Node.ln_Type=NT_INTERRUPT;
g_interrupt.is_Node.ln_Succ=NULL;
g_interrupt.is_Node.ln_Pred=NULL;
g_interrupt.is_Node.ln_Pri=0;
g_interrupt.is_Node.ln_Name=NULL;
g_interrupt.is_Code=InterruptCode;
g_interrupt.is_Data=NULL;
/* and finally link code into server chain: */
AddIntServer(INTB_VERTB,&g_interrupt);
}
/* -------------------------------------------------- */
void PatchOff(void)
{
RemIntServer(INTB_VERTB,&g_interrupt);
SetRGB4(g_viewport_p,COLOUR_REG,g_red,g_green,g_blue);
/* restore colours */
}
/* -------------------------------------------------- */
void  __saveds InterruptCode(void)
{if (!(-g_delay))
   {
   g_delay=DELAY;    /* reset original value */
   if(g_toggle)
       {
          SetRGB4 (g_viewport_p,COLOUR_REG,g_red,
                   g_green,g_blue);
          g_toggle=FALSE;
       }
```

```
        else {
            SetRGB4(g_viewport_p,COLOUR_REG,0,0,0);
            /* set to black */
            g_toggle=TRUE;
            }
    }
    putreg(REG_D0,0);
}
/* ------------------------------------------------ */
```

The Equivalent Assembler Example:

For those of you interested in assembler coding here's a similar *rough and ready* flashing effect routine created using 680x0 assembler. It was assembed with Devpac and makes use of some Devpac specific library access macros (such as CALLGRAF). When using another assembler these calls would need to be replaced with conventional library call code that explicitly specifies the appropriate library base.

Providing you're happy with 680x0 assembler there's little more to mention except that in this example I've hard-coded the delay value (rather than reading the contents of a global delay variable). The overall principles of the routine and its use of the library function calls for installing and removing the interrupt code and getting/setting colour register values are exactly the same as for the example already discussed. Notice however that when we are working at 680x0 coding level it is very easy to ensure that the zero flag is set before the interrupt routine terminates. We just use the instruction:

```
        moveq.l         #0,d0               ;set Z flag
```

Here's the listing of the routine that you find on the program disk:

```
        /*Listing 4.3: A simple 680x0 assembly language interrupt
        colour flashing example*/
        include exec/exec_lib.i
        include exec/interrupts.i
        include exec/types.i
        include hardware/intbits.i
        include graphics/graphics_lib.i
        DELAY       EQU     16
        PRIORITY    EQU     0
                    XDEF    _PatchOn
                    XDEF    _PatchOff
                    XREF    _GfxBase
```

A Flashy Interrupt Trick

```
            XREF    _g_viewport_p
            XREF    _colourtable
*------------------------------------------------------------
*Preserve a6, get colours and then set up the interrupt
*server node before adding to existing vertical blanking
*jobs. Structure is already defined in include files, so
*we can use the pre-calculated offsets:
_PatchOn:   movem.l  a6,-(a7)           ;preserve

            move.l   #_colourtable,a1
            move.w   14(a1),d0          ;get colour
            andi.w   #$0F00,d1          ;isolate red
            lsr.w    #8,d1
            move.b   d1,red
            move.b   d0,d1              ;copy colour
            andi.b   #$00F0,d1          ;isolate green
            lsr.b    #4,d1
            move.b   d1,green
            move.b   d0,d1              ;copy colour
            andi.b   #$000F,d1          ;isolate blue
            move.b   d1,blue
            move.l   #server_node,a1    ;base address
            move.b   #NT_INTERRUPT,LN_TYPE(a1)
            move.b   #PRIORITY,LN_PRI(a1)
            move.l   #_colourtable,IS_DATA(a1)
            move.l   #FLASH_CODE,IS_CODE(a1)
            moveq.l  #INTB_VERTB,d0     ;server node already
                                        ; in a1
            CALLEXEC AddIntServer       ;install
            movem.l  (a7)+,a6           ;restore
            rts                         ;quit
*------------------------------------------------------------*/
            cnop     0,4
_PatchOff:  movem.l  a6,-(a7)           ;preserve
            move.l   #server_node,a1
            moveq.l  #INTB_VERTB,d0
            CALLEXEC RemIntServer
            movem.l  (a7)+,a6           ;restore
            rts                         ;quit
```

```
*   ----------------------------------------------------------------
FLASH_CODE:   movem.l    d2-d3/a6,-(a7)
                         ;preserve registers
              subq.b     #1,count
              bne        FC1
              move.b     #DELAY,count
              bchg       #0,switch        ;alternate value
              beq        CLEAR_REG
SET_REG:      move.b     red,d1           ;prepare colours
              move.b     green,d2         ;for RGB4() call
              move.b     blue,d3
              bra        FC0
CLEAR_REG:    clr        d1               ;clear colours
              clr        d2               ;for RGB4() call
              clr        d3
FC0:          move.l     #7,d0            ;colour reg 7
              move.l     _g_viewport_p,a0
              CALLGRAF   SetRGB4          ;reset colour
FC1:          movem.l    (a7)+,d2-d3/a6   ;restore registers
              moveq.l    #0,d0            ;set Z flag
              rts
/*  ----------------------------------------------------------------*/-
server_node    ds.l    IS_SIZE    ,static declaration
count          dc.b    DELAY
red            ds.b    1          ;space for storing
green          ds.b    1          ;separated colour
blue           ds.b    1          ;values
switch         ds.b    1          ;boolean flash switch
/*  ----------------------------------------------------------------*/
```

An Alternative Amiga-Oriented Solution

On some machines having a piece of code forcibly executed by tying it to an interrupt can be the only way to get a piece of secondary code performed whilst the main program is running. Flashing colours and colour cycling tricks are two typical effects that have frequently required interrupt-based approaches. As we've now seen it is certainly possible to adopt these solutions with the Amiga but is this the best way to tackle such jobs? To be honest the answer is no – because these effects are not actually time-critical enough to warrant their inclusion into the Amiga vertical blanking server chain. Why burden an interrupt chain, that possibly already has a great many important things to do already, by adding yet another complete job? One solution to this dilemma is, in principle at least, simple. Instead of having all of the proposed interrupt driven code attached to the server chain we instead just use a short interrupt routine that sends a *start doing something* signal to another process whenever an interrupt occurs. That removes most of the additional pressure and leads us onto an area of Exec which involves inter-task signalling.

But why stop there? At this point, bearing in mind that the Amiga can multitask, we also need to ask ourselves whether it wouldn't be better to set up totally independent tasks for handling secondary jobs like colour flashing and so on. For the everyday coding problems that most Amiga programmers face, these multiple task approaches turn out to be far more flexible than the corresponding interrupt-based solutions. For two or more tasks to co-operate sensibly they need to communicate and one way of doing this is to use Exec's signalling system. Since these arrangements are important, they get a chapter all to themselves.

5:
Using Exec Signals in Your Own Programs

The Amiga's multi-tasking operating system provides an elegant inter-task signalling system based on the use of sets of signal bits that are stored inside every program's task structure. For each task Exec allocates space for 32 bits of these bits (ie one long word) – the lower 16 bits are for use by Exec itself but the upper 16 bits are available for use by the task in question. These signal facilities are in fact an integral part of the higher level Exec message communications system upon which things like the even higher level Intuition IntuiMessage and ARexx communications systems are built. When dealing with messages at these higher levels the programmer, in most cases, rarely needs to worry about how the underlying signal bits are allocated because Exec-oriented amiga.lib calls such as CreatePort(), Intuition library functions etc, always handle the nitty gritty details automatically. We'll consider some message-oriented ideas in the next chapter but for the moment it is the underlying signalling system that is our main focus of interest.

Because the allocation, handling, and deallocation of signal bits tend to be handled automatically they tend to remain hidden in the background as far as Amiga system resources are concerned. This is a pity because they are not only very useful but they are extremely easy to understand and the purpose of this chapter is to convince you that this is so by showing you a number of useful signal based tricks. First of all though let's start by taking a look at the Exec functions that allow a task to set up and release a signal bit:

Function Name:	AllocSignal()
Description:	Allocate a signal bit
Call Format:	signal_number=AllocSignal(signal_number);
C Prototype:	BYTE=AllocSignal(BYTE);
Registers:	D0=AllocSignal(D0)
Arguments:	signal_number - either a specific signal number or -1 if don't care
Return Value:	allocated number for signal or -1 if function fails
Notes:	Signals should be deallocated before the task terminates.

The actual allocation of user signals is extremely easy to code and one important point is that it is *you* the programmer who decides what the various signal bits are going to mean to your program. We might for instance decide that bit 16 was going to be used as a signal for a program to quit, ie terminate, and so we'd use a #define preprocessor statement to create a suitable definition. When requesting a specific signal bit in this way we can test that the required signal was obtained directly like this:

```
#define QUIT 16
if(AllocSignal(QUIT)==QUIT)
   {
   /* signal available for use here */
   }
```

All allocated signals have to be returned before a program terminates and a FreeSignal() function is available for this purpose. It is used like this:

```
FreeSignal(QUIT);
```

You'll notice that neither the allocation or freeing functions need to know what task is involved. This is deliberate – the calls are task specific and it is not possible to use them to allocate or deallocate the signals of some other task.

Using Exec Signals

Function Name:	**FreeSignal()**
Description:	Free an allocated signal bit
Call Format:	FreeSignal(signal_number);
C Prototype:	void=FreeSignal(BYTE);
Registers:	FreeSignal(D0)
Arguments:	signal_number - signal number of signal to free
Return Value:	None

Once a task has allocated a signal bit other tasks can set this signal by using this Exec Signal() function and again the function is very easy to use. To send the previously mentioned QUIT signal to a task whose Task pointer is contained in the variable called child_task_p we'd use this sort of code:

```
Signal(child_task_p,(1L<<QUIT));
```

Notice that this function does NOT use a signal bit number it uses a long word, ie 32 bit, mask value (which I'll explain about shortly).

Function Name:	**Signal()**
Description:	Signal a task
Call Format:	Signal(task_p,signal_mask);
C Prototype:	void=Signal(struct Task *,ULONG);
Registers:	Signal(A0 D0)
Arguments:	task_p - pointer to the task to be signalled signal_mask - signals to be set
Return Value:	None
Notes:	Tasks can be signalled at any time irrespective of whether they are running, ready to run, or in a wait state. If the task is currently waiting for one of the signals being set it will be made ready to run and a reschedule will occur.

With the Amiga's multitasking system it's important for programs not to use processor time unless really necessary. One common example of when a program should not use processor time is when it needs to wait for user input, eg waiting for a user to hit a gadget or select a menu item. The standard procedure with Amiga programming is to put the program to sleep until such time as something of interest happens and the function which allows this to be done is, for obvious reasons, called Wait():

Function Name:	Wait()
Description:	Wait for one or more signals
Call Format:	signals=Wait(signal_mask);
C Prototype:	ULONG=Wait(ULONG);
Registers:	D0=Wait(D0)
Arguments:	signal_mask - 32 bit mask of signals to wait for
Return Value:	signals which caused the Wait() to be satisfied
Notes:	This is a more generally useful function than Wait Port() because it allows signals from different sources to be combined.

Signal Bits And Masks

The important point with the Signal() and Wait() functions is that they use a 32 bit mask value – not an 8 bit signal bit number as used by AllocSignal() and FreeSignal(). The reason is due to the fact that Signal() and Wait() are designed to work with multiple signals and it is more efficient to provide a mask value rather that a series of bit numbers. The difference between the two representations is easily seen by looking at an example. Let's take the QUIT signal that we defined as bit 16:

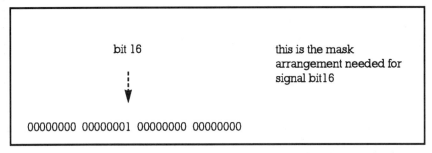

To convert the signal bit value to a mask we simply left-shift the number 1 an appropriate number of times. In C we use the << operator to achieve bit shifting, so typical code might look like this:

```
#define QUIT 16
mask = 1L << QUIT;   Wait(mask);
```

or simply:

```
#define QUIT 16
Wait(1L<<QUIT);
```

The Intuition programmers amongst you will doubtless have seen the single line of succinct, but somewhat obtuse, code used in

Using Exec Signals

many Intuition event handling loops:

```
Wait(1<<g_window_p -> UserPort ->mp_SigBit);
```

What this is doing is identifying the signal bit associated with an Intuition message port, converting it from a signal bit number to a 32 bit mask representation, and then Wait()ing on that mask.

Some Task Signal Communication Mechanics

In order for one task to be able to signal another it needs to know its address and Exec provides a Task search function, called FindTask(), which allows this to be obtained. FindTask() returns zero if it fails and so it is common for coders to combine the tasks name search with a conditional test like this:

```
if(child_task_p=FindTask("some task nameæ"))
    {
    /* if this is executed then task was found */


    }
```

Function Name:	FindTask()
Description:	Find the address of a task's Task control block
Call Format:	task_p=FindTask(task_name);
C Prototype:	struct Task * =FindTask(STRPTR);
Registers:	FindTask(D0 A1)
Arguments:	task_name - name of task to find or NULL to find yourself
Return Value:	pointer to the task structure or NULL if not found

Putting It All Together

What's needed at this point is some runable code and the next two examples, CH5-1.c and CH5-2.c provide a framework that you'll doubtless be able to use for further experimenting. Program CH5-1.c is what you might call the *main* task and its job is to locate program CH5-2 and send it some signals. For example purposes it uses a loop to transmit ten *do something* instructions, and then it sends a QUIT signal which tells the program to quit. CH5-2 is to all intents and purposes a *child* process. It allocates its signal bits and then uses a wait loop to watch for the setting of its two allocated signal bits. The loop exits as soon as a QUIT signal is detected but until that time the program executes the instructions provided in the loop code each time a PERFORM signal is received.

```
/* ============================================================ */
/*Listing 5.1: This program shows you one way to signal a
child process*/
/* Program name: CH5-1.c */
/* ---------------------------------------------------------- */
/* some includes... */
#include <stdio.h>
#include <exec/types.h>
#include <proto/all.h>
/* some prototypes... */
/* some defines... */
#define QUIT    16
#define PERFORM 17
/* ---------------------------------------------------------- */
main(int argc, char *argv[])
{
COUNT i;
struct Task *child_task_p;
if(child_task_p=FindTask("CH5-2"))
      {
      for(i=0;i<10;i++)
         {
         printf("signalling child task to perform\n");
         Signal(child_task_p,(1L<<PERFORM));
         }
      printf("signalling child task to quit\n");
      Signal(child_task_p,(1L<<QUIT));
      }
}
/* ---------------------------------------------------------- */


/* ============================================================ */
/*Listing 5.2: This code illustrates how a child process
can Wait() until a suitable signal is received before
doing anything.*/
/* Program name: CH5-2.c - the child process */
/* ---------------------------------------------------------- */
/* some includes... */
```

```
#include <stdio.h>
#include <exec/types.h>
#include <proto/all.h>
/* some defines... */
#define QUIT    16
#define PERFORM 17
/* some globals... */
/* ------------------------------------------------- */
main(int argc, char *argv[])
{
BOOL exit_flag=FALSE;
ULONG received_signals;printf("started\n");
if(AllocSignal(QUIT)==QUIT)
     {
     printf("quit signal bit allocated\n");
     if(AllocSignal(PERFORM)==PERFORM)
        {
        printf("perform signal bit allocated\n");
        while(!exit_flag)
           {
           received_signals=Wait((1L<<QUIT)|(1L<<PERFORM));
           if(received_signals&(1L<<PERFORM))
                printf("performing\n");
                else exit_flag=TRUE;
           }
        printf("quiting\n");
        FreeSignal(PERFORM);
        }
     FreeSignal(QUIT);
     }
}
/* ------------------------------------------------- */
```

ADT Stack Based Signal Allocation

In programs that use ADT stack resource allocation methods signal bits can be allocated and deallocated as part and parcel of the program setting up and closing down processes. The example CH5-3 code identifies the Workbench screen and then uses the timer device to flash the colour in colour register 3 (an arbitrary choice) using the colour identification and changing scheme similar to that already discussed. The program looks for a QUIT signal from an external program to tell it when to terminate and in this case the signals have been set up in the allocator.c module. Some additional signal bits (defined as ON and OFF) are, incidentally, also allocated and deallocated but these are not used – they were included just to provide further examples of the type of code required. The following pair of routines come from example CH5-3 allocator.c module that you'll find on disk:

```
/* ----------------------------------------------------- */
/*Listing 5.3: An example fragment from a typical alloca-
tor module*/
UBYTE AllocateQuitSignal(void)
{
UBYTE error_number=NO_ERROR;
if(AllocSignal(QUIT)!=QUIT) error_number=STARTUP_ERROR;
else {
      g_function=ReleaseQuitSignal;
      PushStack(g_resource_stack_p,g_function);
      }
return(error_number);
}
/* ----------------------------------------------------- */
void ReleaseOnSignal(void) { FreeSignal(ON);    }
/* ----------------------------------------------------- */
```

The overall plans of the main.c and allocator.c modules, use of the stack ADT etc, will be familiar from earlier discussions but there are a few areas of code that may be of interest in the amiga.c module. Firstly, notice how the program finds the address of its own Task structure by supplying a NULL task name:

```
self_p=FindTask(NULL);
```

The amiga.c module contains what you might call the real 'guts' of the program and this uses a loop which firstly looks to see whether a QUIT signal has been received and, if it hasn't, executes a delay and then switches the colour register contents using the methods described earlier. Because in this case we're not Wait()ing on a signal, some other means has to be used to see whether the QUIT signal has been set. I've done this by looking directly at the tc_SigRecvd field of the program's Task structure, so the basis of the loop ends up looking like this:

```
while(!(self_p->tc_SigRecvd&(1L<<QUIT)))
    {
```

Using Exec Signals

```
        /* do the colour flashing code */
        }
```

Here's the flashing code for the amiga.c module of example CH5-3 so that you can see the overall framework being used:

```c
/* ------------------------------------------------ */
/*Listing 5.4: Part of the example CH5-3 code that you'll
find on disk*/
/* amiga.c - child process code */
#include "general.h"
#define COLOUR_REG   3
UBYTE AmigaProg(void)
{
struct Task *self_p;
UBYTE error_number=NO_ERROR;
UBYTE  red, green, blue, toggle=FALSE;
UWORD  colour_value;
self_p=FindTask(NULL);
colour_value=GetRGB4(g_viewport_p->ColorMap,COLOUR_REG);
red   = (colour_value&0x0F00)>>8;
green = (colour_value&0x00F0)>>4;
blue= colour_value&0x000F;
while(!(self_p->tc_SigRecvd&(1L<<QUIT)))
      {
      SetTimer(DELAY,0);
      if(toggle)
         {
         SetRGB4(g_viewport_p,COLOUR_REG,red,green,blue);
         toggle=FALSE;
         }
      else {
           SetRGB4(g_viewport_p,COLOUR_REG,0,0,0);
           /* set to black */
           toggle=TRUE;
           }
      }
SetRGB4(g_viewport_p,COLOUR_REG,red,green,blue);
/* restore colours */
return(error_number);
```

```
        }
/* ------------------------------------------------------ */
```

When you run example CH5-3 you'll find the borders of the active window on the Workbench will flash. To turn off the effect the program needs to be sent a QUIT signal and program CH5-4 shown in listing 5.5 is a short utility which does just that:

```
/* ====================================================== */
/*Listing 5.5:The test program that signals the child
process*/
/* Program name: CH5-4.c */
/* ------------------------------------------------------ */
/* some includes... */
#include <stdio.h>
#include <exec/types.h>
#include <proto/all.h>
/* some prototypes... */
/* some defines... */
#define    QUIT              18
/* ------------------------------------------------------ */
main(int argc, char *argv[])
{
struct Task *child_task_p;
if(child_task_p=FindTask("Test"))
      {
      printf("signalling child task to quit\n");
      Signal(child_task_p,(1L<<QUIT));
      }
}
/* ------------------------------------------------------ */
```

Aiming For A More General Colour Flashing Solution

Now that you've got to the end of this chapter I've a confession to make – this chapter was really just a stepping stone to greater things because understanding how tasks can communicate via signal arrangements will hopefully make the issues discussed in the next chapter a little easier to get to grips with. Task signalling has many legitimate uses but these signals are effectively just a way of setting Boolean type, ie single bit based, information which obviously limits their usefulness as a general means of program communication.

Using Exec Signals

The examples were contrived to illustrate a point and we got away with flashing Workbench screen colours because both processes were able to identify the Workbench screen address and so determine, and manipulate, the appropriate colour map. For simplicity I hard coded the colour register information, and the delay time, into the program doing the colour flashing but this approach obviously lacks generality.

It would be far better if we could pass to the colour flashing program details of which colour map to use, which register to flash, what time delay value to use and so on. This is what the next chapter is all about.

6: Getting Your Programs to Talk to Each Other

The inter-program communications facilities used by ARexx, the Intuition and Gadtools libraries and so on have all been built upon the general message–based communications arrangements provided by Exec. In this chapter I want to look in detail at these arrangements and show how the messaging system can be used within your own programs. By way of example a background program will be developed which is able to create flashing effects on another programs screen as and when it is asked to do so by appropriate messages. Because the background process will actually be *kicked off*, ie started, by some main program that wants to flash one of its screen colours I'll be talking about the colour flashing program as a *child* process. In short the main program will run the child process and then send it messages that give it the information needed to produce a specified flashing effect (the child process will carry out these necessary colour flashing chores automatically, and quite independently, from the main program). Before the main program terminates it will send a message to the child process telling it that it also should terminate. The benefit of this type of arrangement is flexibility – a single *flash* program can be used by all programs wishing to create flashing colours.

Before examining the code in detail however we need to know something about the Exec messaging system itself. Under the Exec arrangements, information can be sent from one task to another by creating a data packet known as a Message structure and then transmitting it (sending it) to its destination. Messages pass between tasks using another Exec defined structure called a MsgPort, more commonly called a *message port* or just a *port*. Ports are basically software entities whose job, amongst other things, is to act as a receiving station for messages. Before a program can receive a message it must have allocated and initialized a suitable mesage port.

Here's the definition of a port as a C structure:

```
struct MsgPort        {
struct Node      mp_Node;
UBYTE            mp_Flags;
UBYTE            mp_SigBit;
struct Task *mp_SigTask;
struct List mp_MsgList;
};
```

mp_Node is a standard Exec Node structure and mp_MsgList is an Exec list structure used to create a linked list of messages associated with the port. As new messages arrive they are added to the end of the list. As messages are read they are taken from the front (head) of the list. The mp_Flags field is used to indicate various message arrival actions and mp_SigTask field identifies the task to be signalled as messages arrive.

Adding Data To A Message Structure

Messages themselves are based on an extensible length structure with the Exec defined fields being suplemented by additional user defined data. Here's the basic layout.

```
struct Message {
struct Node          mn_Node;
struct MsgPort       *mn_ReplyPort;
UWORD                mn_Length;
};
```

The Node structure is used for port linkage, the mn_ReplyPort field indicates which port the reply will be sent to (see discussion which follows), and the mn_Length field indicates the total length of the message. The real message data is always provided as an extension, usually by defining a new structure in terms of a Message plus other data.

For our example we are interested in creating a program that can handle the job of flashing the colour of a particular colour register associated with a specified ViewPort. To do this we need to know the address of the ViewPort, the frequency with which the colour is to be flashed, and the colour register value. We also need a command field so that, at the very least, the flash effect can be turned on and off and the flash program told when to quit. This is the message structure I chose to adopt for the example program:

```
struct FlashMessage  {
struct Message    flash_Msg; /* standard Message details */
struct ViewPort   *viewport; /* will provide access to a
              *           ColorMap*/
ULONG             frequency; /* colour changes per minute */
UBYTE             colour_reg; /* register to change */
UBYTE             command; /* command to be executed */
};
```

Now that we've seen what messages are in terms of physical blocks of memory let's look at how these structures are used If the main program sends the child program a message it does so by using an Exec system call known as PutMsg(). This adds the message into a linked list of messages which are tied to the child program's port structure. The important point about this process is that the message is *not* copied. In other words it is the memory block associated with the main program's message which is linked into the list of messages present at the child program's message port. Technically this is known as queuing by reference and its main advantage is that the very substantial overhead of creating local copies of each and every message floating around the Amiga system is avoided. In a sense then when the main program allocates, initializes and then sends the child program some message... what the main program is really doing is giving the child program a licence to use part of its memory space.

Now this is all very well but the scheme presents a number of potential difficulties. Let's go over the main program -> child program message passing scenario once more to see what problems can occur. The main program wants to send the child program a message so it allocates some memory for a message, fills in the appropriate details and then *sends* the message to the child program using Exec's PutMsg() function. (The main program will need to know the address of the child program's message port at this time but a system call is available for finding such information). By the time the main program's PutMsg() call has completed we've developed a quite dangerous situation: the main program has allocated some message memory and at some stage it is going to have to deallocate it, ie return it to the system free memory pool. *But*: once the PutMsg() function has 'sent' the message the backward and forward pointing Node fields of the memory block containing the message will have been altered so that the message, is linked into the child program's message list. If the main program terminated, or decided for any other reason to deallocate its message unit, serious problems would arise. In short: the child program's message list would become corrupt and the system would GURU shortly afterwards!

What is needed is a convention which eliminates this type of problem. The method that Exec has adopted is as follows: The main program, in sending a message to the child process, is effectively granting a temporary licence to the child to use part of its memory space (that relating to the message). Once this licence has been granted the main program should not interfer with the message until it is safe to do so. How does it know when its message can be re-used or discarded? Usually the child process will send the message back to the main program using Exec's ReplyMsg() function. This later function links the message (with a suitable reply ID marker) into the main program's message port and, when the main program reads this, it knows that the message is finished with.

The main program is then free to re-use that memory space as it sees fit. Note that the main program in the above scenario, does *not* reply to the message it receives – this is because the main program was the originator of the message. Because the message originator usually needs to be told when a message has been dealt with both communicating programs need their own message ports – despite the fact that, as in the above example, the passage of real information is only going one way.

From a practical viewpoint there are a few things worth mentioning about the routines you'll find described in the function detail box outs. GetMsg() unlinks the first message from a port and after it has been used the associated message is essentially *free floating* and not pointer-linked into the message chain of that port. If the program which receives a message subsequently executes a ReplyMsg() then this of course ties that message into the message list of the program which sent the message in the first place. This has to be removed from the message list like any other message by using the GetMsg() function.

Programs Talking to Each Other

Function Name:	**PutMsg()**
Description:	Send a message to a message port
Call Format:	PutMsg(port_p, message_p);
C Prototype:	void PutMsg(struct MsgPort*, struct Message *);
Registers:	PutMsg(A0, A1)
Arguments:	port_p - pointer to a message port message_p - pointer to a message
Return Value:	None
Notes:	This function can singal tasks and cause software interrupts to occur. The action is dependent on the flags set in the mp_Flags field of the destination port (see RKM manuals for further details).

Function Name:	**ReplyMsg()**
Description:	Send a message back to its reply port
Call Format:	ReplyMsg(message_p);
C Prototype:	void ReplyMsg(struct Message *);
Registers:	ReplyMsg(A1)
Arguments:	message_p - pointer to a message
Return Value:	None
Notes:	This function is a bit like PutMsg() in that it links the message into a message port. To indicate that it is a reply however this function places the NT_REPLYMSG flag into the message's ln_Type field.

Function Name:	**GetMsg()**
Description:	Collect first message queued at message port
Call Format:	message_p=GetMsg(port_p);
C Prototype:	truct Message *GetMsg(struct MsgPort *);
Registers:	D0 GetMsg(A0)
Arguments:	port_p - pointer to a message portReturn
Value:	message_p - pointer to a message
Notes:	This function does not wait. If a message is not available it will return with a NULL value

Now if we add these details to the steps which occur as two programs communicate we end up with this scheme:

Main Program	*Child Process*
1: Allocates memory for message	
2: Fills in relevant field details	
3: Sends Message using PutMsg()	
4:	Collects message using GetMsg()
5:	Extracts data from message
6:	Sends back message using ReplyMsg()
7: Receives reply using GetMsg()	
8: Re-uses/deallocates message	

Table 6.1. Communication Scheme.

You may have noticed that although I have said that one program collects the message that another program sends, nothing has been said about how the receiving program knows that another program has sent it a message. As you have probably guessed from the material in the last chapter this is done using the Exec signalling system. The good news for this chapter is that at the message communications level the nitty-gritty details of signal allocation, deallocation and management are handled automatically by the Exec message support functions. So we don't have to worry about them!

The Use Of Multiple Message Ports

In theory at least it's possible for a program to work with just a single message port but this does not always lead to the best results in practice. The reason is that as messages arrive at a port they get queued up in FIFO (first in first out) order regardless of importance. This can sometimes mean that a message of relatively minor importance could be sitting, waiting for collection, whilst a far more important message was queued up behind it. Usually the delays in handling compound message streams can be kept low but on occasion it might be necessary to open additional ports just for handling messages of particular importance.

The general program framework being used for the examples in this book makes use of an Intuition window that already has two associated message ports – one is used by Intuition and the other (the window's User Port) is used for handling the IntuiMessage and GadTool messages received by the program. To communicate with the Flash program we'll be opening another message port because these messages will be easier to use if they come in as an isolated stream of FlashMessages rather than being possibly mixed up with other classes of message.

Setting Up A Message Port

In order for our main program to communicate with the child colour flashing process, a message port is neeeded for the 'I have finished with the message' reply messages that come back from the child. Since Release 2 of the Amiga's O/S there are both amiga.lib and Exec functions available for creating and deleting message ports and the pair of routines shown in listing 6.1 are the allocator/deallocator functions for a reply port based on the Exec style routines:

```
/* -------------------------------------------------- */
/*Listing 6.1: Functions to allocate and deallocate a
reply port in the main program.*/
UBYTE CreateReplyPort(void)

{
UBYTE error_number=NO_ERROR;

if((g_reply_port_p=CreateMsgPort())==NULL)
       error_number=STARTUP_ERROR;
   else {
       g_function=DeleteReplyPort;
       PushStack(g_resource_stack_p,g_function);
       }
return(error_number);
}
/* -------------------------------------------------- */
void DeleteReplyPort(void){DeleteMsgPort(g_reply_port_p);
}
/* -------------------------------------------------- */
```

Sending a Message

The routine that provides flash control within the main program is going to revolve around the use of just four commands - FLASH_SETUP, FLASH ON, FLASH_OFF and FLASH_QUIT. Of these the first is used only by the main program to indicate that the message needs to be initialised, the remainder are real commands that need to be passed to the external child process that will be doing the colour flashing operations. Listing 6.2 shows a rough plan of the routine that will be used. Listing 6.3 shows the routine in detail (notice that in this example a static structure declaration – static struct FlashMessage flash; – has been used to create the FlashMessage).

```
/* -------------------------------------------------- */
/*Listing 6.2: Skeleton of a routine for sending child
process a 'flash' message.*/
```

```
UBYTE Flash(UBYTE command)
{
if(command==FLASH_SETUP)
        {
        Set up message structure in readiness for
        sending messages
        }
    else {
        Transmit message to child using PutMsg()
        Use the WaitPort() function wait for child to
        confirm use of message
        Use GetMsg() to retrieve reply indicating that
        message is ready for re-use
        }
}
/* -------------------------------------------------- */


/* -------------------------------------------------- */
/*Listing 6.3: An example routine for sending the child
process a 'flash' message.*/
UBYTE Flash(UBYTE command)
{
UBYTE error_number=NO_ERROR;
static struct FlashMessage flash;
if(command==FLASH_SETUP)
        {
        flash.flash_Msg.mn_Length=sizeof(struct
FlashMessage);
        flash.flash_Msg.mn_ReplyPort=g_reply_port_p;
        flash.viewport=g_viewport_p;
        flash.frequency=FLASH_FREQUENCY;
        flash.colour_reg=FLASH_REGISTER;
        }
    else {
        flash.flash_Msg.mn_Node.ln_Type=NT_MESSAGE;
        flash.command=command;
        PutMsg(g_msgport_p,(struct Message *)&flash);
        WaitPort(g_reply_port_p); /* wait for Flash
        program to confirm use */
```

```
            GetMsg(g_reply_port_p); /* message now ready for
            re-use */
            }
    return(error_number);
    }
    /* ------------------------------------------------------- */
```

Some Main Program Coding Issues

For a main program to safely talk a to a child process using FlashMessages we need to allow for the fact that since the child process is a separate entity, ie a runable program in its own right, it may not actually be found when we attempt to run it. The way I tackle this is to include the attempted running of the child process in my normal allocation/deallocation framework and in the CH 6-1 example you'll see this function pointer control block defined:

```
    UBYTE (*display_list[])() = {
            OpenInt,
            OpenGraphics,
            OpenGadtools,
            LockScreen,
            GetVisInfo,
            CreateWindow,
            CreateMenu,
            CreateMenuLayout,
            InstallMenu,
            CreateReplyPort,
            RunFlash
            };
```

Once the library, screen, window, menu and reply port creation jobs have been successfully carried out, the routine shown in listing 6.4 is performed. This tries to run the *flash* program using the DOS SystemTags() function like this:

```
    SystemTags("run FLASH:flash >NIL: <NIL:",TAG_DONE);
```

I've coded this assuming that a logical FLASH: assignment is in place that tells the main program where to find the Flash utility program. If, for example, the flash program was to be placed in the command (c:) directory you would need to use

```
    1> assign FLASH: c:
```

to tell the main program where the flash utility could be found.

How do we tell whether the flash program really does get found and started or not? We just look to see whether its message port can be detected using the Exec FindPort() function like this:

```
Forbid();
g_msgport_p=FindPort(DESTINATION_PORT_NAME);
Permit();
if (!g_msgport_p) error_number=STARTUP_ERROR;
else {
```

Notice here that Exec Forbid() and Permit() calls have been used to sandwich the FindPort() call. This is important because it allows us to lock out other tasks and so prevent any alteration of Exec's port list whilst our program is examining it.

Providing the port is found, which we detect by seeing a non-NULL pointer being returned by the FindPort() function, we set up the fields of the program's FlashMessage structure using a Flash(FLASH_SETUP) call and at this point we know that the child process is up and running. The corresponding deallocation routine just performs the call: Flash(FLASH_EXIT) thereby transmitting a message to the flash program telling it to shut itself down.

```
/* -------------------------------------------------- */
/*Listing 6.4: Checking for the child message port is a
safe way for checking the childs existence.*/
UBYTE RunFlash(void)
{
UBYTE error_number=NO_ERROR;
SystemTags("run FLASH:flash >NIL: <NIL:",TAG_DONE);
Forbid();
g_msgport_p=FindPort(DESTINATION_PORT_NAME);
Permit();
if (!g_msgport_p) error_number=STARTUP_ERROR;
else {
     g_function=KillFlash;
     PushStack(g_resource_stack_p,g_function);
     Flash(FLASH_SETUP);
     }
return(error_number);
}
/* -------------------------------------------------- */
void KillFlash(void){Flash(FLASH_EXIT);}
/* -------------------------------------------------- */
```

The Colour Flashing Program Itself

The child process that performs the colour flashing is an independent program in its own right. From a logical viewpoint it works in much the same way as the colour flashing routines we've already looked with the main difference being that it gets its commands via FlashMessages from an external source. In order to do this the child process must also have a message port available and, as listing 6.5 shows, this is set up in a similar way to that described earlier:

```
/* ------------------------------------------------ */
/*Listing 6.5: Port creation routines for the child
process*/
UBYTE CreateCommandPort()
{
UBYTE error_number=NO_ERROR;
if((g_command_port_p=CreateMsgPort())==NULL)
        error_number=STARTUP_ERROR;
   else {
        g_function=DeleteCommandPort;
        PushStack(g_resource_stack_p,g_function);
        }
return(error_number);
}
/* ------------------------------------------------ */
void DeleteCommandPort(){DeleteMsgPort(g_command_port_p);
}
/* ------------------------------------------------ */
```

In this case however the port needs to be added to Exec's *public ports* list. When the amiga.lib CreatePort() routine is used this is done automatically but with the Exec style functions it has to be done by the program itself using the Exec AddPort() function.

```
/* ------------------------------------------------ */
/*Listing 6.6: Making the command port of the child
process public.*/
UBYTE MakeCommandPortPublic(void)
{
UBYTE error_number=NO_ERROR;
g_command_port_p->mp_Node.ln_Name=COMMAND_PORT_NAME;
AddPort(g_command_port_p);
g_function=RemovePublicCommandPort;
```

```
        PushStack(g_resource_stack_p,g_function);
        return(error_number);
        }
        /* ------------------------------------------------ */
        void RemovePublicCommandPort(void)
        {
        RemPort(g_command_port_p);
        }
        /* ------------------------------------------------ */
```

These routines, like all allocator/deallocator function pairs, are controlled by a function pointer list and for the flash program this looks like this:

```
        UBYTE (*allocator_list[])() = {
                OpenGraphics,
                CreateTimerReplyPort,
                CreateTimerRequestBlock,
                OpenTimer,
                CreateCommandPort,
                MakeCommandPortPublic
                };
```

The graphics library is needed because the GetRGB4() and SetRGB4() are used to get and set colour values. The timer entries are used to set up the Amiga's timer device, and the last two entries produce the command port that we've been discussing. Listing 6.7 shows the code for the complete colour flashing routine:

```
        /* ------------------------------------------------ */
        /*Listing 6.7: The child process colour flashing routine.*/
        /* amiga.c - child process code for colour flashing */
        #include "general.h"
        static UBYTE  red, green, blue, toggle;
        static UWORD  colour_value;
        UBYTE AmigaProg(void)
        {
        UBYTE  colour_reg, command, error_number=NO_ERROR;
        ULONG  secs,microsecs,frequency;
        struct Message *message_p;
        struct ViewPort *viewport_p;
        do {
```

Programs talking ot each other

```
      WaitPort(g_command_port_p);
      while (message_p=GetMsg(g_command_port_p))
          {
          command=((struct FlashMessage *)message_p)->command;
          viewport_p=((struct FlashMessage *)message_p)->
                      viewport;
          colour_reg=((struct FlashMessage *)message_p)-
                      >colour_reg;
          frequency=((struct FlashMessage *)message_p)->
                      frequency;
          ReplyMsg(message_p);
          secs=60/frequency;
          microsecs=(60*1000000/frequency)%1000000;
          switch(command)
              {
              case FLASH_ON:    FlashOn(viewport_p,colour_reg,
                                      secs,microsecs);
                                break;
              case FLASH_OFF:   FlashOff(viewport_p,colour_reg);
                                break;
              case FLASH_EXIT:  FlashOff(viewport_p,colour_reg);
                                error_number=PROGRAM_EXIT;
                                break;
              default:          break;
              }
          }
      }
   while(error_number!=PROGRAM_EXIT);return(
   error_number);
}
/* -------------------------------------------------- */
void FlashOn(struct ViewPort *viewport_p,UBYTE
colour_reg,ULONG secs,ULONG micros)
{
BOOL exit_flag=FALSE;
toggle=FALSE;
colour_value=GetRGB4(viewport_p->ColorMap,colour_reg);
red  = (colour_value&0x0F00)>>8;
green = (colour_value&0x00F0)>>4;
blue= colour_value&0x000F;
while(!exit_flag)
```

```
       {
       if(!IsMsgPortEmpty(g_command_port_p)) exit_flag=TRUE;
       else {
              SetTimer(secs,micros);
              if(toggle)
                 {
                 SetRGB4(viewport_p,colour_reg,red,green,blue);
                 toggle=FALSE;
                 }
          else {
                 SetRGB4(viewport_p,colour_reg,0,0,0);
                 toggle=TRUE;
                 }
              }
       }
}
/* ------------------------------------------------- */
void FlashOff(struct ViewPort *viewport_p,UBYTE colour_reg)
{
SetRGB4(viewport_p,colour_reg,red,green,blue);
}
/* ------------------------------------------------- */
```

Using the Flash Utility

The thing to remember about the approach that we've adopted in this chapter is that the Flash program can now be regarded as a general utility. Any program that needs to use a flashing colour can just set up a reply port, run the flash program and then control the required effects by sending the program the appropriate FlashMessages. For the example associated with this chapter I've just used the routine to flash one of the Workbench screen colours but you'll doubtless be able to think of more interesting uses of this approach in your own projects.

7: Copper Lists: What They Are and How They Work

The Amiga, as you will doubtless know, contains a display co-processor unit, or 'Copper', which can control almost the entire graphics hardware and can manipulate most of the machine's hardware registers. The Copper is able to wait for particular video beam positions and then alter screen colours, re-position sprites, control the blitter and even generate interrupts. What's more it is able to do all of this magic without requiring assistance from the main 680x0 processor because it has DMA (Direct Memory Access) capability.

Copper programs are called Copper lists and they come in two basic forms known as hardware Copper lists and intermediate Copper lists. Hardware Copper lists are the final (usewable) lists of instructions and pointers to these lists are loaded into the Copper registers during vertical blanking interrupt operations. Hardware lists have two important characteristics. Firstly, they have to be held in chip memory because they need to be directly accessed by the Copper. Secondly, they have to be sorted so that the beam co-ordinates of successive instructions are in order of increasing video beam positions since that is the way the hardware expects to find them.

Intermediate Copper lists are effectively just parts of a complete Copper program. The types of instructions they contain are the same as those found in the hardware lists but, because they are not directly read by the

Copper, they do not need to be held in chip memory. These intermediate lists must be merged into a real hardware Copper list before they can be used to create a display. In other words they must be sorted and placed into chip memory! There are a number of functions for achieving this but it is also possible to 'hand craft' your Copper lists by piecing them together, already sorted, directly in chip memory. You sit down with a piece of paper, sketch out the instructions, arrange them in an appropriate order, and write them into your program as data statements if you are an assembler coder, or as, say the contents of a UWORD array if you are coding in C. Hand crafted lists are more difficult, or at least more time consuming, to produce but lots of demo and game coders do this sort of thing to save space. User Copper lists incidentally, which you'll find mentioned in the next chapter, are intermediate Copper lists.

Copper programming is still surrounded by an air of *mystique*. Public domain demos, and there is plenty of good code available, should have been a rich source of Copper list examples but unfortunately much of the documentation for such code is either poor or non-existent. It's a pity because it means that no matter how stunning the effects the code itself, certainly to a newcomer, is unlikely to make much sense. This, to say the very least, can be very frustrating to someone wanting to learn how to write such programs. I'm not going to kid you that the more sophisticated tricks, such as using the Copper to control the blitter, are not complicated. But I do believe however that a brief explanation of the instructions and essential system routines, coupled to some detailed assembler and C examples, will help get you on the right road as far as experimenting goes. This chapter in the main will deal with the underlying ideas and provide an introduction to the assembler side of things. The following chapter will look at a detailed example involving Intuition coding from C.

The Copper Instruction Set

Most people are surprised when they first learn that the Copper has only three instructions, Skip, Wait, and Move. All instructions are two words long and the official documentation tends to label the first word as IR1 and the second as IR2. Here are some instruction details:

SKIP: jump over the next instruction if the video beam has reached a given (x,y) screen position.

Bit 0 of word, IR1, is always set to 1 in a wait instruction. Bits 1-7 hold the horizontal beam co-ordinate and bits 8-15 hold the vertical beam co-ordinate. The instruction skips the next instruction if the beam counter is equal to or greater than the combined 15 bit horizontal + vertical values given in the instruction. The second word, IR2, has bit 0 set to 1. Bits 1-7 are the horizontal beam co-ordinate compare enable bits and bits 8-14 are vertical compare enable bits (these are most commonly used to mask off and so ignore either the vertical or horizontal postion counters). Under most circumstances all enable bits are set to 1. Bit 15 of IR2 is a blitter-finished-disable bit and this is also normally set to 1. Skip is used far less frequently than the other two Copper instructions.

WAIT: wait for a specific (x,y) screen position.

This instruction causes the Copper to wait until the video beam position counters are equal to, or greater than, the (x,y) values specified in the instruction. Bit 0 of word, IR1, is always set to 1 in a wait instruction. Bits 1-7 hold the horizontal beam co-ordinate and bits 8-15 hold the vertical beam co-ordinate. The second word, IR2, has bit 0 set to 0. Bits 1-7 are the horizontal beam co-ordinate compare enable bits and bits 8-14 are vertical compare enable bits (these are most commonly used to mask off and so ignore either the vertical or horizontal position counters). Under most circumstances all enable bits are set to 1. Bit 15 of IR2 is a blitter-finished-disable bit and this is also normally set to 1.

An example? If we wanted the Copper to wait until the display reached line 100 (100=64 hex) we'd use this instruction:

```
dc.w $6401,$ff00 wait until line 100 (ignoring horizontal
counters)
```

MOVE: move some data from chip memory into one of the Amiga's hardware registers.

This instruction causes the Copper to move a specified data value into a register. Bit 0 of word, IR1, is always set to 0 in a move instruction. Bits 1-8 hold the destination address. Bits 9-15 are unused but should be set to zero. The second word, IR2, holds the data being transferred.

Supposing, for example, that we want to load the hardware registers $180, $182, $184 and $186 with the value $000f, $0fff, $00f0, and $0f00 respectively, we'd use these Copper instructions:

```
dc.w $180,$000f
dc.w $182,$0fff
dc.w $184,$00f0
dc.w $186,$0f00
```

Easy enough to do but you're probably thinking that the numbers themselves are not making much sense? At this point we need to talk a little about the Amiga's hardware registers; these are the memory mapped hardware addresses which represent things like the colour registers, bitplane pointers and a host of other control locations. All registers are given symbolic names and the hardware/custom.i include file provides these defined as register address offsets from a base custom chip base address of $dff000.

The $180 value is actually the offset for colour register 0, the base of the Amiga's 32 colour registers and in the hardware/custom.i include file this offset is called *color*. By using this symbolic name we can write the previous example instructions in this more readable fashion:

```
dc.w color+0,$000f
dc.w color+2,$0fff
dc.w color+4,$00f0
dc.w color+6,$0f00
```

In fact with a few well chosen EQUates we can improve things even more:

```
BLUE  EQU   $000f
WHITE EQU   $0fff
GREEN EQU   $00f0
RED   EQU   $0f00


dc.w color+0,BLUE
dc.w color+2,WHITE
dc.w color+4,GREEN
dc.w color+6,RED
```

It's now pretty obvious that what we are doing here is jamming RGB colour values into the hardware colour registers. Each register address is a word apart so the above code is setting register 0 to blue, register 1 to white, register 2 to green and register 3 to red. Copper lists written in this form are relatively easy to fathom out but unfortunately a lot of example code tends to be written just as a series of numbers. This bring us to quite an important part as far as deciphering other coder's Copper lists is concerned – you'll often need to *diassemble* lists and re-write them in more readable fashion just to understand what they mean. To do this you need to be familiar with the general forms of the Copper list instructions in order to work out what each instruction is doing.

Terminating A Copper List

Copper instruction lists, for reasons that we won't go into (but basically it's the only way to stop the thing), *must* terminate with a display position wait that can never occur. A wait for horizontal position 254 on line 255 has been the standard instruction used and as a data statement this looks like this:

```
dc.w $FFFF,$FFFE
```

Getting Things Into Perspective

If you are new to both assembler coding and Copper list creation then learning about both at the same time is a bit like trying to ride a bike at the same time as you are trying to build it. This being so I'm going to devote quite a lot of space to the assembler side of things in the hope that once you've seen how the various pieces of a complete example program fit together you'll be encouraged to pull apart other example programs that you come across. We're going to piece together an example that allocates some display memory and creates a screen for displaying some graphics. In order to do this we'll need to open the graphics library and so library use is the first item on the agenda.

Using Run-Time Libraries From Assembler Code

As you'll doubtless know Exec supports the idea of run time libraries which exist separately and are written in a way which allows any number of different programs to use them simultaneously (or at least appear to do so within Exec's multi-tasking framework) and this obviously makes them much more flexible and efficient.

Programs tell Exec that a library is needed by attempting to *open* it using an OpenLibrary() function. When such a call is made Exec does several things: it searches its lists of libraries which are already open and available. If the library is found then Exec simply returns the address of the library and makes an internal note that another program is now using it. If the library is not already open, Exec passes on the request to AmigaDOS asking it to look for, and then load, the specified library. AmigaDOS looks in the LIBS: logical device (if you boot from the Workbench disk for instance then this logical device will have been assigned to SYS:LIBS, ie the LIBS directory of the Workbench disk). If AmigaDOS finds the library it loads it and tells Exec where it has been placed. Exec then records the fact that the library is now available by adding it to its list of *available* libraries. Exec will never attempt to remove these library modules whilst they are in use but should the last user of a particular active library indicate that they no longer need access to the routines, which they do by executing a CloseLibrary() function, Exec's library manager may then remove the memory copy of library and release the associated memory so that it is free for other use.

As all of this happens a lot of complex operations get carried out but the good news is that from assembler, like C, you don't need to worry about this at all – as far as an applications program is concerned most of these operations are transparent and this is so even at the assembly language programming level. All a program has to do to use a given library is open it using the Exec OpenLibrary() function, and then use the library routines in much the same way that the OpenLibrary() function was itself used. The only thing which the applications program must do is ensure that the OpenLibrary() call was successful and it does this by checking that the address returned is non-NULL (ie not zero). If the address returned has a zero value then the system hasn't been able to open the library.

I've already mentioned that the first stage in using a library is to open it by using the Exec OpenLibrary() function. You may now be wondering how it is possible to open the Exec library in the first place. The simple answer is that you do not need to because the Exec library never has to be opened. Exec's base address, known conventionally as SysBase, is permanently available because it is stored in the long-word memory location whose first byte is at location 4. The four bytes which make up this long word location are called AbsExecBase and because this is loaded with a pointer to the Exec library during system start-up: the Exec library is always alive and kicking from the word go. So, how do we make a library call? By convention we place the base address of the library in register a6, and then make an indirect subroutine call using the appropriate library vector offset (LVO) value to specify the routine to be executed. Indirect subroutine calls of this type are very important on the Amiga and they're used because the arrangement is connected with the way the Amiga library functions are accessed internally (these explanations involve some pretty advanced topics including the use of things called jump tables which are not going to be discussed). What happens as far as the indirect subroutine call with displacement is concerned is that the address in the specified address register gets added to the specified LVO function call displacement and this produces a destination subroutine address that leads us to the right library function.

Now that the mechanics of library function call use has been explained the code which performs the graphics library opening will be easy to understand. I've already mentioned that in the case of the Exec library the base address is already available in AbsExecBase. The bare bones code for an OpenLibrary() Exec call can therefore be written like this:

```
move.l  _AbsExecBase,a6     get base address of Exec library
jsr     _LVOOpenLibrary(a6) make the indirect subroutine call
```

Before this sort of code can be executed it is of course necessary to set up any parameters which the library function needs. If you look back at the OpenLibrary() function you'll see that it needs a pointer to a library name in register a1, and a version number in d0. For the moment I'll be setting the d0 to zero because this tells Exec that *any* library version will do. Closing a Library, incidentally, is just as easy as opening it. You use the same type of indirect subroutine call, but specify the CloseLibrary() function instead:

```
move.l  _AbsExecBase, a6   get base address of Exec library
jsr     _LVOCloseLibrary(a6) make the indirect subroutine
call
```

Failed Open Library Calls

Why would a library fail to open? The system might not have been able to find it on disk, the specified version might not be available, the programmer might simply have spelt its name wrong within the program, or the system might even be running out of memory and have insufficient space to load a new library. The important point is that you must not make any library function calls unless you have got a valid base pointer or you will doubtless get a visit from the Amiga guru!0

Function Name:	OpenLibrary()
Description:	Open a run-time library
Call Format:	base_address=OpenLibrary(library_name, version);
C Prototype:	struct Library *OpenLibrary(STRPTR, ULONG);
Registers:	D0 A1 D0
Arguments:	library_name - the address of a null terminated string version - a library version number
Return Value:	base_address - the address of the base of the library. If the library could not be opened a NULL value is returned.
Notes:	User must not attempt to use any library functions if this function did not succeeded.

Function Name:	CloseLibrary()
Description:	Close a previously successfully opened library
Call Format:	CloseLibrary(base_address);
C Prototype:	void CloseLibrary(struct Library *);
Registers:	A1
Arguments:	base_address - the library base addressReturn
Value:	None
Notes:	User must not make library calls to a library after it has been closed.

Prefixes

You'll notice in the above code fragment that AbsExecBase and the LVO value have underscore prefixes. This stems from an internal C language convention and the underscore used in all assembly language forms has been introduced simply to provide compatibility between C and assembler header files and code. Not all programmers use these underscore arrangements but it's a good habit to cultivate because it will be useful when you come to more advanced coding.

Library Vector Offset (LVO) Values

LVO offset values can be acquired in a number of ways but for the moment we'll be putting LVO definitions at the start of our programs because it is easiest. The LVO value for the Exec OpenLibrary() function is -552, ie -0228 hex and so the assembly language programmer is quite at liberty to define the displacement in this fashion:

```
move.l   _AbsExecBase, a6    get the base address of Exec library

jsr      552(a6)             make the indirect subroutine call
```

The trouble is that with this latter approach however is that you loose the inherent documentation that the LVO references provide. Let's face it the number -552 doesn't, unless you've memorised all of the LVO tables, exactly tell you what library call is being made. The reference _LVOOpenLibrary is much more meaningful.

First Coding Stages

If we can get to the point where all the library opening and closing stuff is in place and most of the code is understandable then the subsequent Copper list code can be discussed in relative isolation and this should make things easier to understand. To get to this first stage we'll need to set up a null terminated text string representing the name of the graphics library. We'll also need a labelled long word location to store the base address of the library once it is open. Here's the sort of pseudo-ops which do the trick:

```
graphics_name dc.b 'graphics.library', NULL

_GfxBase ds.l 1
```

I'll be placing these at the end of my program and between these directives and the initial EQUate definitions will come the real code (the stuff that the assembler will turn into executable instructions). Talking of real code let's identify a suitable plan-of-action: we've got to load the address of the Exec library into register a6, set up the intuition library name pointer and version details, and then make an OpenLibrary() call as explained earlier. If the value returned in d0 is not zero then the graphics library will be open. How do we test d0 to check whether it contains a zero or not? Simple, we use a move instruction to copy the contents of d0 to the location that we've set up to hold the graphics library pointer this move sets or clears the processor's zero flag. Remember that if the library does open successfully we'll need this pointer in order to perform the CloseLibrary() routine before the program terminates. It's important to realise that, if for some reason the library does *not* open then we must *not* use the Exec CloseLibrary() function because there'll be no

Copper Listing

library to close. Similarly we must not make any graphics library calls if the library did not open. As you might guess this calls for a bit of *conditional testing* and the way its done is as follows:

We place a beq instruction immediately after we stored the OpenLibrary() return value and branch in such a way that if the OpenLibrary() return value is zero then we avoid executing the CloseLibrary() routine. We terminate this program with an rts instruction clearing register d0 before returning to system level (to indicate successful completion). Well that's the theory. Example CH7-1.s is the code that handles the graphics library opening and closing. Normally we'd use an assembly language macro for the library opening and closing but for these examples, since macros can tend to hide what's going on, I'm coding all operations so that they are visible:

```
/*Listing 7.1: Some initial skeleton code for the example
progra*/m
* Example CH7-1.s
NULL                 EQU   0
_AbsExecBase         EQU   4
_LVOOpenLibrary      EQU   -552
_LVOCloseLibrary     EQU   -414


start     move.l    _AbsExecBase, a6      get base address of Exec
                                          library
          lea       graphics_name,a1      load pointer to library
                                          name
          moveq     #0,d0                 any version will do!
openlib   jsr       _LVOOpenLibrary(a6)   make the indirect
                                          subroutine call
          move.l    d0,_GfxBase           save returned pointer
          beq       exit                  did library open OK?

open_ok   At this point we can use the graphics library although
          we would need to reinstate exec library base pointer
          before closing

closelib  move.l    _GfxBase,a1           library to close
          jsr       _LVOCloseLibrary(a6)  make the indirect
                                          subroutine call
exit      clr.l     d0
          rts                             logical end of program
```

```
_GfxBase          ds.l 1
       graphics_name dc.b 'graphics.library', NULL
```

Preventing Multitasking

For the current Copper list example we'll be taking over the display and, to prevent interference from other tasks, it's necessary to turn off the Amiga's multitasking by making a call to the Exec Forbid() function. Prior to the example terminating a corresponding Permit() call is made to return the machine to its normal multitasking state. The LVO values for these functions are -132 and -138 respectively and because they are straightforward functions which require no parameters you'll be able to see how they are used directly from the extended listing Example CH7-2.s. I've turned off multitasking shortly after the program starts running and re-instated it before the program finishes. Notice, incidentally, that we do not need to load a6 with the base of the exec library when the Forbid() call is made because this library base is already in register a6.

/*Listing 7.2: The Exec Forbid() function makes sure that we have the machine to ourselves.*/

```
* Example CH7-2.s

NULL             EQU    0
_AbsExecBase     EQU    4
_LVOOpenLibrary  EQU    -552
_LVOCloseLibrary EQU    -414
_LVOForbid       EQU    -132
_LVOPermit       EQU    -138


start    move.l   _AbsExecBase,a6    get base address of Exec
                                     library
         jsr      _LVOForbid(a6)     turn of multitasking
         lea      graphics_name,a1   load pointer to library
                                     name
         moveq    #0,d0              any version will do!
openlib  jsr      _LVOOpenLibrary(a6) make the indirect subrou
                                     tine call
         move.l   d0,_GfxBase        save returned pointer
         beq      exit               did library open OK?
open_ok  Graphics open and our program effectively has the
         machine to itself because no other progams are allowed
         to run!
```

```
closelib  move.l    _GfxBase,a1           library to close
          jsr       _LVOCloseLibrary(a6)  make the indirect
                                          subroutine call
exit      jsr       _LVOPermit(a6)        reinstate multitasking
          clr.l     d0
          rts                             logical end of program
_GfxBase  ds.l 1
graphics_name dc.b 'graphics.library', NULL
```

Creating An Example Copper List

The Copper list has a number of specific jobs to do. For a start the hardware registers that hold the addresses of the display bitplanes need to be set up. Each bitplane pointer is 32 bits long and although the hardware addresses are memory mapped in such a way that 680x0 move.l instructions can store the complete pointer in one go with the Copper it is necessary to store the upper and lower words of each bitplane pointer separately. This is because Copper instructions are word, rather than long word, oriented! Each of the Amiga's hardware bitplane registers are given symbolic names with bpl1pth and bpl1ptl referring to the high and low words of bitplane register 1, bpl2pth and bpl2ptl to the high and low words of bitplane register 2 and so on. We'll be using a 2 bitplane display and so you might be expecting our Copper list to start like this:

```
Copperlist:    dc.w bpl1pth, somevalue
               dc.w bpl1ptl, somevalue
               dc.w bpl2pth, somevalue
               dc.w bpl2ptl, somevalue
```

The fly in the ointment here is that at the time we write the program: we will not know the values of the bitplane pointers. The bitplane memory will be allocated at run time and the bitplane addresses will only be known then. Our code will need to allocate memory and then insert the appropriate addresses into the Copper list. To make this job easier I'm going to write the bitplane instructions in a way that allows us to identify the word locations that will hold those addesses.

```
Copperlist:    dc.w bpl1pth       bitplane 1
p1h:           dc.w 0
               dc.w bpl1ptl
p1l:           dc.w 0
               dc.w bpl2pth       bitplane 2
p2h:           dc.w 0
```

```
                dc.w bpl2ptl
p21:            dc.w 0
```

We also need to tell the system how many bit planes are being used and there is a hardware register called bplcon0 (bitplane control register 0) that is used for this purpose. Bits 12-14 are used as a bitplane count. Bit 9 is also usually set as this enables composite video colour on some machines (A1000) so for our example we'll be using this instruction:

```
    dc.w bplcon0,$2200        2 bitplanes
```

The next thing to do is set up the colour registers and we've already seen some suitable example code for this. Providing these equates are in place:

```
    BLUE    EQU    $000f
    WHITE   EQU    $0fff
    GREEN   EQU    $00f0
    RED     EQU    $0f00
```

our instructions for loading the four colour registers needed for a 2 bitplane display are:

```
    dc.w color+0,BLUE
    dc.w color+2,WHITE
    dc.w color+4,GREEN
    dc.w color+6,RED
```

These colour values are of course completely arbitrary. We could have chosen any colours we liked.

There are a few other control registers that have to be set up in order including the registers that position the display. Register diwstrt (display window start) controls the starting position of the display with the upper byte of data word IR2 representing the vertical start position and the lower byte the horizontal start position. Because of the way raster scan devices work a 320 x 256 pixel display normally needs a top left position of (129,41) to centre it on the monitor and if you add the 320 widths and 256 height to these values you get a bottom right co-ordinate of (448,296) so diwstop needs to represent co-ordinate (449,297). The diwstop register uses an implied upper bit for its vertical component so the value written actually corresponds to (449,297-256), ie (449,41) so in hex form the result is that diwstrt needs a value of $2981 and dwstop of $29C1 and the corresponding Copper instructions are:

```
    dc.w diwstrt,$2981
    dc.w diwstop,$29C1
```

Two other registers called ddfstrt and ddfstop also need to be set because these govern how many data words are displayed per line. The normal low res display values are:

    dc.w ddfstrt,$38

    dc.w ddfstop,$D0

Two modulo registers, which govern the amount added on to the bitplane pointers at the end of each screenline, need to be cleared using these instructions:

    dc.w bpl1mod,0

    dc.w bpl2mod,0

Do remember incidentally that the object of the exercise is simply to provide an overview of what coders do when they *hit the hardware*. It's impossible to provide full details of the use and purposes of all the various hardware registers in the space available but this information is of course readily available from the official Addison Wesley Amiga Hardware manual.

The last instruction in our Copper list is the everlasting wait instruction mentioned earlier:

    dc.w $ffff,$fffe   end of list

Now if we piece all the above ideas together we end up with this set of instructions:

```
Copperlist:dc.w    bpl1pth              bitplane 1
p1h:       dc.w    0
           dc.w    bpl1ptl
p1l:       dc.w    0
           dc.w    bpl2pth              bitplane 2
p2h:       dc.w    0
           dc.w    bpl2ptl
p2l:       dc.w    0
           dc.w    bplcon0,$2200        2 bitplanes
           dc.w    color+0,BLUE
           dc.w    color+2,WHITE
           dc.w    color+4,GREEN
           dc.w    color+6,RED
           dc.w    diwstrt, $2981
           dc.w    diwstop,$29C1
           dc.w    ddfstrt,$38
           dc.w    ddfstop,$D0
           dc.w    bpl1mod,0
           dc.w    bpl2mod,0
           dc.w $ffff, $fffe            end of list
```

Allocating Display Memory

For simplicity I'll be using a display with just two bitplanes and to allocate this the exec library AllocMem() function will be used. This requires the amount of memory to be specified in register d0 and the memory type to be in register d1. The returned memory pointer needs to be saved, in order to return the memory before the program terminates, and it also needs to be tested to see that the allocation was successful. Here's the code that does the job:

```
        move.l   #40*256*2,d0            lowres 256 lines 2 planes
        move.l   #MEMF_CHIP|MEMF_CLEAR,d1
        jsr      _LVOAllocMem(a6)
        move.l   d0,screen
        beq      closelib
```

and this is the code that will return that memory:

```
        move.l   _AbsExecBase,a6         Exec library base
        move.l   screen,a1               screen address
        move.l   #40*256*2,d0            amount allocated
        jsr                              _LVO FreeMem(A6)
```

Setting the Bitplane Pointers

Once the display memory has been allocated we can store the bitplane pointers into the designated Copper list locations. Since there are only two bitplanes involved in this example I've opted for the simple approach of loading the screen address and storing each part in turn (this constitutes bitplane 1), and then repeating the process after re-loading the address and adding an amount equal to the size of a single bitplane:

```
        move.l   screen,d0
        move.w   d0,p1l
        swap     d0
        move.w   d0,p1h
        move.l   screen,d0
        add.l    #40*256,d0
        move.w   d0,p2l
        swap     d0
        move.w   d0,p2h
```

Because this code is executed whilst d0 contains the screen address the first instruction in the above sequence will not be needed in the program itself (it was just shown for clarity in the above fragment).

Using The Copper List

We load the address of the custom chips into register a5 (any address register could have been used) and the base of the graphics library into a6. Then we turn off the Copper DMA by writing to the DMA control register like this:

```
move.w    #$80,dmacon(a5)           Copper dma off
```

and having done that we save the old Copper list pointer and install the one associated with our program:

```
move.l    LOFlist(a6),old_list      save existing Copper list
move.l    #Copperlist,LOFlist(a6)   install new list
```

The LOFlist offset (actually $32) is the location within the GfxBase structure that points to the LOFlist Copper list and it is this pointer, after saving it, that we replace with our own. Once the pointer is in place Copper DMA is turned back on again like this:

```
move.w    #$8080,dmacon(a5)         Copper dma on
```

so, if we put these ideas together, we get the section of code that installs our new list:

```
lea       CUSTOM,a5                 custom chip base
move.l    _GfxBase,a6               graphics base
move.w    #$80,dmacon(a5)           Copper dma off
move.l    LOFlist(a6),old_list      save existing Copper list
move.l    #Copperlist,LOFlist(a6)   install new list
move.w    #$8080,dmacon(a5)         Copper dma on
```

All we need now is a loop to check for an exit condition and I've opted for the user hitting the ESCape key. The following code *busy loops* waiting for screen line 255 ($ff) to be reached then it reads the keyboard and checks to see if it is an ESCape character. The moment such a keypress is detected the old LOFlist pointer is re-instated in readiness for the program to terminate. Here's what this section of the code looks like:

```
loop:   move.b    vhposr(a5),d0           get scanline
        cmp.b     #$ff,d0                 line $ff?
        bne.s                             loop

;                 could do something here!

        move.b    $bfec01,d0              read keyboard
        eor.b     #$ff,d0                 decode byte
        ror.b     #1,d0
        cmp.b     #$45,d0                 ESCape key?
        bne.s     loop                    keep going
```

```
            move.w      #$80,dmacon(a5)        Copper dma off
            move.l      old_list,LOFlist(a6)   re-install old list
            move.w      #$8080,dmacon(a5)      Copper dma on
```

Busy waiting like this shouldn't really be done with Amiga programs but it makes for a simple to understand loop and, since our program has disabled multitasking anyway, it doesn't really matter. The good news is that we've now got a completed program and if all of the Copper list and display related fragments are now added to our assembler source code along with the extra definitions required to allow assembly we get this finished result:

/*Listing 7.3: The completed program with Copper list in place*/

```
        * Example CH7-3.s

            section code,code_c
NULL                    EQU   0
_AbsExecBase            EQU   4
_LVOOpenLibrary         EQU   -552
_LVOCloseLibrary        EQU   -414
_LVOForbid              EQU   -132
_LVOPermit              EQU   -138
_LVOAllocMem            EQU   -198
_LVOFreeMem             EQU   -210

MEMF_CHIP               EQU   1<<1
MEMF_CLEAR              EQU   1<<16
CUSTOM                  EQU   $DFF000

BLUE                    EQU   $000f
WHITE                   EQU   $0fff
GREEN                   EQU   $00f0
RED                     EQU   $0f00

color                   EQU   $180
LOFlist                 EQU   $32

bplcon0                 EQU   $100
```

bpl1mod		EQU $108	
bpl2mod		EQU $10A	
bpl1pth		EQU $E0	
bpl1ptl		EQU $E2	
bpl2pth		EQU $E4	
bpl2ptl		EQU $e6	
diwstrt		EQU $8E	
diwstop		EQU $90	
ddfstrt		EQU $92	
ddfstop		EQU $94	
dmacon		EQU $96	
vhposr		EQU $6	
start	move.l	_AbsExecBase,a6	get base address of Exec library
	jsr	_LVOForbid(a6)	turn of multitasking
	lea	graphics_name,a1	load pointer to library name
	moveq	#0,d0	any version will do!
openlib	jsr	_LVOOpenLibrary(a6)	make the indirect subroutine call
	move.l	d0,_GfxBase	save returned pointer
	beq	exit	did library open OK?
open_ok	move.l	#40*256*2,d0	lowres 256 lines 2 planes
	move.l	#MEMF_CHIP+MEMF_CLEAR,d1	
	jsr	_LVOAllocMem(a6)	
	move.l	d0,screen	
	beq	closelib	
	move.w	d0,p1l	install bit plane pointers
	swap	d0	
	move.w	d0,p1h	
	move.l	screen,d0	
	add.l	#40*256,d0	

```
            move.w    d0,p2l
            swap      d0
            move.w    d0,p2h
            lea       CUSTOM,a5

            move.l    _GfxBase,a6              graphics base
            move.w    #$80,dmacon(a5)          Copper dma off
            move.l    LOFlist(a6),old_list     save existing Copper list
            move.l    #Copperlist,LOFlist(a6)  install new list
            move.w    #$8080,dmacon(a5)        Copper dma on

loop:       move.b    vhposr(a5),d0            get scanline
            cmp.b     #$ff,d0                  line $ff?
            bne.s     loop

;                     could do something here!

            move.b    $bfec01,d0               read keyboard
            eor.b     #$ff,d0                  decode byte
            ror.b     #1,d0
            cmp.b     #$45,d0                  ESCape key?
            bne.s     loop                     keep going

            move.w    #$80,dmacon(a5)          Copper dma off
            move.l    old_list,LOFlist(a6)     re-install old list
            move.w    #$8080,dmacon(a5)        Copper dma on

            move.l    _AbsExecBase,a6          base address of Exec
                                               library
            move.l    screen,a1                screen address
            move.l    #40*256*2,d0             amount allocated
            jsr       _LVOFreeMem(a6)

closelib    move.l    _GfxBase,a1              library to close
            jsr       _LVOCloseLibrary(a6)     make the indirect subrou
                                               tine call
exit        jsr       _LVOPermit(a6)           reinstate multitasking
            clr.l     d0
```

```
            rts           logical end of program

_GfxBase  ds.l 1
screen    ds.l 1
old_list  ds.l 1
graphics_name dc.b 'graphics.library', NULL

          even

Copperlist:dc.w   bpl1pth              bitplane 1
p1h:      dc.w    0
          dc.w    bpl1ptl
p1l:      dc.w    0
          dc.w    bpl2pth              bitplane 2
p2h:      dc.w    0
          dc.w    bpl2ptl
p2l:      dc.w    0
          dc.w    bplcon0,$2200        2 bitplanes

          dc.w    color+0,BLUE
          dc.w    color+2,WHITE
          dc.w    color+4,GREEN
          dc.w    color+6,RED
          dc.w    diwstrt,$2981
          dc.w    diwstop,$9CC1
          dc.w    ddfstrt,$38
          dc.w    ddfstop,$D0
          dc.w    bpl1mod,0
          dc.w    bpl2mod,0
          dc.w $ffff,$fffe             end of list
```

When this program runs you'll get a display that is just showing the (blue) background colour and when you press the ESCape key the program will terminate. It's actually very easy now to show you how the Copper list can be modified to alter the display because, since all the underlying 680x0 code framework is now in place, we only need concern ourselves with the Copper list issues.

Let's say we want to divide the screen into four background colours, blue, green, red and white. To split the screen into four equal parts on a $FF (ie 256) line screen the line numbers which we'll need to wait for are $3F, $7F, and $BF. But our screen is starting from a vertical position of $29 (remember the value placed in register distrt) so the values actually waited for are going to be $3F+$29, $7F+$29, and $BF+$29.

With the current Copper list the display background colour (colour register 0) starts off blue. What we need to do now therefore is wait for the above screenline positions and as they occur change the value of colour register 0 to green, red and finally white. There's a minor complication with the horizontal wait position calculation and it turns out that you need to wait for position $E in order to get the color register changed during the time that the beam is away from the visible display area but accepting this the overall ideas are realtively straightforward. Here are the instructions needed:

```
        dc.w    $3F0F+$2900,$fffe    wait for this line
        dc.w    color+0,GREEN        and change colour reg 0
        dc.w    $7F0F+$2900,$fffe    ditto
        dc.w    color+0,RED
        dc.w    $BF0F+$2900,$fffe    ditto
        dc.w    color+0,WHITE
```

If we add these instructions to our existing Copper list we get the following four colour display example:

```
/*Listing 7.4: Changing effects by altering the Copper
instructions is easy once the main framework of the pro-
gram is in place.*/

* Example CH7-4.s


            section code,code_c
NULL                EQU     0
_AbsExecBase        EQU     4
_LVOOpenLibrary     EQU     -552
_LVOCloseLibrary    EQU     -414
_LVOForbid          EQU     -132
_LVOPermit          EQU     -138
_LVOAllocMem        EQU     -198
_LVOFreeMem         EQU     -210

MEMF_CHIP           EQU     1<<1
MEMF_CLEAR          EQU     1<<16
CUSTOM              EQU     $DFF000
```

```
BLUE            EQU     $000f
WHITE           EQU     $0fff
GREEN           EQU     $00f0
RED             EQU     $0f00

color           EQU     $180
LOFlist         EQU     $32

bplcon0         EQU     $100

bpl1mod         EQU     $108
bpl2mod         EQU     $10A

bpl1pth         EQU     $E0
bpl1ptl         EQU     $E2
bpl2pth         EQU     $E4
bpl2ptl         EQU     $e6

diwstrt         EQU     $8E
diwstop         EQU     $90
ddfstrt         EQU     $92
ddfstop         EQU     $94
dmacon          EQU     $96
vhposr          EQU     $6

start    move.l  _AbsExecBase,a6         get base address of Exec
                                         library
         jsr     _LVOForbid(a6)          turn of multitasking
         lea     graphics_name,a1        load pointer to library
name
         moveq   #0,d0                   any version will do!
openlib  jsr     _LVOOpenLibrary(a6)     make the indirect
                                         subroutine call
         move.l  d0,_GfxBase             save returned pointer
         beq     exit                    did library open OK?

open_ok  move.l  #40*256*2,d0            lowres 256 lines 2 planes
```

```
            move.l      #MEMF_CHIP+MEMF_CLEAR,d1
            jsr         _LVOAllocMem(a6)
            move.l      d0,screen
            beq         closelib

            move.w      d0,p1l                  install bit plane point-
    ers
            swap        d0
            move.w      d0,p1h
            move.l      screen,d0
            add.l       #40*256,d0
            move.w      d0,p2l
            swap        d0
            move.w      d0,p2h


            lea         CUSTOM,a5

            move.l      _GfxBase,a6             graphics base
            move.w      #$80,dmacon(a5)         Copper dma off
            move.l      LOFlist(a6),old_list    save existing Copper list
            move.l      #Copperlist,LOFlist(a6) install new list
            move.w      #$8080,dmacon(a5)       Copper dma on

loop:       move.b      vhposr(a5),d0           get scanline
            cmp.b       #$ff,d0                 line $ff?
            bne.s       loop

;                       could do something here!

            move.b      $bfec01,d0              read keyboard
            eor.b       #$ff,d0                 decode byte
            ror.b       #1,d0
            cmp.b       #$45,d0                 ESCape key?
            bne.s       loop                    keep going

            move.w      #$80,dmacon(a5)         Copper dma off
            move.l      old_list,LOFlist(a6)    re-install old list
            move.w      #$8080,dmacon(a5)       Copper dma on
```

Copper Listing

```
            move.l    _AbsExecBase,a6      base address of Exec
                                           library
            move.l    screen,a1            screen address
            move.l    #40*256*2,d0         amount allocated
            jsr       _LVOFreeMem(a6)

closelib    move.l    _GfxBase,a1          library to close
            jsr       _LVOCloseLibrary(a6) make the indirect
                                           subroutine call
exit        jsr       _LVOPermit(a6)       reinstate multitasking
            clr.l     d0
            rts                            logical end of program


_GfxBase   ds.l 1
screen     ds.l 1
old_list   ds.l 1
graphics_name dc.b 'graphics.library', NULL
              even

Copperlist: dc.w    bpl1pth              bitplane 1
p1h:        dc.w    0
            dc.w    bpl1ptl
p1l:        dc.w    0
            dc.w    bpl2pth              bitplane 2
p2h:        dc.w    0
            dc.w    bpl2ptl
p2l:        dc.w    0
            dc.w    bplcon0,$2200        2 bitplanes
            dc.w    color+0,BLUE
            dc.w    color+2,WHITE
            dc.w    color+4,GREEN
            dc.w    color+6,RED
            dc.w    diwstrt,$2981
            dc.w    diwstop,$9CC1
            dc.w    ddfstrt,$38
            dc.w    ddfstop,$D0
            dc.w    bpl1mod,0
```

```
        dc.w    bpl1mod,0
        dc.w    bpl2mod,0
        dc.w    $3F0F+$2900,$fffe       wait for this line
        dc.w    color+0,GREEN           and change colour reg 0
        dc.w    $7F0F+$2900,$fffe       ditto
        dc.w    color+0,RED
        dc.w    $BF0F+$2900,$fffe       ditto
        dc.w    color+0,WHITE
        dc.w $ffff,$fffe                end of list
```

With both example programs I've incuded my own definitions of register names and so on and this has been done firstly so that they're visible as you look at the program, and secondly so that the examples can be assembled without requiring the official includes. Most programmers however would include the appropriate Amiga system includes and use those definitions rather that duplicating them in the code itself.

The High-Level Alternative

The examples I've dealt with so far have been extremely simple ones and were written just to show you how such code is constructed. Trust me, much more work is needed to create useful programs of this nature and it should be apparent that this approach leaves much to be desired as far as the effort/results ratio is concerned. Taking over the display, disabling multitasking etc, are all frowned upon by Commodore and most sensible coders and in fact there are much easier and more system friendly ways of adding many Copper list effects to your programs. What's equally important is that you don't need to use assembly language either because C programmers have a number of macros for generating Copper instructions. I won't be using these macros until the next chapter but since their uses and formats are related to all our previous Copper list discussions they are best dealt with now.

Function Name: CWAIT()	
Description:	to add a wait instruction to a user copper list
Call Format:	CWAIT(copper_list_p, vertical, horizontal)
C Prototype:	void CWAIT(struct UCopList *, WORD, WORD);
Registers:	CWAIT(A1, D0, D1)
Arguments:	copper_list_p - pointer to a UCopList structure vertical - vertical beam position horizontal - horizontal beam position
Return Value:	None
Notes:	Horizontal value must not be greater than 222

Copper Listing

Function Name:	**CMOVE()**
Description:	Macro to add a move instruction to a user copper list
Call Format:	CMOVE(copper_list_p, hregister, hvalue)
C Prototype:	void CMOVE(struct UCopList *, void *, WORD);
Registers:	CMOVE(A1, D0, D1)
Arguments:	copper_list_p - pointer to a UCopList structure hregister - target hardware register hvalue - value to be placed in register
Return Value:	None

There is another macro provided called CINIT() and this allows the C programmer to allocate/initialize a user Copper list:

Function Name:	**CINIT()**
Description:	Macro to initialize a user Copper list
Call Format:	ucl_p=CINIT(c_p, n)
C Prototype:	struct UCopList *CINIT (struct UCopList *, UWORD);
Registers:	D0 = CINIT(A0, D0)
Arguments:	c_p- pointer to a UCopList structure n - number of copper instructions being used
Return Value:	ucl_p - pointer to an initialized list to hold user Copper list instructions
Notes:	The official documentation for this function is not as clear as it might have been. It seems that the original idea of the routine was that if a user provided a NULL c_p UCopList pointer CINIT() would do ALL necessary structure/buffer allocations and would return a pointer to a freshly allocated UCopList structure (for use in subsequent Copper list operations). This doesn't now appear to be the case and to allocate a new list the routine actually needs to be passed a twelve byte block of MEMF_PUBLIC|MEMF_CLEAR memory (ie an 'uninitialized' UCopList structure). Normally then subsequent operations should use the c_p UCopList structure supplied to CINIT() routine and ignore the returned ucl_p pointer.

Function Name	**CEND()**
Description:	Macro to terminate a copper list
Call Format:	CEND(copper_list_p)
C Prototype:	void CEND(struct UCopList *copper_list_p);
Arguments:	copper_list_p - pointer to a UCopList structure
Return Value:	None

Intuition

Copper list examples which build an Amiga display from the ground upwards are all very well but many of you will I suspect be working in the Intuition environment and will be more interested in this side of the coin. The point here is that if you have opened an Intuition screen then all the low-level system structures, and the Copper list instructions which describe the display, are already in place – they have been set up by Intuition itself.

The good news now is that a mechanism exists whereby a programmer can add additional Copper instructions via a separate *user* Copper list. These were mentioned at the start of this chapter and it is these entites, coupled with the use of the high-level CWAIT, CMOVE and CINIT macros that the C programmer needs to come to terms with. The basic idea is that the user sets up a suitable list of the extra commands, an intermediate Copper list, and then asks the system to remake its own lists so that it incorporates the new user list instructions. Having done that the system is asked to use the *re-made* hardware Copper lists. The benefit of knowing how to do this in an Intuition compatible way is that the programmer can get the best of both worlds – low-level style display tricks can be used from within an easily handled high-level Intuition environment.

When Intuition sets up a screen display it uses a complex data block called a Screen structure. If you look at this structure you'll see that it contains a number of sub-structures including one called a ViewPort structure. It is this latter entity which describes the screen display and, if you look in the graphics/view.h header file you will see this type of layout:

```
struct ViewPort {
struct ViewPort *Next;
struct ColorMap *ColourMap;
struct CopList  *DspIns;
struct CopList  *SprIns;
struct CopList  *ClrIns;
struct UCopList *UCopIns;   /* user Copper list pointer */
SHORT   DWidth, DHeight;
SHORT   DxOffset, DyOffset;
UWORD   Modes;
UBYTE   SpritePriorities;
UBYTE   reserved;
struct RasInfo *RasInfo;
};
```

As might be expected there is a lot of information about ViewPorts in the RKM manuals. For our present purposes however all that we need to know is that the ViewPort structure contains space for a pointer to a user Copper list. Our task then (at least on the face of it) is simple; create a user Copper list, place the start address in the UCopIns field of the screen's ViewPort structure, and then tell the system to make use of the new instructions. This involves a number of operations including the merging and sorting of the instruction lists. Luckily, at the Intuition level, a system routine called MakeScreen() does all the hard work for us:

Function Name:	**MakeScreen()**
Description:	This function forces (in an Intuition compatible way) a complete remake of the screens ViewPort data.
Call Format:	MakeScreen(screen_p)
C Prototype:	void MakeScreen(struct Screen *);
Registers:	MakeScreen(A0)
Arguments:	screen_p - pointer to a screen structure
Return Value:	None
Notes:	If a user copper list has been added to the ViewPort this routine will incorporate it.

With the new ViewPort data in place all that has to be done is tell the system to take notice of it. Intuition contains a routine especially made for the purpose:

Function Name:	**RethinkDisplay()**
Description:	Routine will completely reconstruct the Intuition display
Call Format:	RethinkDisplay()
C Prototype:	void RethinkDisplay(void);
Registers:	None
Arguments:	None
Return Value:	None
Notes:	This routine can take several milliseconds to run but it is by far the easiest way to incorporate user copper list code into the Intuition environment.

That then, in terms of the main instructions and function calls, is the basic scenario for what might be called high-level Copper list programming. For the C programmer, incidentally, it is the hardware/custom.h include file which provides the register address offsets needed to hit the hardware directly

The more difficult task, deciding exactly what Copper instructions need to be used, still has to be carried out and the instructions obviously depends on what it is you wish to do. The best thing to do here is provide a detailed example and that is what the next chapter is all about.

8: Copper List Shading Effects

Copper list shading tricks are used in hundreds of demos and in quite a few commercial programs as well. To be honest I could give you half a dozen lines of C or assembler code and say this is how you can do it. I could; but that approach is really only of use if you know what the hardware does and know how to generate the colour values anyway. I'll assume that you don't know about such things and, because it's not going to be that obvious how the final code works, I'll tackle the explanations right from first principles. The main problem actually has little to do with the Copper or the Amiga at all – it is to do with working out how to generate series of cycling numbers. Admitedly these numbers, at the end of the day, will be jammed into colour registers – but as far as the underlying ideas go that is neither here nor there. Essentially we need to step through the lines of the display changing the colour as we go, using a scheme like this:

```
for ( i = 0; i<SCREENLINES; i=i+1 )
    {
    Identify new colour 'j' to
    be used
    Set line 'i' to colour 'j'
    }
```

The variable j must be kept within the range of colour numbers suitable for the screen. The obvious choice is to combine the changing value of i with a modulo function so that we generate a value of j which will always stay within the chosen limits like this:

```
for ( i = 0; i<SCREENLINES; i=i+1 )
   {
   j = i % m
   Set line 'i' to colour 'j'
   }
```

If m is set to 5 then j will take values from 0 to 4 and the colours used down the screen will follow this pattern: 0 1 2 3 4 0 1 2 3 4 0 1 2 3 4 etc. In practice it's usually better to produce an oscillating sequence rather than a direct cycling sequence and so instead of generating the above pattern we'd opt for one based on a 0 1 2 3 4 3 2 1 0 1 2 type of arrangement. To do this we have to modify the generating function slightly. Figure 8.1 shows one arrangement, in Warnier diagram form, which does the trick:

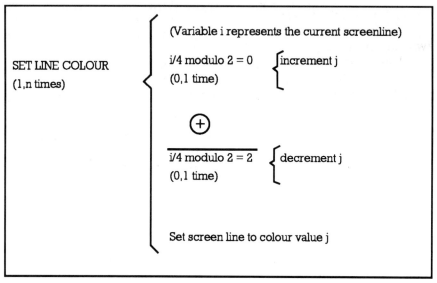

Figure 8.1. Warnier diagram description of what we are trying to do to produce a colour shading effect.

The ideas translate to this type of C code:

```
for (i=0; i<SCREENLINES; i=i+1)
   {
   if ((i/4) %2 == 0 ) { j=j+1; } else { j=j-1; }
   Set line 'i' to colour 'j'
   }
```

Whilst the above fragment does produce the required result, most C programmers would tend to use C's increment/decrement operators combined with an implied i test, so they'd write the loop like this:

```
for (i=0; i<SCREENLINES; i++)
    {       if ((i/4) % 2) {j—;} else {j++;}
    Set line 'i' to colour 'j'
    }
```

Even this form can be improved by using the ternary operator ? to select the operation performed on j:

```
for (i=0;i<SCREENLINES;i++)
    {
    ((i/4) % 2) ? j— : j++;
    Set line 'i' to colour 'j'
    }
```

That then is one way of generating a set of colour register values. Now all we need to worry about is how to set a screen line to a particular colour. One approach, and from a purely design viewpoint there would be nothing wrong with it, would be to use some standard line drawing function. We could use the graphics function SetAPen() to set the pen colour for drawing, then use Move() to position the pen at the start of a screen line, and finally use the Draw() function to perform the actual line filling operation.

If we added this type of code to our existing loop we'd end up with a typical shading routine – this following example uses a screen's rastport pointer to completely fill a screen display with an oscillating colour pattern:

```
for (i=0;i<SCREENLINES;i++)
{ (i/4) % 2 ? j— : j++;            /* j selects the colour
                                       register */
SetAPen(rastport_p,j);             /* set APen to the
                                       required colour */
Move(rastport_p, 0, i);            /* move to the start of
                                       the line */
Draw(rasport_p,SCREENWIDTH, i);    /* draw the line */
}
```

You can of course modify the amplitude of the oscillation range – the expression (i/n) % 2 ? j— : j++; will oscillate between 0 and n inclusive. Secondly, you can add a fixed amount to the final j value produced – so that any given oscillating function can be made to select any chosen range of colour numbers.

Making the Most of the Amiga's Hardware

On the Amiga we don't have to use routines like Move() and Draw() at all because we can use the Copper to jam colour values into the appropriate colour registers as the video beam moves down the screen. Why bother? There are two reasons: firstly, it is faster. Secondly, once the Copper list has been created the display is created automatically and the program itself doesn't have to worry about it. Now that the basic mechanism for creating cycling numbers has been discovered the, crux of the remaining problem is working out how to build a suitable list of Copper instructions (which is then linked into the viewport associated with the screen). Inevitably we do start tangling with the hardware now, but don't forget we have already decided what operations are need so the preliminary analysis has made life somewhat easier for us.

The Copper has three instructions – WAIT, MOVE and SKIP. WAIT is used to wait for the video beam to reach a particular screen line so I'll obviously use that to specify a screenline. I'll use MOVE instructions to force the calculated colour value into the colour registers, but rather than cycling through many different colours I'll be using the generated cyclic values as colour intensities and jamming these into a single colour register. There are obviously a number of system specific code issues involved and the following notes will illustrate the basic details:

First we need some space for a UCopList structure. In the following fragment I am using an AllocMem() call:

```
user_copperlist_p=AllocMem(sizeof(struct UCopList),
MEMF_PUBLIC|MEMF_CLEAR);
```

Next, we use the system macro CINIT to initialise our Copper list memory:

```
CINIT(user_copperlist_p,SCREENHEIGHT*2+1);
```

Now we need the Copper instructions themselves. To put things in perspective Figure 8.2 shows a preliminary Warnier sketch of what we are trying to do:

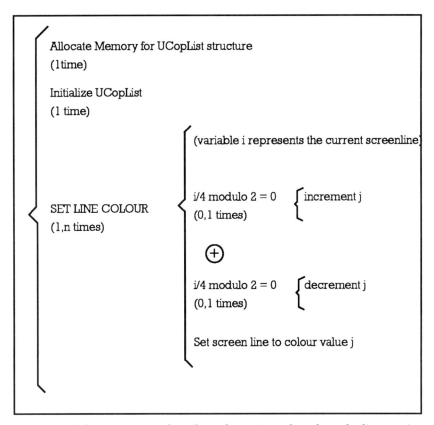

Figure 8.2. A first attempt at describing the actions of a colour shading routine.

Is Figure 8.2 right? No, not quite; the UCopList memory allocation could fail so we ought to make a check to see that memory was obtained:

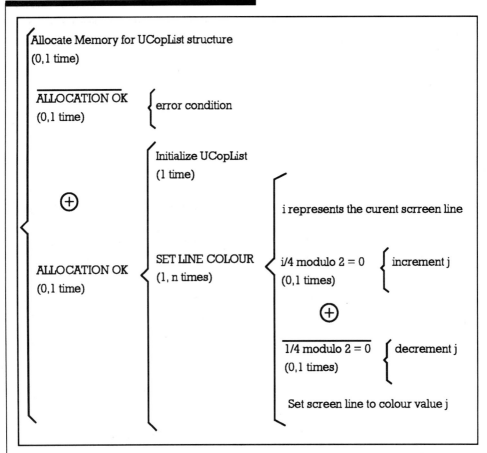

Figure 8.3. An improved Warnier sketch of the operations that need to be carried out to produce a Copper list colour shading effect.

I ought to point out that the UCopList initialization process is handled by a system macro call that allocates the chip memory which holds the Copper instructions. I've not dealt with this because the allocation and the deallocation (which includes the handing back of the UCopList structure memory which we've allocated) is handled transparently.

The Amiga system conventions require three other actions. We must terminate the Copper list with an impossible wait (you'll have to see the Amiga hardware manual for details of why), we must link this newly-created list into the appropriate viewport structure, and we must remake the display so that our Copper list gets incorporated. Don't forget that these constraints have been found by digging around in the RKM manuals – that digging, plus some thought about what we were trying to do colour-wise, allowed me to sketch a suitable plan of action. This logical description of what is needed is now complete and it is provided in figure 8.4 below:

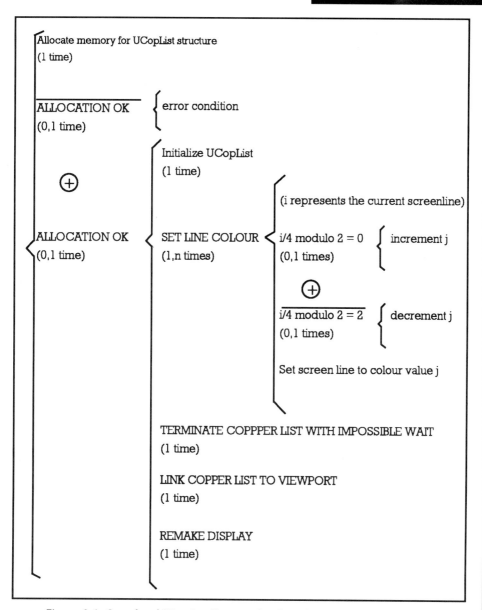

Figure 8.4. Completed Warnier diagram for the colour shading operations.

Now let's look at some example code that will put these ideas into context:

```
if (user_Copperlist_p=AllocMem(sizeof(struct
UCopList),MEMF_PUBLIC|MEMF_CLEAR))
    {
    CINIT(user_Copperlist_p,SCREENHEIGHT*2+1);
    for (i=0;i<SCREENHEIGHT;i++)
        {
```

```
            (i/15) % 2 ? Intensity- : Intensity++;
            CWAIT(user_Copperlist_p,i,0L);
            CMOVE(user_Copperlist_p,custom.color[0],Intensity);
            }
        CEND(user_Copperlist_p);
        global_viewport_p->UCopIns=user_Copperlist_p;
        MakeScreen(global_screen_p); RethinkDisplay();
        }
```

I'm using a loop which works out the necessary instructions for each screenline, calculating the colour with a function similar to the oscillating function discussed earlier. The CWAIT system macro creates Copper instructions which say *wait for the video beam position to reach co-ordinates (j,0)*. The CMOVE macro produces the instructions which jams the colour I've calculated into the background colour register (register 0). The result of the following loop is therefore a list of Copper instructions which continually change the value of colour register 0 as the electron beam moves down the screen. Finally we terminate the Copper list with an impossible wait instruction (that's what the CEND system macro does), link our newly created Copper list into the viewport, and remake the display.

So that's it: Grab some memory for a UCopList structure, get the system to initialize it and allocate its internal list space, use a loop to generate some *wait and jam a value into a colour register* instructions, link the list into the viewport, and then remake the display. Once you know what you're doing you can actually squash the whole *Copper list generation* thing into three or four lines of C code; so don't let anyone kid you that there's anything inherently difficult about it. Having said that it is always best to take a bit more coding space and lay it such code in what will hopefully be an understandable fashion. Listing 8.1 shows some more code, this time written as a call-able routine which returns a TRUE error flag if it is unable to install the designated background shading. To be honest the routine is not particularly flexible but it is sufficient to illustrate the principles. The routine installs a blue band shading Copper list into the Amiga background colour register:

```
/*Listing 8.1: A typical Copper list based routine for
producing shading effects*/

BOOL InstallBlueBackgroundShading(void)

{

BOOL error_flag=TRUE; /* guilty until proven innocent
                                approach */

struct UCopList *user_Copperlist_p=NULL;

COUNT j;
```

```
        if (user_Copperlist_p=AllocMem(sizeof(struct
    UCopList),MEMF_PUBLIC|MEMF_CLEAR))
          {
          error_flag=FALSE;
          CINIT(user_Copperlist_p,SCREENHEIGHT*2+1);
          for (j=0;j<SCREENHEIGHT;j++)
             {
             (j/15) % 2 ? Blue— : Blue++;
             CWAIT(user_Copperlist_p,j,OL);
             CMOVE(user_Copperlist_p,custom.color[0],Blue);
             }
          CEND(user_Copperlist_p);
          global_viewport_p->UCopIns=user_Copperlist_p;
          MakeScreen(global_screen_p);
          RethinkDisplay();
          }
       return(error_flag);
       }
```

Obviously now that the approach is available many similar routines become possible. Listing 8.2 shows a useful modification which toggles the shading (ie turns it on and off) with alternate calls. The idea is very simple: first we look at the user Copper list pointer to see whether a user list is already present. If the list exists then the shading effect is already in place and in this case we remove it and set the user Copper list pointer back to zero. If on calling the routine the user list pointer is zero then there is no user list installed – so we install one! It's a relatively small extension of the routine just dealt with although it does involve a number of addtional system calls (see Includes & Autodocs RKM manual for full details of the system calls):

```
/*Listing 8.2: A shading routine that alternately switches
on and removes a Copper list shading effect with each
call*/
BOOL ColourShading(UBYTE colour_number, UBYTE
colour_shade)
{
BOOL error_flag=TRUE; /* guilty until proven innocent
approach */
static struct UCopList *user_Copperlist_p=NULL;
COUNT j;
UBYTE Intensity=0;
```

```
            if(global_viewport_p->UCopIns==NULL)
               {
               if (user_Copperlist_p=
                   AllocMem(sizeof(struct UCopList),MEMF_PUBLIC|
                   MEMF_CLEAR))
                  {
                  error_flag=FALSE;
                  CINIT(user_Copperlist_p,SCREENHEIGHT*2+1);
                     for (j=0;j<SCREENHEIGHT;j++)
                        {
                        (j/15) % 2 ? Intensity-- : Intensity++;
                        CWAIT(user_Copperlist_p,j,0L);
                        CMOVE(user_Copperlist_p,
                        custom.color[colour_number],Intensity<<
                        colour_shade);
                        }
                     CEND(user_Copperlist_p);
                     global_viewport_p->UCopIns=user_Copperlist_p;
                     MakeScreen(global_screen_p);
                     RethinkDisplay();
                     }
                  }
            else {
                  global_viewport_p->UCopIns=NULL;
                  MakeScreen(global_screen_p);
                  RethinkDisplay();
                  FreeCopList(user_Copperlist_p->FirstCopList);
                  FreeMem(user_Copperlist_p,sizeof(struct UCopList));
                  user_Copperlist_p=NULL;
                  }
            return(error_flag);
            }
```

As mentioned earlier once you understand the basic principles of cycling number generation you can modify the ideas to your heart's content. As one last example listing 8.3 shows a routine that generates and installs (or removes) a shading effect involving a specified Amiga style RGB colour value, a colour register. Internally the routine isolates these red, blue and green components making use of static cycle and minimum shading value variables to control the style of the shading.

```c
/*Listing 8.3: Yet another colour shading routine modifi-
cation*/
BOOL ColourShading(UBYTE colour_number, UWORD
colour_shade)
{
BOOL error_flag=TRUE; /* guilty until proven innocent
approach */
static struct UCopList *user_Copperlist_p=NULL;
COUNT j;
UBYTE brightness=0x5; /* must be between 0 and 15 */
UBYTE cycle_max=10,intensity=0;
UBYTE base_red,red,base_blue,blue,base_green,green;
if(g_viewport_p->UCopIns==NULL)
     {
     if (user_Copperlist_p=
         AllocMem(sizeof(struct UCopList),MEMF_PUBLIC|
         MEMF_CLEAR))
       {
       error_flag=FALSE;
       base_red=(colour_shade&0x0F00)>>8;
       base_green=(colour_shade&0x00F0)>>4;
       base_blue=colour_shade&0x000F;
       CINIT(user_Copperlist_p,WINDOW_HEIGHT*2+1);
       for (j=0;j<WINDOW_HEIGHT;j++)
          {
          (j/cycle_max) % 2 ? intensity-- : intensity++;
          red=(base_red*intensity)/cycle_max;
          if (red<brightness) red=brightness;
          green=(base_green*intensity)/cycle_max;
          if (green<brightness) green=brightness;
          blue=(base_blue*intensity)/cycle_max;
          if (blue<brightness) blue=brightness;
          CWAIT(user_Copperlist_p,j,0L);
          CMOVE(user_Copperlist_p,
          custom.color[colour_number],(red<<8)|(green<<4)
          |blue);
          }
       CEND(user_Copperlist_p);
       g_viewport_p->UCopIns=user_Copperlist_p;
```

```
            MakeScreen(g_public_screen_p);
            RethinkDisplay();
            }
        }
    else {
        g_viewport_p->UCopIns=NULL;
        MakeScreen(g_public_screen_p);
        RethinkDisplay();
        FreeCopList(user_Copperlist_p->FirstCopList);
        FreeMem(user_Copperlist_p,sizeof(struct UCopList));
        user_Copperlist_p=NULL;
        }
    return(error_flag);
    }
```

Making It Up As You Go Along

Perhaps the most important thing to be gleaned from this chapter is an understanding of how a series of cycling numbers can be generated. Remember incidentally that you may not always need to opt for the dynamic list generation technique that I've discussed. Sometimes when you know exactly what colours you want you can just use a static list of colour register data or perhaps even the equivalent static Copper list instructions. A programmer who uses 680x0 assembler however might well consider it worthwhile to write a C language Copper list generating untility that stores the instructions as a series of 680x0 style data statements. This would allow shading effect data to be read directly into 680x0 source code files. Similarly the C programmer might wish to have done all the colour register calculations before the program is run. Listing 8.4 is the code for a colour register value generating utility. It's based loosely on the previous shading routine, that produces a C style array containing a set of horizontal band shading values but instead of using the generated colour register values it just writes them to stdout:

```
/* -------------------------------------------------- */

/*Listing 8.4: A colour shade value generating utility*/

/* Shading effect colour-value generator for use in Copper
lists */

/* This utility generates a UWORD c[] colour register data
array   using this format...

                <line count> {<colour values>}
*/
```

```c
/* ------------------------------------------------ */
#include <stdio.h>
#include <exec/memory.h>
#define LINE_COUNT 255
void GenerateColourShadingList(UWORD colour_shade);
/* ------------------------------------------------ */
main()
{
GenerateColourShadingList(0x0F0);    /* green shading */
}
/* ------------------------------------------------ */
void GenerateColourShadingList(UWORD colour_shade)
{
UBYTE j;
UWORD colour_value;
UBYTE brightness=0x0; /* must be between 0 and 15 */
UBYTE cycle_max=15,intensity=0;
UBYTE base_red,red,base_blue,blue,base_green,green;
base_red=(colour_shade&0x0F00)>>8;
base_green=(colour_shade&0x00F0)>>4;
base_blue=colour_shade&0x000F;
printf("UWORD c[] = {\n");       /* c[] array declaration */
printf("0x%.4x,",LINE_COUNT); /* line count */
for (j=0;j<LINE_COUNT;j++)
        {
        (j/cycle_max) % 2 ? intensity-- : intensity++;
        red=(base_red*intensity)/cycle_max;
        if (red<brightness) red=brightness;
        green=(base_green*intensity)/cycle_max;
        if (green<brightness) green=brightness;
        blue=(base_blue*intensity)/cycle_max;
        if (blue<brightness) blue=brightness;
        colour_value=(red<<8)|(green<<4)|blue;
        if(j<LINE_COUNT-1)
           {
           printf("0x%.4x,",colour_value);
           if (!((j-2)%4)) printf("\n");
```

```
                    }
                    else printf("0x%.4x\n",colour_value);
                }
        printf("};\n"); /* terminal brace */
        }
        /* ------------------------------------------------ */
```

The sort of output that the program given in listing 8.4 produces looks like this:

```
/*Listing 8.5: Typical output from the generator utility
program shown in listing 8.4*/
UWORD c[] = {
0x00ff,0x0010,0x0020,0x0030,
0x0040,0x0050,0x0060,0x0070,
0x0080,0x0090,0x00a0,0x00b0,
0x00c0,0x00d0,0x00e0,0x00f0,
0x00e0,0x00d0,0x00c0,0x00b0,
0x00a0,0x0090,0x0080,0x0070,
0x0060,0x0050,0x0040,0x0030,
0x0020,0x0010,0x0000,0x0010,
0x0020,0x0030,0x0040,0x0050,
0x0060,0x0070,0x0080,0x0090,
0x00a0,0x00b0,0x00c0,0x00d0,
0x00e0,0x00f0,0x00e0,0x00d0,
0x00c0,0x00b0,0x00a0,0x0090,
0x0080,0x0070,0x0060,0x0050,
0x0040,0x0030,0x0020,0x0010,
0x0000,0x0010,0x0020,0x0030,
0x0040,0x0050,0x0060,0x0070,
0x0080,0x0090,0x00a0,0x00b0,
0x00c0,0x00d0,0x00e0,0x00f0,
0x00e0,0x00d0,0x00c0,0x00b0,
0x00a0,0x0090,0x0080,0x0070,
0x0060,0x0050,0x0040,0x0030,
0x0020,0x0010,0x0000,0x0010,
0x0020,0x0030,0x0040,0x0050,
0x0060,0x0070,0x0080,0x0090,
0x00a0,0x00b0,0x00c0,0x00d0,
```

```
0x00e0,0x00f0,0x00e0,0x00d0,
0x00c0,0x00b0,0x00a0,0x0090,
0x0080,0x0070,0x0060,0x0050,
0x0040,0x0030,0x0020,0x0010,
0x0000,0x0010,0x0020,0x0030,
0x0040,0x0050,0x0060,0x0070,
0x0080,0x0090,0x00a0,0x00b0,
0x00c0,0x00d0,0x00e0,0x00f0,
0x00e0,0x00d0,0x00c0,0x00b0,
0x00a0,0x0090,0x0080,0x0070,
0x0060,0x0050,0x0040,0x0030,
0x0020,0x0010,0x0000,0x0010,
0x0020,0x0030,0x0040,0x0050,
0x0060,0x0070,0x0080,0x0090,
0x00a0,0x00b0,0x00c0,0x00d0,
0x00e0,0x00f0,0x00e0,0x00d0,
0x00c0,0x00b0,0x00a0,0x0090,
0x0080,0x0070,0x0060,0x0050,
0x0040,0x0030,0x0020,0x0010,
0x0000,0x0010,0x0020,0x0030,
0x0040,0x0050,0x0060,0x0070,
0x0080,0x0090,0x00a0,0x00b0,
0x00c0,0x00d0,0x00e0,0x00f0,
0x00e0,0x00d0,0x00c0,0x00b0,
0x00a0,0x0090,0x0080,0x0070,
0x0060,0x0050,0x0040,0x0030,
0x0020,0x0010,0x0000,0x0010,
0x0020,0x0030,0x0040,0x0050,
0x0060,0x0070,0x0080,0x0090,
0x00a0,0x00b0,0x00c0,0x00d0,
0x00e0,0x00f0,0x00e0,0x00d0,
0x00c0,0x00b0,0x00a0,0x0090,
0x0080,0x0070,0x0060,0x0050,
0x0040,0x0030,0x0020,0x0010,
0x0000,0x0010,0x0020,0x0030,
0x0040,0x0050,0x0060,0x0070,
0x0080,0x0090,0x00a0,0x00b0,
```

```
            0x00c0,0x00d0,0x00e0,0x00f0
        };
```

Needless to say this colour register data, if directed to a temporary file, can be subsequently loaded into a C program and the line count and RGB-content values used directly. In this case the shading routine is simpler because it only has to read the array items and use them to build a user Copper list. No colour value generating code is required. Listing 8.6 provides a typical example that places data from a given array into a specified colour register:

```
/* ----------------------------------------------- */
/*Listing 8.6: Routines that make use of pre-generated
colour register data are easier to code.*/
BOOL ColourShading(UBYTE colour_number,UWORD a[])
{
static struct UCopList *user_Copperlist_p=NULL;
COUNT i=0;
if(g_viewport_p->UCopIns==NULL)
        {
        if(user_Copperlist_p=
            AllocMem(sizeof(struct UCopList),MEMF_PUBLIC|
            MEMF_CLEAR))
            {
            CINIT(user_Copperlist_p,2*a[0]+1);
            for (i=0;i<a[0];i++)
                {
                CWAIT(user_Copperlist_p,i,0);
                CMOVE(user_Copperlist_p,custom.color
                    [colour_number],a[i+1]);
                }
            CEND(user_Copperlist_p);
            g_viewport_p->UCopIns=user_Copperlist_p;
            MakeScreen(g_public_screen_p);
            RethinkDisplay();
            }
        }
    else {
        g_viewport_p->UCopIns=NULL;
        MakeScreen(g_public_screen_p);
        RethinkDisplay();
        FreeCopList(user_Copperlist_p->FirstCopList);
```

```
            FreeMem(user_Copperlist_p,sizeof(struct
            UCopList));
            user_Copperlist_p=NULL;
            }
    return(0);
    }
    /* ------------------------------------------------ */
```

There is an infinite number of variations of these types of techniques and, as always, the suitability of a particular approach will depend on exactly what you are trying to do. In the main I tend to use the dynamic generation approach because during development it is more flexible than the alternatives – it's possible to change colours, change generating functions and so on without having to worry about the exact form of the resulting Copper lists. Whatever pathways you tread in these areas do make no mistake about one thing – as far as all of these shading effects are concerned the key to success is to understand the underlying principles of generating the appropriate values in the first place!

9: How Viruses Get at the Amiga Library Functions

There seems, at the moment, to be quite a lot of interest in how some Amiga programs are able to both alter selected Amiga operating system routines at will (especially when many of the routines are held in ROM) and monitor data passed to system routines by other programs. Obviously one of the reasons why these topics interest, and to some extent scare, a lot of users is because many computer viruses do these types of things. There are of course a number of legitimate reasons why a program might want to monitor, or alter, certain Amiga system routines but in order to understand both the *virus* and the *legitimate use* connections we need to take a few steps backwards and talk about how the Amiga library system works. As you'll probably already know the Amiga's library system is extremely flexible with some library routines being held in read only memory (ROM) and others being transparently loaded into RAM as required.

Programs tell Exec that a library is needed by attempting to *open* it using an OpenLibrary() function. When such a call is made Exec does several things beginning by searching its lists of libraries which are already open and available. If the library is found then Exec simply returns the address of the library and makes an internal note that another program is now using it. If the library is not already open Exec passes on the request to AmigaDOS asking it to look for, and then load, the specified library. AmigaDOS looks in the LIBS: logical device (if you boot from the Workbench disk for instance then this logical device will have been assigned to SYS:LIBS, ie the LIBS directory of the WorkBench disk). If AmigaDOS finds the library, it loads it and tells Exec which then duly records the fact that the library is now available. Exec incidentally will never attempt to remove these library modules whilst they are in use but when the last user of a particular library indicates that it is no longer needed, which they do by executing a CloseLibrary() function, Exec's library manager may then remove the memory copy of library and release the associated memory so that it is free for other use.

As far as, say, an applications program is concerned, most of these operations are transparent. All a program has to do to use a given library is open it using the Exec OpenLibrary() function, and then use the library routines in much the same way that the OpenLibrary() function itself is used. Applications programs which follow this protocol never need to concern themselves with where the library routines are in memory, nor with the fact that other programs may also be using the very same routines.

How Library Access Really Works

A library is basically just a collection of routines. These routines are not however called directly, they're accessed via a jump table which is a table consisting of entries that contain JMP instructions coupled to corresponding target addresses. The base address returned by the OpenLibrary() call is the address in memory of the start of a Library structure and this base location actually sits between this structure and other library specific data (Figure 9.1 provides a schematic illustration of what this data looks like once set up in memory).

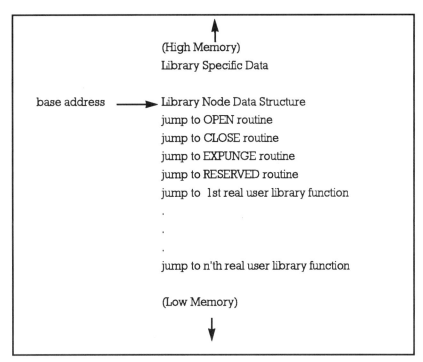

Figure 9.1. The 'in-memory' library access arrangements.

The first four function jump entries OPEN, CLOSE, EXPUNGE and RESERVED are for system only use. OPEN is an entry point called when the library is opened and is the routine responsible for incrementing the count of the number of users of a particular library. CLOSE is a corresponding routine which decreases the user count and, when the count gets to zero (ie the last library user indicates that the library is no longer needed) it may perform an EXPUNGE operation to prepare the library for removal. The RESERVED vector is, incidentally, currently unused.

To execute a particular library routine you use the opened library's base address in conjunction with a negative displacement that indicates which routine you wish to jump to (these offsets are called library vector offsets or LVO values). In a sense then you can associate these LVOs values with the corresponding *in memory jump table* as Figure 9.2 illustrates.

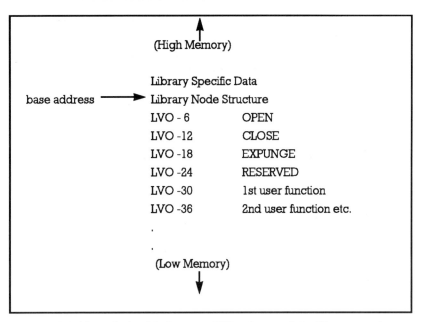

Figure 9.2. The relationship between LVO values and the library routines.

To call a library function on the Amiga you place the base address of the library in register a6, and then make an indirect subroutine call using the appropriate library vector offset (LVO) value. Let's take a concrete example. As you'll doubtless know, Intuition contains a DisplayBeep() function which can be used to *flash* an Intuition screen and the bare bones code for a DisplayBeep() call will look something like this:

```
move.l   _IntuitionBase, a6
jsr      _LVODisplayBeep(a6)
```

and would result in program control branching to the _LVODisplayBeep table entry of the library-structure/jump-table unit which was set up in memory when the Intuition library was opened. The jump table entry then branches to the *real* library routine.

Vanishing Vectors!

So, access to *all* Amiga library routines, whether they exist in RAM, or ROM, occurs indirectly using a series of library specific RAM-based jump table vectors. Once the purpose of these jump tables is understood the mechanisms used to modify system functions become almost obvious because in order to appear to change or replace a library routine, all you need to do is alter the appropriate jump table vector!

Let's get one thing clear: these types of changes do have legitimate uses and the 1.3 SetPatch function for instance made such changes in order to replace some bugged system functions. On a less official level a Workbench 1.3 based program might choose to replace the DisplayBeep() routine so that an audible beep rather than a screen flash was provided. The Amiga's Exec library does in fact contain a SetFunction() routine which allows a program to reset a library vector in this way and if for example I wanted to replace the Intuition DisplayBeep() function (which has an LVO value of -0x0060) with some alternative routine called MyF(), I'd do it like this:

```
old_p=SetFunction(IntuitionBase,-0x0060,(APTR)MyF);
```

and from that point on any program which called DisplayBeep() would end up executing my routine, called MyF(), instead.

As SetFunction() changes a library vector it returns the address of the original routine and this means that the original DisplayBeep() routine could be re-instated using this type of code:

```
SetFunction(IntuitionBase,-0x0060,old_p);
```

Function Name:	SetFunction()
Description:	Changes a function vector in a library
Call Format:	old_function=SetFunction(library_p,offset, =entry_point)
C Prototype:	APTR SetFunction(struct Library *, LONG, APTR);
Registers:	A0 A1 A0 D0
Arguments:	library_p - library base pointer offset - LVO offset of function to be replaced entry_point - pointer to the 0/new function
Return Value:	old_function - pointer to function that was replaced.

To appreciate the whole picture we need to look at a potential replacement routine and by way of example listing 9.1 shows a simple 68k patch that *double calls* the Intuition DisplayBeep() function. It executes DisplayBeep() in the normal fashion, waits for one second (using AmigaDOS's Delay() function), and then executes DisplayBeep() again. By using SetFunction() to insert a vector to this routine in the Intuition library's jump table the routine would then be entered by *all* programs and system functions that make a DisplayBeep() library call.

The result in this case is harmless – all programs calling the DisplayBeep() Intuition function would end up flashing the screen twice, when they thought they were flashing it once!

Listing 9.1: A 68k assembler patch which fools other programs into double calling the DisplayBeep() function.*/

```
_LVODelay    equ    -$00c6
             xdef   _MyF
             xref   _old_p
             xref   _DOSBase
```

```
            xref     _DOSBase
_MyF:       move.l   a0,screen       save screen address
            movea.l  _old_p,a1       real DisplayBeep() function
                                     address
            jsr      (a1)            do first DisplayBeep()
            jsr      delay           wait 1 second
            movea.l  screen,a0
            movea.l  _old_p,a1
            jsr      (a1)            do second displayBeep()
rtsdelay:   move.l   a6,-(sp)        preserve _IntuitionBase
            movea.l  _DOSBase,a6
            move.l   #50,d1          d1 = 50 ticks = 1 second
            jsr      _LVODelay(a6)
            move.l   (sp)+,a6        restore _IntuitionBase
rtsscreen:  dc.l     1
```

Although replacing the original DisplayBeep() vector would, in this particular example, serve little purpose, the general implications of such changes are extremely important. In this case, once the replacement routine is in place, other programs will think they are using the DisplayBeep() function as originally written when they are not!

Equally disconcerting of course is the fact that those programs can do nothing to avoid calling the modified routine. A lot of virus programs use exactly this approach to redirect important function calls, like Exec's DoIO(), through their own routines and such routines obviously have access to all the 680x0 register information provided for the original function call. All however is not lost and in fact most virus check programs do look at the most important jump table vectors, such as those relating to the Exec library and trackdisk device, to ensure that they are not changed in this way.

10: Music, Midi, and the MPX File Connection

This chapter is the first of two that concern Midi files and Midi serial port use. Just in case you are not yet Midi literate I'm going to start with a few preliminary notes on Midi itself. That way you'll be able to appreciate the general ideas even if the subject itself is new to you.

From a purely technical viewpoint Midi is a communications scheme that has been designed to allow standardized messages to be passed between pieces of musical equipment (synthesizers, drum machines etc). What this means in practice however is that Midi allows you to connect together all sorts of different pieces of musical equipment (from any number of manufacturers) and, providing a few ground rules are followed, they'll all work together quite happily. That in itself is quite an achievement but Midi has done far more than this: it has allowed computers to be used to read, store, edit and replay those messages (acting like a digital message tape-recorder) and this has led to a development which has turned the music world upside down. I'm talking here about the Midi sequencer. Not only has sequencing made life easier for the competent musician but it has opened the doors for everyone else. It is no exaggeration to say that the sequencer has made it possible for *anyone* with the slightest ear for music to play things that sound good without having to spend years mastering a musical instrument. In many ways then the sequencer is to the music world what the word-processor is to the secretary. Midi, as I've already mentioned, is a serial communications standard and Midi messages are sent as streams of pulses (much like the data that is passed through a printer cable or a modem). Each eight bit *byte* is sent as a start bit, eight data bits, and a stop bit at a speed of 31.25 KiloBaud. That's about one byte of Midi information every 320 millionths of a second. Midi equipment usually has two or three *five pin* DIN sockets. The terminal marked Midi-In is where the equipment receives its Midi data, that marked Midi-Out is where data is transmitted. Usually you'll also find a Midi-Thru socket and this provides a duplicate of whatever is being received at the Midi-In terminal. Not all types of equipment will understand all types of messages, nor does every piece of Midi equipment send every type of message but this doesn't usually cause much in the way of problems – providing you know what types of messages your particular equipment is capable of sending and understanding.

Midi messages are sent then as streams of eight bit numbers and it is the Midi standard which has defined their meaning. The first byte of a Midi message is called a status byte and it acts as a message identifier, ie it enables the receiving equipment to tell what type of message is coming in. Subsequent bytes of the message, if indeed they exist, are known as data bytes. How does Midi distinguish between status bytes and data bytes? It has opted for using the uppermost bit of each byte. Status bytes *always* have the high bit (bit 7) set so these numbers can range from 10000000 binary to 11111111 binary (decimal 128 to decimal 255). Because bit 7 is effectively used as a status byte indicator all data bytes are restricted to values ranging from 00000000 binary to 01111111 binary (decimal 0 to decimal 127).

Midi recognizes the existence of 16 separate channels and a large class of Midi messages, known as Channel messages, contain a channel number encoded within the status byte of the message. Pieces of equipment can therefore be selective about the messages they make use of and the result is that it is possible to have drummers, sequencers, synthesizers etc, all attached to each other via a single Midi communications cable loop. By setting up each unit to respond to a different Midi channel all of the Midi messages can be sent down the same set of cables with each unit responding to only those messages that have the matching channel number identification.

It's a bit like someone writing a letter to you, sticking it in a addressed envelope and posting it – the letter, along with thousands of others, gets carried around the postal system but, as far as reading the contents goes, it is essentially ignored until it arrives at your front door, ie its final destination. You know the letter is for you because it has got your name and address on it – Midi units know when a channel message has arrived for them because they will have a suitable channel number built into the message's status byte. So, Midi messages are streams of numbers whose meanings have been defined by the Midi standard. When do these numbers get transmitted? It's usually when you do something, touch a control knob or press a note on a keyboard etc. On a synthesizer, streams of numbers which represent such things as the notes being played and controller information, will be transmitted at the Midi-Out terminal. Other types of Midi equipment send similar streams of numbers and because the meanings of the numbers are standardized one piece of Midi equipment is able to understand another piece of equipment's messages. To get one unit to *talk* to another you simply use a Midi lead to connect them together using the appropriate Midi In/Out terminals. When you hit a note on a synthesizer keyboard for instance three pieces of Midi data actually get transmitted: a status byte which says 'here comes a message about a note being hit', a number representing the particular note in question, and lastly a number which indicates how hard the note was hit. The status byte includes details of which Midi channel is being used so after a program has read these three pieces of *data* it will be able to tell firstly that you've hit a note on the keyboard, secondly which Midi channel you're using, thirdly which note you hit and lastly it will be able to measure of its *loudness* (ie it will know how hard you hit the key).

Unfortunately all commerical sequencer programs tend to adopt their own file format arrangements for storing Midi information to disk and so to aid users in moving sequencer data between different sequencers a *Standard Midi File* format has been designed which nowadays most sequencers also support.

Standard Midi and MPX Format Files

Midi files come in three flavours, called types 0, 1 and 2. Type 0 is essentially a single stream of events that is meant to be played in much the same way as a single track of sequencer data. They are actually ideal for *playing* because only a small amount of translation work has to be done by the player program. Type 1 Midi files were designed for transferring multiple track Midi sequences between sequencer programs. Programs which *play* type 1 files have to be more sophisticated because the events from the various track chunks have to be rearranged to place them into the right order for playback. Type 2 Midi file files are quite rare – they were designed to allow the storage of multiple related sequences (eg the separate verses and choruses of a song could be stored in a type 2 file) but do not seem to be used much.

Top end Amiga sequencers like Blue Ribbon's Bars & Pipes Professional and Dr T's KCS, whilst being great packages for editing sequences, are expensive, *memory hungry*, beasts whose power is totally wasted when it comes to playing back completed compositions. To be honest all you need for Midi file playback purposes is a reliable, reasonably priced and easy to use product that is capable of reading and playing back the contents of a Midi file.

One would perhaps have thought that plenty of Midi file player utilities would have appeared in the public domain. Unfortunately this does not seem to have been the case and the main reason is that the parsing (ie reading and interpreting) and playing of a Midi file in real time is not a particularly easy a job. Needless to say adding Midi file playing capability to your own programs is likewise not easy, but there is an alternative approach based on the use of a much simpler file format that I've adopted called MPX, and this works like a dream.

MPX files start with a header event that looks like this:

```
8 byte Header:  <4 bytes MPX1 header>
                <4 bytes spare>
```

followed by a set of events that have this format:

```
8 byte Data:   <4 bytes absolute event time (microseconds)>
               <1 byte Midi message length>
               <Midi message itself>
```

Each event is padded to 8 bytes in length and for efficiency all duplicate status bytes will have been removed from consecutive Midi messages with message lengths adjusted accordingly. At the end of the day the Midi events in an MPX format file are just a stream of times plus real events that can *played* by reading the event time, executing a suitable delay, reading the event's length, and then transmitting the appropriate number of bytes via the serial port. Having sent one event you then read the next time value, do the next delay, and transmit the next event ad infinitum until the end of the file is reached. In order to play a file in this way you do of course need to be able to convert a Midi file into MPX format and that's where the following utility comes in handy.

MidiWriteX

This Shell utility, which you'll find on the disks accompanying the book, will convert a Midi file into its equivalent MPX form. It uses this sort of template:

```
MidiWriteX <source_filename destination_filename>
```

So if you want to translate a Midi file called mysong.mid on drive df0: into an MPX file called mysong.mpx you'd do it like this:

```
MidiWriteX df0:mysong.mid df0:mysong.mpx
```

The .mpx filename extension isn't a requirement – MPX files will be recognised whatever you decide to call them. Renaming files with an .mpx extension is however a useful convention to adopt because you'll then be able to recognise these files very easily. The corresponding MPX files produced are, incidentally, always larger than the Midi files from which they are derived but despite the size penalty they do have a big advantage of being easy to play because all the difficult Midi File event unpacking has already been done. Consequently adding MPX file playing capability to a program is, as we shall see shortly, a very easy thing to do. In order to play Midi data out through the Amiga's serial port however you do of course need to know how to use the Amiga's serial device.

Devices - An Introduction

Exec is said to provide standardized *device independent* I/O. A better description would be that it tries to make the I/O operations as uniform and as device independent as possible given the differing physical and electronic characteristics of the various bits of hardware involved. It's achieved by providing library routines which work with standardized blocks of data called I/O request structures. Device commands themselves fall into two categories: firstly, there are the standard commands, ie those which are designated as being common to all devices. Secondly come the commands which are device-specific.

All I/O requests are handled by setting up a data block which contains information relative to the request. The basic I/O request structure is called an IORequest and it looks like this:

```
struct IORequest   {
   struct Message  *io_Message;
   struct Device   *io_Device;
   struct Unit     *io_Unit;
   UWORD           io_Command;
   UBYTE           io_Flags;
   BYTE            io_Error;
};
```

The io_Message field points to a message header used by the device, io_Device points to a Device structure and io_Unit to a particular instance of the device. Units share the same device structures, code modules etc, but they operate independently. A typical example are the Amiga's floppy drives – each drive is represented as an independent unit of the same device where one device structure and one set of code modules support all the drives present. The io_Command field must be set to one of the allowable device commands and neither this, nor the ReplyPort which the device uses to communicate with your program, are changed by the servicing of the request – this facilitates the repeated use of the request block. io_Flags is used to indicate special options, and the last field io_Error is used to return the request's success/failure indicator (field is set to zero if the request was successfully carried out and to a non-zero error value if a problem occurred). A number of devices use an expanded request unit based on this IOStdReq structure:

```
struct IOStdReq    {
   struct Message  *io_Message;
   struct Device   *io_Device;
   struct Unit     *io_Unit;
   UWORD           io_Command;
   UBYTE           io_Flags;
   BYTE            io_Error;
   ULONG           io_Actual;  /* bytes actually transferred*/
   ULONG           io_Length;  /* number of bytes to be transferred*/
   APTR            io_Data;    /* pointer to a data transfer buffer*/
   ULONG           io_Offset;  /* an offset field used by some devices*/
};
```

The serial device uses these type of entities but it adds serial device specific data using this IOExtSer structure:

```
struct IOExtSer   {
   struct   IOStdReq IOSer;/* field discussed earlier*/
   ULONG    io_CtlChar;     /* control characters */
   ULONG    io_RBufLen;     /* serial port read buffer length */
   ULONG    io_ExtFlags;    /* additional, extension, flag set */
   ULONG    io_Baud;        /* baud rate of serial transmission */
   ULONG    io_BrkTime;     /* duration of break signal */
   struct   IOTArray io_TermArray; /* terminal character set */
   UBYTE    io_ReadLen;     /* bits per read character */
   UBYTE    io_WriteLen;    /* bits per write character */
   UBYTE    io_StopBits;    /* number of stop bits */
   UBYTE    io_SerFlags;    /* Serial Flag set */
   UWORD    io_Status;      /* see devices/serial.h for details */
};
```

Most of these fields are set to reasonable default values by the OpenDevice() function so in general you'll only need to worry about actually setting a parameter if you need to use a value which is different to the default value. Here for reference though are some details of the fields which may be set/altered: io_CntChar – this four byte field specifies the control character bytes to use for XON, XOFF, INQ and ACK although at present INQ/ACK handshaking is NOT supported. io_RBufLenField specifies the size of the buffer to be used for collecting incoming data. It *must* have a size of at least 64 bytes and should not be changed whilst the device is receiving data (the device will almost certainly discard the contents of the old buffer as it installs the new buffer).

io_ExtFlags

This can be used to select mark or space parity (see RKM manuals for further details). If not used the whole of this field *must* be set to zero.

io_Baud

Any value, from 1 to over 4 million, can be placed here but if the value cannot be supported by the hardware then the device will reject it. Baud rates over 19,200 need a few special tricks to ensure that data does not get lost – special corner-cutting provisions for Midi data (which uses a 31,250 baud rate) are provided.

io_Brk

TimeThis allows the user to define (in microseconds) how long a serial line break condition lasts.

io_TermArray

This is a nice flexible array-based approach to End-Of-File character collection. You fill the array with up to eight different EOF terminators (because of the way the array is searched these have to be arranged in *descending* order). The two things to bear in mind are: firstly, that you do have to provide eight entries so if, for instance, you only want to define one EOF value you'll need to set eight identical values in this array. Secondly, the EOFMODE flag must be set in the serial flags field because of this is not done the serial device ignores the io_TermArray altogether.

io_ReadLen/io_WriteLen

These tell the serial device how many bits should be present per character on the data being read and transmitted (normal values are 7 or 8).

io_StopBits

Tells the device how many stop bits should be produced when writing serial data (and expected when reading serial data). Normally set to either 1 or 2.

io_SerFlags

The devices/serial.h system header file provides a number of flag definitions which are recognized by the serial device. The default values of *all* of these flags is zero (ie not set):

SERF_EOFMODE : If you want the serial device to check io_TermArray then you will need to set this flag. It is incidentally the only flag that can be set/reset directly (ie without using the conventional *set parameters* function described later).

SERF_PARTY_ODD: Selects odd parity. Default (flag clear) condition selects even parity.

SERF_PARTY_ON: If this flag is set parity usage and checking is enabled.

SERF_QUEUEBRK: If set then all break commands will be queued. The default setting is that this flag is clear and in this case any break command received will take precedence over other serial output already queued.

SERF_RAD_BOOGIE: What a great name for a flag. If you set it the serial device will use a high-speed mode which by-passes some of its internal data checking operations. There are however some do's and don'ts associated with the use of this flag because: you *must* have disabled parity checking, you *must* have disabled XON/XOFF checking, you *must* be reading/writing 8-bit characters, and you *should not* expect to test for break signals!

SERF_SHARED: By default the serial device opens assuming that the user wants exclusive access. Setting this flag *before* opening the serial device will allow other tasks serial device access. In general this is not a wise move but it could be useful in some *carefully controlled* multi-program environments.

SERF_XDISABLED: If set this flag disables XON/XOFF handshaking.

SERF_7WIRE: Forces the device to use seven-wire handshaking for RS232C communications instead of the default three-wire arrangement (based on pins 2, 3 and 7). Flag *must* be set before device is initially opened.

Device Commands

Exec devices in general are expected to respond to at least eight standard commands. The term respond however does not mean execute properly – if a device cannot carry out one of these commands (and you would not, for instance, expect to be able to read data from a printer device) the device should return a suitable error code. The following commands are defined in the exec/io.h system file:

CMD_CLEAR

This clears all internal device buffers (*without* doing a CMD_UPDATE first). All existing data is lost.

CMD_FLUSH

This command aborts *all* queued I/O requests.

CMD_READ

This command will try to read a number of bytes, as specified in the request block's io_Length field, into the data buffer. The number of bytes actually read will be returned in the io_Actual field (this field should be checked to ensure that the expected number of bytes were read).

CMD_RESET

This command initializes a device returning any parameters to their default settings. Any impending requests are aborted and all buffers etc, are effectively cleared.

CMD_START

Used to re-start a device after a CMD_STOP command. I/O request handling then continues as per normal with any requests that may have been queuing being handled first.

CMD_STOP

This command stops the device at the earliest opportunity. I/O requests continue to queue but are not serviced.

CMD_UPDATE

This command forces the device's internal memory buffers to be written to the physical device – under normal circumstances the device should perform such operations automatically anyway.

CMD_WRITE

This command will try to write a number of bytes, as specified in the request block's io_Length field, from the data buffer. The number of bytes actually written will be returned in the io_Actual field (again this field should be checked to ensure that the expected number of bytes were read).The serial device supports seven of the standard device commands – CMD_CLEAR, CMD_FLUSH, CMD_READ, CMD_RESET, CMD_START, CMD_STOP and CMD_WRITE.

It also supports these three non-standard commands.

SDCMD_BREAK

This is used to send a break signal (results in the serial line being held low for a user-defined, relatively long, period.

SDCMD_QUERY

This command returns a snapshot of the serial port's lines and registers. Details can be obtained from the RKM serial device autodocs.

SDCMD_SETPARAMS

This enables the serial port parameters to be changed. Within the MidiPlayX program you'll find a routine called SetHighSpeedSerial() that uses this command, in conjunction with a DoIO() call that I'll discuss later, to set up the serial device for Midi transmission. The required Midi values are set up and a SDCMD_SETPARAMS command issued like this:

```
g_serial_request_p->io_SerFlags=SERF_SHARED|SERF_XDIS-
ABLED| SERF_RAD_BOOGIE;
g_serial_request_p->io_RBufLen=BUFFER_SIZE;
g_serial_request_p->io_Baud=Midi;
g_serial_request_p->io_ReadLen=8;
g_serial_request_p->io_WriteLen=8;
g_serial_request_p->io_StopBits=1;
g_serial_request_p->IOSer.io_Command=SDCMD_SETPARAMS;
if((DoIO((struct IORequest *)g_serial_request_p))!=NULL)
etc.
```

Opening and Closing A Device

As mentioned Exec I/O is *always* performed using I/O request blocks. Before I/O can be successfully achieved however the blocks must be properly initialized (by both the system and the user). Providing this has been done the device can be opened and this is done in much the same way as one would open a library. The Exec system function which performs this is called OpenDevice() and, since all devices opened by a program must be closed before the program terminates, Exec also provides a corresponding CloseDevice() function.

Function Name:	**OpenDevice()**
Description:	This function opens the specified device unit (completing any further initialization of the request block as it does so).
Call Format:	error=OpenDevice(name_p, unit, io_request_p, flags);
C Prototype:	BYTE OpenDevice(char *, ULONG, struct IORequest *, ULONG);
Registers:	D0 OpenDevice(A0, D0, A1, D1)
Arguments:	name_p - pointer to device name
	unit - unit number of the device to open
	io_request_p - pointer to a request block
	flags - additional info (device specific)
Return Value:	error - success/failure indicator
Notes:	when specifying a device name you should bear in mind that Exec filenames are case sensitive!

Music, Midi, and the MPX File Connections

Function Name:	**CloseDevice()**
Description:	This function closes a specified device unit.
Call Format:	CloseDevice(io_request_p);
C Prototype:	void CloseDevice(struct IORequest *);
Registers:	CloseDevice(A1)
Arguments:	io_request_p - pointer to a request block
Return Value:	None
Notes:	All outstanding I/O requests must have been completed (or aborted) *before* closing the device.

The function calls are perfectly straightforward to use and, needless to say, I place these operations into my standard stack based allocation scheme. Listing 10.1 shows the device opening function you'll find me using within the example code along with the corresponding closing routine.

```
/*Listing 10.1: Allocator based device opening and closing
code*/
UBYTE OpenSerialDevice()
{
UBYTE error_number=NO_ERROR;
g_serial_request_p->io_SerFlags=SERF_SHARED;
if((OpenDevice(SERIALNAME,0,(struct IORequest
*)g_serial_request_p,0))!=NULL)
error_number=STARTUP_ERROR;
else {
     g_function=CloseSerialDevice;
     PushStack(g_resource_stack_p,g_function);
     }
return(error_number);
}
void CloseSerialDevice()
{
CloseDevice((struct IORequest *)g_serial_request_p);
}
```

Amiga Lib Support Functions

The basic ideas of opening a device, using it via a combined set of standard and non-standard commands, and closing it when you've finished using it are simple enough. In practice the issues are complicated by the fact that a fair amount of initialization has to be done and that includes setting up a reply port so that the device has somewhere to deliver its messages to. Fortunately four additional functions are provided in the amiga.lib library that make life that much easier. The first two simplify the creation and deletion of message ports, the second two allow you to create and delete extended IORequest structures:

Function Name:	**CreatePort()**
Description:	Set up (allocate and initialize) a message port
Call Format:	port_p=CreatePort(name_p, priority);
C Prototype:	struct MsgPort *CreatePort(char *, LONG);
Arguments:	name_p - pointer to NULL terminated string
	priority - priority value (used to position the port in the public port list).
Return Value:	port_p - pointer to a new message port.
Notes:	If a NULL name is provided the port is not added to Exec's public port list. Since such ports cannot be found by using the Exec FindPort() function they are termed 'private'.

Function Name:	**DeletePort()**
Description:	Delete a message port
Call Format:	DeletePort(port_p);
C Prototype:	void DeletePort(struct MsgPort *);
Arguments:	port_p - pointer to the message port.
Return Value:	None

Again the use of these functions is very straightforward as you'll see from the MidiPlayX source listing. Reply port creation for instance is done like this:

```
/*Listing 10.2: Allocator based reply port creation*/
UBYTE CreateSerialReplyPort(void)
{
UBYTE error_number=NO_ERROR;
if((g_serial_reply_port_p=CreatePort(SERIALNAME,0))==NULL)
error_number=STARTUP_ERROR;
else {
     g_function=DeleteSerialReplyPort;
```

Music, Midi, and the MPX File Connections

```
            PushStack(g_resource_stack_p,g_function);
        }
    return(error_number);
    }
```

[Note: If you look in the official literature you will incidentally find that there are CreateMsgPort() and DeleteMsgPort() functions available in the exec library (from V36 onwards). The advantage of using these functions is that you do not have to link with amiga.lib.]

Function Name:	**CreateExtIO()**
Description:	Create an IORequest based structure
Call Format:	io_request_p=CreateExtIO(reply_port_p, size);
C Prototype:	struct IORequest *CreateExtIO(struct MsgPort *, ULONG);
Arguments:	reply_port_p - pointer to an INITIALIZED message port size - size of the I/O request block needed
Return Value:	io_request_p - pointer to the new I/O request structure or NULL if function failed.
Notes:	Normally size is determined by using sizeof() in conjunction with the extended device specific structures defined in the system headers.

Function Name:	**DeleteExtIO()**
Description:	Delete an IORequest based structure
Call Format:	DeleteExtIO(io_request_p);
C Prototype:	void DeleteExtIO(struct IORequest *);
Arguments:	io_request_p - pointer to an I/O request block.
Return Value:	None

[Note: Again, if you look in the official literature you will incidentally find that there are CreateIORequest() and DeleteIORequest() functions now available in the exec library (from V36 onwards).]

Device Use Summary

If you extract the general ideas from the previous discussions you'll see that a recognisable pattern is emerging for the use of Amiga devices:

1. Use CreatePort() or the equivalent exec function to create a reply port for the device to send its messages to.

2. Allocate and initialize a suitable device I/O request structure by using CreateExtIO() or the equivalent exec function .

3. Open the device using the OpenDevice() function.
4. Use the device for as long as required via any standard or non-standard device calls which are available.
5. Close the device using the CloseDevice() function.
6. Delete the I/O request structure using DeleteExtIO() or the equivalent exec function.
7. Delete the reply port using DeletePort() or the equivalent exec function.

The setting up and closing of the various entities can seem a bit like hard work. Luckily once the device is up and running sending commands to it is easy.

The DoIO() Standard Interface Function

There are a number of Exec functions reponsible for interfacing I/O requests and these operate independently of the particular device in question (essentially they deal with the request block as a whole and ignore the contents of the block). The one that I'll be using in this chapter is called DoIO():

Function Name:	DoIO()
Description:	This initiates an I/O request and waits for it to complete. In other words it performs synchronous I/O.
Call Format:	error=DoIO(io_request_p);
C Prototype:	BYTE DoIO(struct IORequest *);
Registers:	D0 DoIO(A1)
Arguments:	io_request_p - pointer to an initialized I/O request block
Return Value:	error - NULL if operation was successful otherwise the returned value is a (device specific) error number.
Notes:	This function asks the device driver to perform the requested I/O operation and then waits until the operation is complete (it will try to use quick I/O if possible).

Timer Device

The Amiga's timer device use follows the same broad plan as any other device and it is necessary to set up a reply port and a request block before opening the device. You'll see from the accompanying listings that there is a lot of common ground between serial device and timer device code during the initial setting up stages. I'll be setting the timer device up in what's called UNIT_MICROHZ mode using a TR_ADDREQUEST command coupled with DoIO() call. This results in the timer device waiting for the specified time period before replying to my time interval request. The timer device use within the MidiPlayX program will be quite easy to follow but the timer device is capable of much more sophisticated uses. For more complete details of timer device use you should consult the official Amiga literature.

MidiPlayX

With the device related issues now safely out of the way we can now talk sensibly about the overall structure of MidiPlayX – an AmigaDOS style command that can play MPX format files. By looking at the coding for this utility you should be able see what has to be done to incorporate MPX playing into your own code.

The command itself uses this command template:

```
MidiPlayX <filename>
```

The program uses my conventional resource allocation method, in this case setting up and opening serial and timer devices using an allocation list that looks like this:

```
UBYTE (*display_list[])() = {
    CreateSerialReplyPort,
    CreateSerialRequestBlock,
    OpenSerialDevice
    SetHighSpeedSerial,
    CreateTimerReplyPort,
    CreateTimerRequestBlock,
    OpenTimer
};
```

Providing the allocation stages are successful the program simply calls a PlayFile() routine passing to it the name of the file that was provided on the Shell command line. Once the PlayFile() routine terminates, the program deallocates its resources in the usual fashion. Here's the loop that provides control of the startup, file playing and closing down operations:

```
if(!AllocateResource(DISPLAY_COUNT,display_list))
    {
    if(PlayFile(argv[1])) printf(MISSING_SOURCE);
    }
while(!PopStack(g_resource_stack_p,g_function)) g_function();
KillStack(g_resource_stack_p);
}
```

File playing, as I've already mentioned, is straightforward because of the simple structure of MPX files. Accurate timing however is obviously of paramount importance if the song being played is to sound right and so one of the first things that the PlayFile() routine does is bump up the MidiPlayX task priority like this:

```
g_task_priority=SetTaskPri(FindTask(0),BUMPED_PRIORITY);
```

The specified file is then opened and checked for suitable header info using this sort of code:

```
file_id=Read4BytesFromChunk(source_p);
if(file_id==ID_MPX1)
{ etc.
```

Event handing itself is also easy. We use a loop that reads each 8 byte event and works out the required time delay by subtracting the event time of the current event from the event time of the previously read event and then, after any time delay required, transmits the message via the serial port using a conventional DoIO() command.

Here's the framework of the loop that you'll find in the PlayFile() routine:

```
while(fread(g_Midi_message,8,1,source_p))
{
delay=*((ULONG *)g_Midi_message)-g_absolute_time;
g_absolute_time=*((ULONG *)g_Midi_message);
if(delay)
    {
    Do a time delay (see later source for details)
    }
TransmitMessage((UBYTE)g_Midi_message[4]);
}
```

This PlayFile() routine is simple and short and all a program has to do to incorporate MPX file playing capability is to incorporate this code along with the SetTimer(), TransmitMessage() and Read4BytesFromChunk() support routines (obviously the serial and timer device handling code needs to be present as well). Set up and open the serial and timer devices and then just pass the name of the file to be played to the PlayFile() routine. The MidiPlayX utility was written primarily to show you what needs to be done and since it is relatively small here to finish this chapter is, for ease of reference, the complete source for the program:

```
/* ======================================================= */
/* Module name: Midiplayx.c - contains the MidiPlayX pro-
gram code
/* ------------------------------------------------------- */
#define ALLOCATE_GLOBALS
#include "general.h"
```

```c
#define MakeID(a,b,c,d)  ( (LONG) (a)<<24L | (LONG) (b)<<16L | (c)<<8 | (d) )
#define ID_MPX1    MakeID('M','P','X','1')
#define DISPLAY_COUNT 7
__buffsize=MidiFILE_BUFFER_SIZE;
UBYTE (*display_list[])() = {
     CreateSerialReplyPort,
     CreateSerialRequestBlock,
     OpenSerialDevice,
     SetHighSpeedSerial,
     CreateTimerReplyPort,
     CreateTimerRequestBlock,
     OpenTimer
     };
main(int argc, char *argv[])
{
UBYTE error_number=NO_ERROR;
printf(SIGN_ON);
if(!(g_resource_stack_p=CreateStack(void *))) error_number=NO_STACK;
else {
     /* attempt to allocate resources... */
     if(!AllocateResource(DISPLAY_COUNT,display_list))
          {
          if(PlayFile(argv[1])) printf(MISSING_SOURCE);
          }
     while(!PopStack(g_resource_stack_p,g_function))
     g_function();
     KillStack(g_resource_stack_p);
     }
return(0);
}
 /* Logical end of program */
/* -------------------------------------------------- */
UBYTE AllocateResource(UBYTE count,UBYTE (*list[])())
{
UBYTE i, error_number;
for (i=0;i<count;i++)
```

```c
            {
            if(error_number=list[i]())
                {
                printf("%s %d\n",CANNOT_ALLOCATE,i);
                i=count; /* force exit from loop */
            }
            }
    return(error_number);
    }
    /* ------------------------------------------------ */
    UBYTE CreateSerialReplyPort(void)
    {
    UBYTE error_number=NO_ERROR;
    if((g_serial_reply_port_p=CreatePort(SERIALNAME,0))==NULL)
            error_number=STARTUP_ERROR;
    else {
        g_function=DeleteSerialReplyPort;
        PushStack(g_resource_stack_p,g_function);
        }
    return(error_number);
    }
    /* ------------------------------------------------ */
    void DeleteSerialReplyPort(void)
    {
    DeletePort(g_serial_reply_port_p);
    }
    /* ------------------------------------------------ */
    UBYTE CreateSerialRequestBlock()
    {
    UBYTE error_number=NO_ERROR;
    g_serial_request_p=(struct IOExtSer *)
            CreateExtIO(g_serial_reply_port_p,sizeof(struct
            IOExtSer));
    if (g_serial_request_p==NULL) error_number=STARTUP_ERROR;
    else {
        g_serial_request_p->IOSer.io_Data=(APTR)&g_Midi_mes
        sage[5];
        g_function=DeleteSerialRequestBlock;
```

```
        PushStack(g_resource_stack_p,g_function);
        }
return(error_number);
}
/* -------------------------------------------------- */
void DeleteSerialRequestBlock()
{
DeleteExtIO((struct IORequest *)g_serial_request_p);
}
/* -------------------------------------------------- */
UBYTE OpenSerialDevice()
{
UBYTE error_number=NO_ERROR;
g_serial_request_p->io_SerFlags=SERF_SHARED;
if((OpenDevice(SERIALNAME,0,(struct IORequest *)
g_serial_request_p,0))!=NULL)error_number=STARTUP_ERROR;
else {
     g_function=CloseSerialDevice;
     PushStack(g_resource_stack_p,g_function);
     }
return(error_number);
}
/* -------------------------------------------------- */
void CloseSerialDevice()
{
CloseDevice((struct IORequest *)g_serial_request_p);
}
/* -------------------------------------------------- */
UBYTE SetHighSpeedSerial()
{
UBYTE error_number=NO_ERROR;
g_serial_request_p->io_SerFlags=SERF_SHARED|SERF_XDIS-
ABLED|SERF_RAD_BOOGIE;
g_serial_request_p->io_RBufLen=BUFFER_SIZE;
g_serial_request_p->io_Baud=Midi;
g_serial_request_p->io_ReadLen=8;
g_serial_request_p->io_WriteLen=8;
g_serial_request_p->io_StopBits=1;
```

```
            g_serial_request_p->IOSer.io_Command=SDCMD_SETPARAMS;
            if((DoIO((struct IORequest *)g_serial_request_p))!=NULL)
                    error_number=STARTUP_ERROR;
            else {
                g_serial_request_p->IOSer.io_Command=CMD_WRITE;
                }
            return(error_number);
            }
            /* ------------------------------------------------- */
            UBYTE CreateTimerReplyPort()
            {
            UBYTE error_number=NO_ERROR;
            if((g_timer_reply_port_p=CreatePort(TIMERNAME,0))==NULL)
                    error_number=STARTUP_ERROR;
            else {
                g_function=DeleteTimerReplyPort;
                PushStack(g_resource_stack_p,g_function);
                }
            return(error_number);
            }
            /* ------------------------------------------------- */
            void DeleteTimerReplyPort()
            {
            DeletePort(g_timer_reply_port_p);
            }
            /* ------------------------------------------------- */
            UBYTE CreateTimerRequestBlock()
            {
            UBYTE error_number=NO_ERROR;
            g_timer_request_p=(struct timerequest *)
                    CreateExtIO(g_timer_reply_port_p,sizeof(struct
                    timerequest));
            if (g_timer_request_p==NULL) error_number=STARTUP_ERROR;
            else {
                g_function=DeleteTimerRequestBlock;
                PushStack(g_resource_stack_p,g_function);
                }
            return(error_number);
```

```
}
/* -------------------------------------------------- */
void DeleteTimerRequestBlock()
{
DeleteExtIO((struct IORequest *)g_timer_request_p);
}
/* -------------------------------------------------- */
UBYTE OpenTimer()
{
UBYTE error_number=NO_ERROR;
if((OpenDevice(TIMERNAME,UNIT_MICROHZ,(struct IORequest
*)g_timer_request_p,0))!=NULL)
        error_number=STARTUP_ERROR;
else {
     g_timer_request_p->tr_node.io_Command=TR_ADDREQUEST;
     g_function=CloseTimer;
     PushStack(g_resource_stack_p,g_function);
     }
return(error_number);
}
/* -------------------------------------------------- */
void CloseTimer()
{
CloseDevice((struct IORequest *)g_timer_request_p);
}
/* -------------------------------------------------- */
void __regargs TransmitMessage(ULONG size)
{
BYTE io_error;
g_serial_request_p->IOSer.io_Length=size;
if(io_error=DoIO((struct IORequest *)g_serial_request_p))
   printf("%s %x\n",SERIAL_IO_ERROR,io_error);
}
/* -------------------------------------------------- */
void __regargs SetTimer(ULONG seconds, ULONG microseconds)
{
BYTE io_error;
g_timer_request_p->tr_time.tv_secs=seconds;
```

```c
            g_timer_request_p->tr_time.tv_micro=microseconds;
            if(io_error=DoIO((struct IORequest *)g_timer_request_p))
                  printf("%s %x\n",TIMER_IO_ERROR,io_error);
            }
            /* ---------------------------------------------- */
            UBYTE __regargs PlayFile(TEXT *source_name_p)
            {
            BYTE io_error;
            FILE *source_p;
            UBYTE error_number=NO_ERROR;
            ULONG delay, file_id;
            g_absolute_time=0;
            g_task_priority=SetTaskPri(FindTask(0),BUMPED_PRIORITY);
            if(source_p=fopen(source_name_p,"rb"))
                  {
                  file_id=Read4BytesFromChunk(source_p);
                  if(file_id==ID_MPX1)
                     {
                     Read4BytesFromChunk(source_p); /* read over blank
                           space */
                     while(fread(g_Midi_message,8,1,source_p))
                        {
                        delay=*((ULONG *)g_Midi_message)-
                              g_absolute_time;
                        g_absolute_time=*((ULONG *)g_Midi_message);
                        if(delay)
                              {
                              g_timer_request_p-
                                    >tr_time.tv_secs=delay/1000000;
                              g_timer_request_p-
                                    >tr_time.tv_micro=delay%1000000;
                              if(io_error=DoIO((struct IORequest
                                    *)g_timer_request_p))
                              printf("%s %x\n",TIMER_IO_ERROR,io_error);
                              }
                        TransmitMessage((UBYTE)g_Midi_message[4]);
                        }
                     }
                  else error_number=BAD_FILE;
```

```
            fclose(source_p);
           }
       else error_number=NO_SOURCE;
SetTaskPri(FindTask(0),g_task_priority);
return(error_number);
}
/* ------------------------------------------------- */
ULONG __regargs Read4BytesFromChunk(FILE *source_p)
{
ULONG value; UBYTE i;
value=(ULONG)fgetc(source_p);
for(i=0;i<3;i++) value=(value<<8)+fgetc(source_p);
return(value);
}
/* ------------------------------------------------- */
void __regargs __chkabort(void)
{
}
/* ------------------------------------------------- */
```

11: The Workbench MidiPlayer Program

Midi sequencer packages are designed primarily for the creation and editing of Midi sequences and whilst they offer playback facilities as part and parcel of this process they use their own (proprietary) data formats internally and are therefore not usually geared up for direct playback of Midi files. This lack of direct Midi file playing support can be a pain. Suppose for example you have a library of sequences and songs which, for reasons of portability, you keep in Midi file form. To listen to any of the data you'd have to load a sequencer and then import the sequence or song before you could play it. When you've got hundreds of songs or sequences these import operations can take a lot of time. Alternatively, ask any musician who uses a Midi sequencer on live gigs and they'll also confirm that sequencers in general are not geared for ease-of-use as playback devices. They have too many controls and are nowadays large *memory hungry* programs (memory that with a smaller program could be used for storing Ram-based, and therefore rapidly accessed, sequences). What's needed in these, and many other, *playback only* situations is some sort of small utility that can handle Midi files directly. I was never able to find one and so, to cut a long story short, I wrote my own called the MidiPlayer. At the time of writing two versions of the program are available, a Workbench version and a Shell command version. Before we do anything else then here are some brief details of the utilities that you'll find on the disk accompanying the book.

MidiPlayer 1.30 is the Workbench 2.04+ runable form of a utility for playing Type 0 *and* Type 1 Midi files. It can also examine and display general details concerning the contents of Midi files and in this case any type of Midi file, including Type 2, can be loaded for examination. How do you use it? Well you'll find the full docs file on disk but basically you just connect your Midi gear to an Amiga via a Midi interface and double click on the MidiPlayer icon. Use the Project Menu's *Select File* option to open the file requester and choose a Midi file.

When you click on OK the file will be loaded and analysed after which you will be able to use the Display menu to examine a number of file characteristics. In particular you'll be able to see if the file contains any Sysex or sequencer specific *meta* events, and be able to see the general Midi message events present and the channels being used. This should help make setting up easier when attempting to play files created by other users. The Play File menu is used for playing, or cancelling, the selected file. All Notes Off messages are sent as soon as a play operation is cancelled so most equipment should therefore turn off any hanging notes very quickly. As a precaution real Note Off messages then also get sent for every note on every channel. This is because some Midi units refuse to recognise All Notes Off commands. The Utility menu provides a similar *Kill Notes* option that can be used at any time.

The AmigaDOS Style MidiPlayer Command

This, as the name suggests, is a version of the MidiPlayer that can be used to play Midi files from a Shell window or an AmigaDOS or ARexx script. The command itself is used like this:

```
MidiPlayer <filename>
```

To play a file called myfile.mid present on a disk in drive df0: for instance you would type the command:

```
MidiPlayer df0:mysong.mid
```

As usual if you want to suppress the program's sign-on text etc, you just redirect its output to NIL:

```
MidiPlayer >NIL: <filename>
```

I ought to at this stage mention that I am not going to provide an in-depth line-by-line analysis of how I designed and coded these Midi file playing programs – this would take a book in itself. What I do want to do however is cover the important areas and detail with a number of issues that illustrate important general coding points. To start with it should be pretty obvious that the key to writing any file processing utility is to understand, in detail, the relevant file format. This means of course that it is necessary for

The Workbench MidiPlayer Program

you also to know a little about Midi files in order to appreciate the ideas that are about to be discussed.

Overview Of The Standard Midi File Structure

At the highest level Midi files consist of blocks of data called *chunks*. Each chunk consists of a 4 byte identifier followed by a 32 bit number which provides the byte-length of the data held in the chunk. At the time of writing only two types of chunks are defined: Header chunks which have a *MThd* identifier, and track chunks which have a *MTrk* identifier. The idea of files consisting of identifiable chunks which may be used or skipped over is of course similar to that used by Electronic Art's IFF format. There are however two important differences: firstly, the Midi file arrangement doesn't support the idea of nested chunks. Secondly, Midi file chunks are not padded to an even number of bytes like IFF files.

Midi file chunks can be arranged in three ways and this, as indicated in the previous chapter, leads to three types of files. Type 0 files contain a header chunk followed by a single track chunk – this is the most portable of all Midi file arrangements and is used for storing a sequence or song as a single stream of events. Type 1 files have a different use – they allow multiple simultaneous track sequences to be stored. Type 1 files contain a header chunk followed by a number of separate track chunks intended to represent tracks to be played simultaneously.

Format 2 files are different again because they've been developed to allow sets of independent sequences to be stored. A sequencer might save the individual sequences (intro, verse, bridge etc) which make up a complete song as a single format 2 type file. For a Midi file player program the most convenient format is the type 0 arrangement but since most companies that produce commercial Midi file compositions tend to provide type 1 format files, a player program ideally needs to be able to read and play these as well as type 0 format files.

MThd header chunks are always the first chunk in a MIDI file and, like all Midi file chunks, they start with the identifier followed by a 32 bit chunk size value. Header chunks currently have six bytes of data: the first word gives the file format (0, 1, or 2), the second tells you how many track chunks are present in the file, and the last contains timing/division information. The chunk contents therefore take this form:

```
4 Bytes MThd identifier
4 Bytes Size in bytes of following data (currently 6)
2 Bytes Midi file type (0, 1 or 2)
2 Bytes Number of Track Chunks (will be 1 for file type 0)
```

2 Bytes Division information

The *division* field's contents and format may vary but if bit 15, ie the most significant bit, is zero then bits 14-0 give a 15 bit number which specifies how many delta-time ticks make up a crotchet and this information is used to adjust the overall event playback speed.

Track chunks start with a 4 byte identifier *MTrk* and a 32 bit length field which shows how many bytes the chunk contains. Following that come the data events themselves – these all start with a field that specifies the amount of time which should pass before the specified event occurs (this is the so called *delta time*). Track chunk events can be one of three types: Midi Events (which are defined as being any Midi channel message), Sysex events (which in a Midi file can be represented in two different ways), and a collection of non-Midi events known as *Meta Events*.

Midi events are obviously going to be of interest to the player program and I'll deal with the issues related to these events later. I'm not going to deal with Sysex events in any great detail because most musicians do not include them in their Midi files. However, because these events have to be properly skipped over we do need to know how to both identify them and measure their size. Here are the general Sysex event formats:

```
Sysex event 1:    <delta-time>    <F0>    <byte-count>    <sysex-data-bytes>
Sysex event 2:    <delta-time>    <F7>    <byte-count>    <sysex-data-bytes>
```

Only two Meta events will directly concern us although again general format details are needed in order to properly skip over any unused events as they are encountered. Meta events take this general format:

```
Meta Event  <delta time> <FF hex> <meta-event type> <length> <data bytes>
```

In other words all of them start with an FF hex Meta event identifier, followed by a *type* field, a byte count, and the data itself. The type field is a 1 byte value between 0 and 127 and the length field is stored in the same variable length format as is used for delta-time values. The two Meta events of interest are those that allow the end of a track, or a change in tempo, to be recognised (See table 11.1). A whole collection of other Meta events have been defined and many are used for embedding text material (eg sequence or track names, lyrics and Copyright notices).

The Workbench MidiPlayer Program

Description	Type (Hex)	Length	Details
End Of Track	2F	0	This event *must* be used so that an exact ending point can be specified for a track. It's use is non-optional!
Set Tempo	51	3	A 24 bit number which represents microseconds per quarter note. These events should ideally only occur at positions where real Midi clocks could be located.

Table 11.1. Two example meta events

Delta Times

These time fields are an integral part of the syntax of all Midi file events and, like a number of other Midi file items, their values are stored in a variable length format containing 7 real bits per byte. The most significant bit (bit 7) is used to indicate either the continuation, or the end, of the number:

1st Byte   2nd Byte   n'th Byte
1xxx xxxx   1xxx xxxx   0xxx xxxx

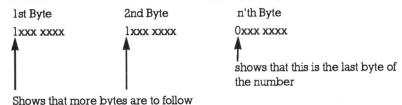

shows that this is the last byte of the number

Shows that more bytes are to follow

You may be wondering why Midi files do not use say a simple fixed 4 byte event time field. The reason is to do with efficiency because with the variable length approach inter-event times which are less than 128 (the majority of the time values) can be stored using just a single byte. The number 126 for example can be stored simply as binary 0111 1110. Once we get above 127 however, ie 0111 1111, more bytes will be needed to store the number.

Table 11.2. Time fields.

So that then is the basis of the Midi file standard. It's worth mentioning that something called *running status*, the use of implied status bytes is allowed in Midi file data much as it is allowed in real time Midi data streams. It's a trick used for improving the efficiency of the Midi system and is based on the pretty obvious fact that pieces of music will invariably contain many sections that consist of just note on and note off messages. Because of this the Midi standard has allowed notes to be turned off using note on messages with zero velocity bytes. These sections can therefore be completely transmitted using just note on status bytes. A normal note on message as we saw in the last chapter consists of three bytes but when the running status arrangement is used most of the note playing events can be sent as just the two data bytes (because the status byte is unchanged). Running status can therefore reduce by up to 1/3rd the number of bytes that need to be transmitted!

Although this running status scheme is also allowed to occur within Midi file data it is only permitted within a stream of Midi events – it must not be carried across non-channel events. So, if a stream of running status Midi messages are interrupted by one or more Meta or Sysex events in a Midi file then a new status byte must be present in the first of any Midi messages which follow.

A Matter Of Design

The initial program development stages, as might be expected, revolved around the use of a collection of techniques whose aim was to map out in detail the overall structure of the program. I used Warnier diagramming techniques for the initial program design but there are plenty of other, equally useful, techniques available that could have been used. In general the two most important points to make are that firstly you should use some kind of systematic design approach, and secondly that you should feel comfortable with the techniques you adopt!

Having studied the Midi file standard in detail its logical structure was mapped out to give me a clear picture of the formats of the allowable data items. There is always a very strong connection between the file structure and final program structure in these type of file parsing programs and in fact the descriptions of many of the player program routines were created directly from my Midi file structure diagrams. I found it convenient to split the development into two parts producing first a (high-level) *chunk reader* whose job was to identify individual Midi file track chunks. Don't get fooled into thinking that these early design stages are just a matter of sketching a program structure and getting stuck into the coding - it's more an *iterative cycle* that involves you thinking about what you're doing, perhaps changing some ideas in light of further thought, modifying the design and so on. For example, as the development proceeded, one question that arose with the high-level chunk reader was how to check that any supplied filename actually constituted a Midi file. In this instance the standard gave the necessary clues – the program must read the header chunk and see if the *MThd* identifier is present because only if a valid header chunk is found must the program attempt to read the header items described in the standard. Other thoughts involved the incorporation of a dummy *destination file* for receiving output data – although not needed for the player program itself I knew that this file output hook would prove valuable in a number of related Midi file applications. With my planning approaches all of this type of

The Workbench MidiPlayer Program

detail gets eventually embedded into the program design diagrams. As an example Figure 11.1 shows a Warnier sketch of the chunk reader part of the player program. Notice that I've allowed for the fact that, at some later stage in the development of the Midi standard, some new (and therefore unrecognised) fields might be added to the header. What does the final code look like in relation to the diagram forms? Listing 11.1 shows a code sketch that was developed from the VALID FILE area of the Figure 11.1 framework during the early development stages:

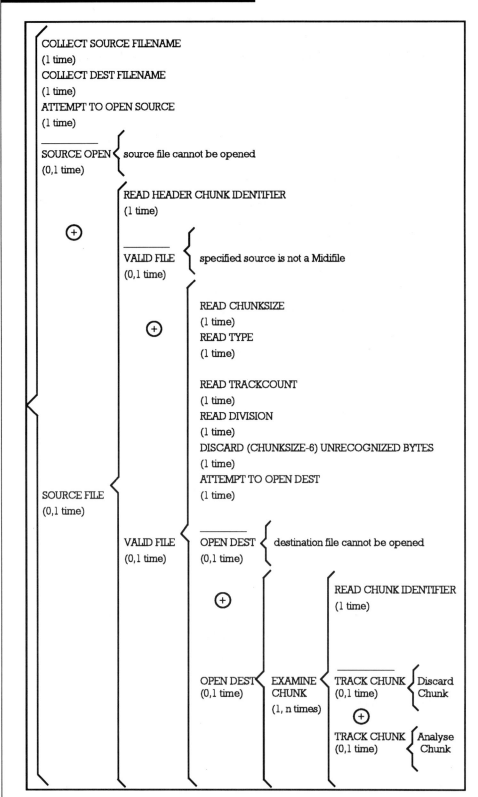

Figure 11.1. Part of the Warnier description of the high-level chunk reader.

```c
/*Listing 11.1: Part of some preliminary chunk reader code
for the player program*/
UBYTE OpenSourceOK(FILE *source_p, TEXT *dest_name_p)
{
variable declarations
identifier=Read4BytesFromChunk(source_p);
if(identifier!=ID_HEADER) error_number=BAD_HEADER;
else {
    chunksize=Read4BytesFromChunk(source_p);
    type=fgetc(source_p); type=(type<<8)+fgetc(source_p);
    trackcount=fgetc(source_p); trackcount=(track
    count<<8)+fgetc(source_p);
    g_division=fgetc(source_p); g_division=(g_divi
    sion<<8)+fgetc(source_p);
    g_microsecs=g_tempo/g_division;
    bytes_to_discard=chunksize-3*sizeof(UWORD);
    error_number=DiscardBytes(bytes_to_discard,source_p);
    if(error_number==NO_ERROR)
       {
      if (!(dest_p=fopen(dest_name_p,"wb")))
         error_number=NO_DEST;
        else {
            for (i=0;i<trackcount;i++)
                {
                error_number=ExamineChunk(source_p,
                dest_p, dest_name_p);
                if(error_number!=NO_ERROR) i=track
                count; /* force exit */
                } /* end of loop processing */
            fclose(dest_p);
            } /* end of successful
                fopen(dest_name_p,"wb") processing */
      } /* end of if(error_number==NO_ERROR) processing*/
    } /* end of (identifier==ID_HEADER) processing */
fclose(source_p);
return(error_number);
}
```

Chunk Analysis

The high-level reader just described will happily skip through a Midi file on a chunk by chunk basis. The next stage involved the creation of a (low-level) chunk analyser whose job was to perform the detailed track chunk examination. Again a lot of preliminary planning was carried out and the resulting design diagrams used to produce the final code. The chunk analyser routine has to be involved with the detailed structure of possible events present in a Midi file and we know from the Midi file standard that every event has an associated delta time value and that events are either Sysex, Meta or Midi events. The overall formats of Sysex and Meta events are reasonably simple and have already been discussed. Midi events, the disk file equivalent of a Midi message, are a little more complicated because there are seven separate classes.

A channel MIDI message consists of a status byte (bit 7 set high) followed by either one or two trailing data bytes whose values can only be between 0 and 0x7F. The status byte itself need not be sent if the previous message had the same status byte (this is called running status and it is used to avoid unnecessary status byte duplication). The status bytes have a MIDI channel number (shown as n) embedded in the lower four bytes and this 0x0-0xF value corresponds to MIDI channels 1-16. Channel message types and sizes are shown below:

NOTE_OFF	0x8n	NOTE_OFF_SIZE	2
NOTE_ON	0x9n	NOTE_ON_SIZE	2
POLYPHONIC_AT	0xAn	POLYPHONIC_AT_SIZE	2
CONTROL_CHANGE	0xBn	CONTROL_CHANGE_SIZE	2
PROGRAM_CHANGE	0xCn	PROGRAM_CHANGE_SIZE	1
CHANNEL_PRESSURE	0xDn	CHANNEL_PRESSURE_SIZE	1
PITCHBEND	0xEn	PITCHBEND_SIZE	2

The bottom line here for all file events is that, having read the delta time value and executed an appropriate delay, we must identify the event type. In the corresponding code these Sysex and Meta event classifications are handled by a switch statement and all other bytes, which should be either Midi status bytes or Midi data bytes are dealt with by a separate MidiHandler() routine that checks/sets any status changes using a switch statement to identify the various message categories. Listing 11.2 shows a skeleton version of the routine which handles the event identification.

Midi messages vary in size and in order to transmit the right number of bytes it's necessary to distinguish between the various classes. This again is easily handled in C by using a switch statement and listing 11.3 should give the general idea. Transmission of each message is achieved by the serial device oriented TransmitMessage()function shown in listing 11.4.

```
/*Listing 11.2: Skeleton form of the program section that
identifies event classes.*/
UBYTE AnalyseChunk(FILE *source_p, FILE *dest_p)
{
do {
   delta_time=ReadVarLen(source_p);
   if(delta_time)
         {
         real_delay=delta_time*g_microsecs;
         g_timer_request_p->tr_time.tv_secs=
         real_delay/1000000;
         g_timer_request_p->tr_time.tv_micro=
         real_delay%1000000;
         DoIO((struct IORequest *)g_timer_request_p);
         }
current_byte=fgetc(source_p); /* read first byte of this
event */
switch(current_byte)
      {
      case SYSEX_EVENT1: handle this type of event
      case SYSEX_EVENT2: ditto
      case META_EVENT: ditto
      default:
               pass item to MidiHandler()
               break;
      }
   }while(!(exit_flag|g_break_flag));
return(error_number);
}


/*Listing 11.3: The switch section code that built the
Midi messages*/
switch(current_status)
{
case NOTE_OFF:          g_midi_message[2]=fgetc(source_p);
                        TransmitMessage(NOTE_OFF_SIZE);
                        break;
```

```
        case NOTE_ON:           g_midi_message[2]=fgetc(source_p);
                                TransmitMessage(NOTE_ON_SIZE);
                                break;
        case POLYPHONIC_AT:     g_midi_message[2]=fgetc(source_p);
                                TransmitMessage(POLYPHONIC_AT_SIZE);
                                break;
        case CONTROL_CHANGE:    g_midi_message[2]=fgetc(source_p);
                                TransmitMessage(
                                CONTROL_CHANGE_SIZE);
                                break;
        case PROGRAM_CHANGE:    TransmitMessage(
                                PROGRAM_CHANGE_SIZE);
                                break;
        case CHANNEL_PRESSURE: TransmitMessage(
                                CHANNEL_PRESSURE_SIZE);
                                break;
        case PITCHBEND:         g_midi_message[2]=fgetc(source_p);
                                TransmitMessage(PITCHBEND_SIZE);
                                break;
        default:current_status=BAD_CHUNK_DATA;break;
        }
        Listing 11.4: Serial request code for sending a Midi
        Message*/



        void TransmitMessage(ULONG size)

        {

        g_serial_request_p->IOSer.io_Data=(APTR)g_midi_message;

        g_serial_request_p->IOSer.io_Length=size;

        g_serial_request_p->IOSer.io_Command=CMD_WRITE;

        DoIO((struct IORequest *)g_serial_request_p);

        }
        Listing 11.5: A generalised routine used to skip over
        unwanted file events*/



        UBYTE DiscardBytes(ULONG count, FILE *source_p)

        {

        UBYTE error_number=NO_ERROR;

        while(count—)

           {
           if (fgetc(source_p)==EOF) {error_number=BAD_CHUNK_DATA;
           count=0;} /* force exit */
```

```
        }
    return(error_number);
}
```

The first version of the MidiPlayer I produced was Shell based and could play only type 0 files. It used my stack based resource allocation methods for timer and serial device control in much the same way as the MidiPlayX utility dealt with in the last chapter. The only difference was that before a Midi file event could be played it had to be identified, and its delta time value had to be unpacked. Unused events, like Meta and Sysex events, were discarded using the generalised routine shown in listing 11.5. There's no doubt that the key to producing this piece of software was a complete and thorough understanding of the Midi file standard. In fact for many months I deliberately lived and breathed the Midi file standard in order to develop a very clear mental picture of their contents. I also spent a lot of time with the program design stages and made sure that my code corresponded very closely to the design diagrams I had produced.

There were incidentally very clear reasons for creating a Shell based version initially. As file reading programs go the Midi file parsing routines used were relatively complex and because of this they needed to be tested in the simplest *environment* possible. The Shell version which coupled the Midi file parsing routines to the minimum amount of resource allocation/deallocation code needed to produce a runable program in effect provided a *testbed* that allowed me to confirm that the underlying file parsing design ideas were sound. I tested this program for about a year just to ensure that there were no major problems.

Having got to this stage, producing a version of the program that uses windows, gadgets and menus is relatively easy. Intuition provides all the building blocks needed and nowadays the Release 2 GadTools facilities and things like the ASL file requester library, which I use in MidiPlayer version 1.30, have made things even easier. I began the Workbench conversion phase by sketching out some possible display layouts and thinking about whether there were any additional *goodies* that I could bolt onto the code. What sort of extras did I have in mind? For my own interest I was keen to identify files that contain hidden *sequencer specific* Meta event messages. Why? It's because the International Midi Association, the body that nowadays controls the Midi file standard, has for many years suggested that software houses make the contents of such data packets public knowledge. Most software houses do not do this as a matter of course (simply because most users wouldn't be interested anyway). I am, and it seemed to me that if I knew which files contained such messages I'd be in a better position to 'encourage' the appropriate software houses to release some extra info. There were also some more practical considerations to bear in mind – like knowing what Midi channels are being used in a given file. When you are playing a Midi file that you didn't create yourself it is often necessary to reset the channel assignments of your Midi gear in order to hear anything. For similar reasons it is of interest to know whether a Midi file contains program change or Sysex messages.

Now in theory this type of information could be obtained and displayed during the time the file was actually playing. Time-keeping would however clearly suffer as more detailed analysis functions were added to the program. Since I expect that such functions would continue to grow (and get more complex) in later versions of the program I've chosen right from the start to handle the display-oriented file analysis functions separately Event detection code is extremely simple – I just use a set of array-based indicator variables and as events of importance are detected the appropriate event flags are set to TRUE like this:

```
case NOTE_ON:    g_channel_detected[f(NOTE_ON)]
                 [current_channel]=TRUE;
                 break;
```

By the time the Midi file has been read a flag set is available that tells us exactly what events have been encounted and this data is then used to update the display seen by the user. Before reading a new file all event indicators do of course need to be cleared (set to 0). This again is very straightforward and just involves the use of a few 'for' loops (see listing 11.6).

```
/*Listing 11.6: Before a new Midi file is examined the
arrays which hold the detected/not-detected flags for the
various event classes must be re-initialised.*/
void ClearDetectedFlags(void)
{
UBYTE i,j;
for (i=0;i<C_TYPE_COUNT;i++)
    {
    for (j=0;j<16;j++) g_channel_detected[i][j]=FALSE
    }
for (i=0;i<S_TYPE_COUNT;i++) g_sysex_detected[i]=FALSE;
for (i=0;i<M_TYPE_COUNT;i++)  g_meta_detected[i]=FALSE;
}
```

Adopting a Modular Approach

There are a number of well-defined areas which the Intuition version of the MidiPlayer program needed to tackle including of course the handling of the Intuition based display seen by the user. There was also the Midi file parsing operations discussed earlier and the resource allocation/deallocation routines that had to be extended to cope with the new Intuition-oriented program requirements like opening windows and setting up menus. I coded each of these areas as separate program modules making as much use of existing pre-written code as possible.

I'm not going to discuss the structure of my resource handling code because this has been dealt with in earlier chapters. The function pointer set shown in listing 11.7 however provides a list of the operations that have to be carried out.

```
/*Listing 11.7: This list of function pointers controls
the MidiPlayer startup operations.*/
UBYTE (*display_list[])() = {
        OpenInt,
        OpenGraphics,
        OpenGadtools,
        OpenAsl,
        LockScreen,
        GetVisInfo
        CreateWindow,
        CreateMenu,
        CreateMenuLayout,
        InstallMenu,
        CreateFileRequest,
        CreateSerialReplyPort,
        CreateSerialRequestBlock,
        OpenSerialDevice,
        SetHighSpeedSerial,
        CreateTimerReplyPort,
        CreateTimerRequestBlock,
        penTimer
    };
```

The Intuition Angle

The Intuition related aspects of the MidiPlayer code may be of interest and these fall roughly into three areas: the program uses a window that opens in the Workbench screen and under Release 2 this screen has to be locked during the time a window is set up and opened. Menus also have to be installed and this must obviously only be done if the window itself is successfully opened. Area one then concerns the Intuition related resource allocation and deallocation tasks and these of course can be handled in exactly the same way as any other system resource.

In the latest version I have incidentally opted for using the GadTools Library rather than the older style Intuition approaches and this is primarily for simplicity – things like menus are far easier to set up using the GadTools arangements. You'll be able to see this from the menu definition shown in listing 11.8. The GadTools library is able to convert this description directly into the menu that appears on the screen!

There are a number of well-defined areas which the Intuition version of the MidiPlayer program must tackle including of course the handling of the Intuition based display seen by the user. There are the Midi file parsing operations (which were discussed earlier) and the resource allocation/deallocation routines that must now be extended to cope with the new Intuition-oriented program requirements like opening windows and setting up menus. Ive coded each of these areas as separate program modules making as much use of existing pre-written code as possible.

The second area of Intuition related code concerns the handling of gadget and menu events passed back to the program from Intuition. This type of code may look frightening when you first see it, but the basic principles are very easy to understand. The program executes a Wait() or WaitPort() which puts it to sleep (ie puts it on hold so that it stops requiring processor time) until the user hits a gadget or makes a menu selection. At this time it is Intuition that's doing all the *event recognition* work and having identified a particular user action it sends the program an *IntuiMessage*. The first thing that your program knows about all this is when Exec wakes it up and tells it that the signal that it is waiting on has been satisfied. The program then knows that a message has arrived and so it collects the message, looks in the message's Class field to identify its type, and *returns* the message using a reply function (which lets the sender know that the message has been dealt with and can be deallocated or re-used). Having done all that it must then perform whatever action is suitable for the particular message in question. My MidiPlayer event handling uses a preliminary routine to identify the general type (gadget or menu) and then, for menu messages, I send a copy of the Code field to a dedicated menu message routine.

When GadTools entities are being used it is necessary to use the GT_GetIMessage() function to collect the IntuiMessages generated by menu/gadget use. The overall event handling schemes are however structurally identical to those used with say Workbench 1.3, and listings 11.9 and 11.10 show the type of event collection loops that were implemented. There was one snag that I hadn't really thought about until I started coding. I needed to find a way to allow a user to quit playing a file at any time via a normal menu selection operation. The difficulty was of course that, once a Midi file is being played, program control passes away from the main Intuition event-collection loops. What I needed was a quick way of seeing whether any IntuiMessages were queued at the Window's UserPort. The approach I adopted involves a preliminary check to see whether any messages were present at all followed by some more conventional message handling code that is only ever executed if the message port is non-empty (see listing 11.11). The IsMsgPortEmpty() function shown in listing 11.11 is a system macro which can be found in the exec/lists.h system header file.

Lastly of course, there are the general display-oriented Intuition connections to consider: beeping the screen when errors occur, putting up messages that provide information to the user and so on. MidiPlayer uses a relatively simple display and text items are placed on screen using IntuiText structures and the PrintIText() Intuition function. Listing 11.12 for example shows the definition of the text array that is used to tell the user that their currently selected Midi file contains Sysex data:

```
/*Listing 11.8: Together the NewMenu structure and the
GadTools library have greatly simplifed the creation of
Intuition menu definitions.*/

struct NewMenu menu1[] =
{
        {NM_TITLE,"PROJECT"                 0 ,0,0,0,},
        {NM_ITEM, "Select File..  .",       "S",0,0,0,},
        {NM_ITEM, "Quit to Workbench",      "Q",0,0,0,},
        {NM_TITLE,"PLAYFILE ",              0 ,0,0,0,},
        {NM_ITEM, "Play    file... ",       "P",0,0,0,},
        {NM_ITEM, "Cancel play...  ",       "C",0,0,0,},
        {NM_TITLE,"DISPLAY  ",              0 ,0,0,0,},
        {NM_ITEM, "Channel Data... ",       "O",0,0,0,},
        {NM_ITEM, "Sysex Data...   ",       "F",0,0,0,},
        {NM_ITEM, "Custom Data...  ",       "M",0,0,0,},
        {NM_TITLE,"UTILITY  ",              0 ,0,0,0,},
```

```
            {NM_ITEM, "Kill Notes...    ",      "K",0,0,0,},
            {NM_END, NULL,                       0, 0,0,0,},
};
*/Listing 11.9: MidiPlayer's high-level Intuition event
collection loop.*/
port_mask=(1<<g_window_p->UserPort->mp_SigBit);
do {
   Wait(port_mask);
   while (message_p=(struct Message *)GT_GetIMsg(
   g_win   dow_p->UserPort))
         {
         error_number=IntuitionEvent((struct IntuiMessage*)
         message_p);
         }
   }while(error_number!=PROGRAM_EXIT);
return(error_number);
}
/*Listing 11.10: Each Intuition event gets passed to the
appropriate handler.*/



UBYTE IntuitionEvent(struct IntuiMessage *message_p)
{
UBYTE error_number=NO_ERROR;
UWORD code;
ULONG class;class=message_p->Class;
code= message_p->Code;
GT_ReplyIMsg(message_p);
switch (class)   {
                case IDCMP_CLOSEWINDOW:
                error_number=PROGRAM_EXIT;
                break;
                case IDCMP_MENUPICK:
                error_number=MenuEvent(code,
                INTUITION_CALL); break;
                default: error_number=PROGRAM_EXIT;
                break;
                }
return(error_number);
```

```
}
/*Listing 11.11: The tricky job of checking to see if user
wants to quit whilst a Midi file is being played is han-
dled by quickly checking to see if any messages are queued
up at the Window's UserPort  message port.*/



if (!(IsMsgPortEmpty(g_window_p->UserPort)))
   {
   message_p=GT_GetIMsg(g_window_p->UserPort);
   code=message_p->Code;
   GT_ReplyIMsg(message_p);
   if (code!=MENUNULL)
      {
WriteBoxText(&intuitext3,XPOS3,LINEPOS3,PANIC_KILL,GREY,BI
G_OFFSET);
   KillSounds();
   ClearBoxText(&intuitext3,BLUE,BIG_OFFSET);
WriteBoxText(&intuitext3,XPOS3,LINEPOS3,FUNCTION_COM-
PLETE,GREY,BIG_OFFSET);
   Delay(DELAY);
   ClearBoxText(&intuitext3,BLUE,BIG_OFFSET);
   exit_flag=TRUE;
   }
}
/*Listing 11.12: MidiPlayer uses simple static text arrays
like this for its on-screen messages!*/



TEXT *g_sysex_text[]={
"    ********** SYSTEM EXCLUSIVE ********    ",
"                                             ",
"       This file contains Sysex data!        ",
"                                             ",
"    At the present time MidiPlayer reads     ",
"    but does NOT transmit this information   ",
"                                             ",
"    *************************************    "
};
```

```
/*Listing 11.13: This 'makefile' automatically controls
all MidiPlayer compiling and linking operations.*/



# ==========================================================
#MidiPlayer smake file
# ----------------------------------------------------------
MidiPlayer:     allocator.o amiga.o midiplayer.o images.o
                sc:c/slink FROM LIB:c.o "allocator.o"
                "amiga.o" \
                "midiplayer.o" "stack_adt.o" "images.o" \
                TO MidiPlayer LIB LIB:sc.lib+LIB:amiga.lib
allocator.o:    allocator.c display_position.h general.h
                prototypes.h
                sc:c/sc allocator.c
amiga.o:        amiga.c amiga.h display_position.h
                general.h prototypes.h
                c:c/sc amiga.c
midiplayer.o:   midiplayer.c display_position.h general.h
                prototypes.h
                sc:c/sc midiplayer.c
images.o:       images.c
                sc:c/sc images.c
# ==========================================================
```

12: Colour Cycling

The Amiga, as many of you will doubtless know, uses a pixel colouring scheme known as *colour indirection*. Instead of the bitplane data in a given position representing a particular colour it represents a colour register number and it is the value in each colour register which determines the on-screen colours.

Let's consider, for example, a screen with two bitplanes. If we fill all the bytes of the bitplanes with zeros then the two bits (one bit from the corresponding display positions of each bitplane) which define the colour register numbers of the corresponding screen locations will be 00 binary, ie zero, in all cases. This means that the display would be filled with the single colour defined by colour register 0. If this register was set to the RGB triplet value 0x000F then the colours of the pixels would be blue. If register 0 held value 0x0FFF the colours of each pixel would be white. If, however, we had filled the bytes of both bitplanes with 0xFF values (so that all bits in all bitplanes were set to '1's) then each position on the screen would be using the colour register corresponding to 11 binary, ie register 3.

Irrespective of the actual contents of a given colour register one thing should now be obvious. To change the on-screen colour of all pixels associated with a particular colour register all we have to do is change the value in that register. If, for arguments sake, you were displaying a two bitplane image of a red box on a blue background where colour register 1 held a red colour 0x0F00 and register 0 was 0x000F (ie blue) then to change the red box to a green box we'd just need to write 0x00F0 (ie green) into colour register 1. Similarly to change the background colour we would change the value in colour register 0.

The important thing with the above scenario is that the contents of the bitplanes themselves do not need to be changed. The benefit of colour indirection then is that you can re-map the colours of an image very quickly, and very easily, without having to alter the image data itself. Colour cycling on the Amiga makes use of this colour indirection effect and it works by moving around the colour values held in a set of colour registers so that the associated pixels take on the colours of each of the colour registers in turn. With a two bitplane display, colour register 0 to 3 will be in use, so if we wanted to cycle all of these colours this is what we would do:

```
copy the contents of register 0 to a temporary store
copy the contents of register 1 to register 0
copy the contents of register 2 to register 1
copy the contents of register 3 to register 2
copy temporary store to register 3
```

Each time this set of operations were performed the colour values would move cyclically to the next position and by the time the operations had been done four times the register values will be back to their original positions. In general then, if we want to cycle a set of registers we can use this sort of loop based scheme:

```
copy the contents of the lower register (1) to a temporary store
for i = 1 to h-1
copy contents of register i to register (i+1)
next i
copy temporary store to register h
```

And that, as far as the basic idea of colour cycling goes, is all there is to it although in practice a little more detail has to be considered.

The Intuition Connection

To scroll the colours associated with an Intuition screen you need to make a copy of the colour register values of the associated viewport. These values are held in a block of memory called a colour table which is arranged as a set of words where the lowest 12 bits of each word corresponds to the so called RGB triplet values (4 bit red, 4 bit green and 4 bit blue). To get the address of this RGB colour table array it is necessary to look at the screen's ColorMap structure. The ColorMap definition has incidentally undergone a number of changes since it was first defined but the two fields that

Colour Cycling

we are interested in, namely the address of the colour table entries and the count of the number of entries in the colour table, are present in all forms of the ColorMap structure. From C this would be the sort of code required to isolate the necessary data given the screen's viewport:

```
g_count=viewport_p->ColorMap->Count;
/* number of RGB triplets in table */

cm_p=viewport_p->ColorMap->ColorTable;
/* pointer to start of colour table */
```

We do in fact need to make two copies of the colour map data values – one set will be used for altering the colours and one set, which we'll leave unchanged, for reinstating the colours when we've finished. In the example program I use a loop which reads a triplet and the increments the colour table pointer so that it points to the next entry like this:

```
for (i=0;i<g_count;i++)
{ /* copy colour map details */
g_cm_copy[i]=g_cm[i]=*cm_p++;
}
```

Once the colour table data is available the cycling process is, as already mentioned, very easy to accomplish. The following loop cycles the register between two chosen limits (lower_reg and upper_reg) and then uses the graphics library LoadRGB4() function to install the rearranged colours into the display:

```
temp=g_cm_copy[lower_reg];
for (i=0;i<3;i++)
{
g_cm_copy[i]=g_cm_copy[i+1];
}
g_cm_copy[upper_reg]=temp;
LoadRGB4(viewport_p,g_cm_copy,g_count);
```

Function Name:	**LoadRGB4()**
Description:	Load RGB colour table into a given viewport's colour map
Call Format:	LoadRGB4(viewport_p,colour_table_p,count);
C Prototype:	void LoadRGB4(struct ViewPort * viewport_p, UWORD * colour_table_p,WORD count);
Registers:	LoadRGB4(a0, a1, d0:16)
Arguments:	viewport_p - pointer to viewport colour_table_ p - pointer to start of RGB colour table count - number of entries in table
Return value:	None
Notes:	RGB colour table entries are UWORDs which correspond to 4 bit red, green and blue components stored like this:
	colour reg 0 0x0RGB (background colour)
	colour reg 1 0x0RGB
	colour reg 2 0x0RGB.etc.one UWORD per entry

To restore the colours to their original positions we can do one of two things. Always arrange to cycle the colours enough times to bring them back to their original positions before terminating the cycling operations, or reinstate the original colour map from a copy of the colour table that has been held unchanged. I've adopted the second solution and use a routine like this to reinstate the original display colours:

```
void CycleOff(struct ViewPort *viewport_p)
{
LoadRGB4(viewport_p, g_cm, g_count);
}
```

To turn these ideas into a usable routine we need to be able to choose a set of colour registers, read their contents (from the colour map), cycle them and load the new arrangement into the viewport, wait a while, cycle and update the colours again, continuing until we decide to stop and reinstate the original colour map contents. As far as executing a time delay is concerned there are a number of possibilities available: we could use an interrupt based routine tied to the Amiga's vertical blanking server chain, or we could use the dos library Delay() function, or have Intuition send us intuitick messages, and arrange for a program to cycle its own registers at the appropriate time. I'm going to adopt what will at first sight appear a more complicated solution but it's one that eliminates the need for the program itself to concern itself with the job of cycling its colour register values. What I'll be doing of course is creating a separate program which is able to produce colour cycling effects on another program's screen as and when it is asked to do so by appropriate messages. Communications-wise this colour cycling program will be based on similar ideas to chapter six's flash program and because the background process will actually be *kicked off*, ie started, by some main program that wants to cycle its screen colours I'll again be talking about the colour cycling program as a *child* process.

In short the main program will run the child process and then send it messages that give it the information needed to produce a specified cycle effect (the child process will carry out these necessary colour cycling chores automatically, and quite independently, from the main program). Before the main program terminates it will send a message to the child process telling it that it also should terminate. The benefit of this type of arrangement is flexibility – a single *cycle* program can be used by all programs wishing to create these effects. Another reason why I've adopted this message based arrangement is that it gives you another chance to see how easy it is to use the Exec messaging system in your own programs.

CycleMessages and Their Use

We saw in chapter 6 that Exec messages are based on an extensible length structure with the Exec defined fields being supplemented by additional user defined data. For this chapter's example we are interested in creating a program that can handle the job of cycling the colours, in particular colour registers associated with a specified ViewPort. To do this we need to know the address of the ViewPort, the frequency with which the colours are to be cycled, and the colour registers concerned. We also need a command field so that, at the very least, the effect can be turned on and off and the program told when to quit. This is the message structure I chose to adopt for the example program:

```
struct CycleMessage         {
struct Message     cycle_Msg; /* standard Message details */
struct ViewPort    *viewport; /* will provide access to a
                                 ColorMap*/
ULONG              frequency; /* colour changes per minute */
UBYTE              lower_reg; /* lower register of range */
UBYTE              upper_reg  /* upper register of range */
UBYTE              command;   /* command to be executed */
};
```

Let's go over how these messages are used. When the main program sends the child program a message using PutMsg() the message gets sends the child program a message using PutMsg() the message gets linked into a list of messages which are tied to the child program's port structure. The important point about this process is that the message is *not* copied – it is the memory block associated with the main program's message which is linked into the list of messages present at the child program's message port. In a sense then when the main program allocates, initializes and then sends the child program some message. what the main program is really doing is giving the child program a licence to use part of its memory space.Once this licence has been granted the main program should not interfere with the message until it is safe to do so. How does it know when its message can be re-used or discarded? Usually the child process will send the message back to the main program using Exec's ReplyMsg() function. This later function links (with a suitable reply ID marker) the message into the main program's message port and, when the main program reads this, it knows that the message is finished with. The main program is then free to re-use that memory space as it sees fit. Note that the main program in the above scenario, does *not* reply to the message it receives – this is because the main program was the originator of the message. Because the message originator usually needs to be told when a message has been dealt with, both communicating programs need their own message ports – despite the fact that, as in the above example, the passage of real information is only going one way. The net result, as we saw in Chapter 6, is that two programs communicate using this type of scheme:

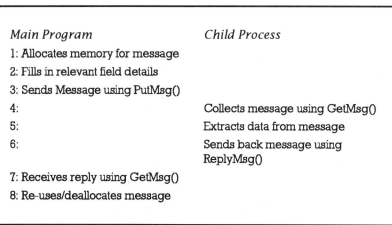

Main Program	Child Process
1: Allocates memory for message	
2: Fills in relevant field details	
3: Sends Message using PutMsg()	
4:	Collects message using GetMsg()
5:	Extracts data from message
6:	Sends back message using ReplyMsg()
7: Receives reply using GetMsg()	
8: Re-uses/deallocates message	

Table 12.1. Process communication.

The general program framework being used for the examples in this book makes use of a Intuition window that already has two associated message ports – one is used by Intuition and the other (the window's User Port) is used for handling the IntuiMessage and GadTool messages received by the program. To communicate with the Cycle program we'll be opening another message port because these messages will be easier to use if they come in as an isolated stream of CycleMessages rather than being possibly mixed up with other classes of message.

Setting Up A Message Port

In order for our main program to communicate with the child colour cycling process a message port is needed for the 'I have finished with the message' reply messages that come back from the child. Since Release 2 of the Amiga's O/S there are both amiga.lib and Exec functions available for creating and deleting message ports and the pair of routines shown in listing 12.1 are the allocator/deallocator functions for a reply port based on the Exec style routines:

```
/* -------------------------------------------------- */
/*Listing 12.1: Functions to allocate and deallocate a
reply port in the main program.*/
UBYTE CreateReplyPort(void)
{
UBYTE error_number=NO_ERROR;
if((g_reply_port_p=CreateMsgPort())==NULL)
   error_number=STARTUP_ERROR;
else {
    g_function=DeleteReplyPort;
    PushStack(g_resource_stack_p,g_function);
    }
return(error_number);
}
/* -------------------------------------------------- */
void DeleteReplyPort(void){DeleteMsgPort(g_reply_port_p);
}
/* -------------------------------------------------- */
```

Sending a Message

The routine that provides colour cycling control within the main program is going to revolve around the use of four commands – CYCLE_SETUP, CYCLE_ON, CYCLE_OFF and CYCLE_QUIT. Of these the first is used only by the main program to indicate that the message needs to be initialised, the remainder are real commands that need to be passed to the external child process that will be doing the colour cycling operations.

Listing 12.2 shows a rough plan of the routine that will be used. Listing 12.3 shows the routine in detail (notice that in this example a static structure declaration – static struct CycleMessage cycle; – has been used to create the CycleMessage).

```
/* ------------------------------------------------------ */
/*Listing 12.2: Skeleton of a routine for sending child
process a 'cycle' message.*/
UBYTE Cycle(UBYTE command)

{
if(command==CYCLE_SETUP)

      {
      Set up message structure in readiness for sending
      messages
      }
else {
      Transmit message to child using PutMsg()

      Use the WaitPort() function wait for child to confirm
      use of message

      Use GetMsg() to retrieve reply indicating that
      message is ready for re-use

      }
}
/* ------------------------------------------------------ */


/*Listing 12.3: An example routine for sending the child
process a 'cycle' message.*/
/* ------------------------------------------------------ */
UBYTE Cycle(UBYTE command)

{
UBYTE error_number=NO_ERROR;
static struct CycleMessage cycle;
if(command==CYCLE_SETUP)

      {
      cycle.cycle_Msg.mn_Length=sizeof(struct
      CycleMessage);
      cycle.cycle_Msg.mn_ReplyPort=g_reply_port_p;
      cycle.viewport=g_viewport_p;
      cycle.frequency=CYCLE_FREQUENCY;
      cycle.lower_reg=LOWER_REG;
      cycle.upper_reg=UPPER_REG;
      }
  else {
      cycle.cycle_Msg.mn_Node.ln_Type=NT_MESSAGE;
```

```
            cycle.command=command;
            PutMsg(g_msgport_p,(struct Message *)&cycle);
            WaitPort(g_reply_port_p); /* wait for cycle program
            to confirm use */
            GetMsg(g_reply_port_p); /* message now ready for re-
            use */
            }
      return(error_number);
      }
      /* -------------------------------------------------- */
```

Some Main Program Coding Issues

For a main program to safely talk to a child process using CycleMessages we need to allow for the fact that since the child process is a separate entity, ie a runable program in its own right, it may not actually be found when we attempt to run it. As you should now expect, the way I tackle this job is to include the attempted running of the child process in my normal allocation/deallocation framework. In the CH 12-1 example then you will see this function pointer control block defined:

```
      UBYTE (*display_list[])() = {
         OpenInt,
         OpenGraphics,
         OpenGadtools,
         LockScreen,
         GetVisInfo,
         CreateWindow,
         CreateMenu,
         CreateMenuLayout,
         InstallMenu,
         CreateReplyPort,
         RunCycle
         };
```

Once the library, screen, window, menu and reply port creation jobs have been successfully carried out the routine shown in listing 12.4 is performed. This tries to run the *cycle* program using the DOS SystemTags() function like this:

```
      SystemTags("run CYCLE:cycle >NIL: <NIL:",TAG_DONE);
```

I've coded this assuming that a logical CYCLE: assignment is in place that tells the main program where to find the Cycle utility program. If, for example, the cycle program was to be placed in the command (c:) directory you would need to use

```
1> assign CYCLE: c:
```

to tell the main program where the cycle utility could be found.

How do we tell whether the cycle program really does get found and started or not? We just look to see whether its message port can be detected using the Exec FindPort() function like this:

```
Forbid();
g_msgport_p=FindPort(DESTINATION_PORT_NAME);
Permit();
if (!g_msgport_p) error_number=STARTUP_ERROR;
else {
```

Notice here that Exec Forbid() and Permit() calls have been used to sandwich the FindPort() call. This is important because it allows us to lock out other tasks and so prevent any alteration of Exec's port list whilst our program is examining it.

Providing the port is found, which we detect by seeing a non-NULL pointer being returned by the FindPort() function, we set up the fields of the program's CycleMessage structure using a Cycle(CYCLE_SETUP) call and at this point we know that the child process is up and running. The corresponding deallocation routine just performs the call: Cycle(CYCLE_EXIT) thereby transmitting a message to the cycle program telling it to shut itself down.

```
/* -------------------------------------------------- */
/*Listing 12.4: Checking for the child message port is a
safe way for checking the child's existence.*/
UBYTE RunCycle(void)
{
UBYTE error_number=NO_ERROR;
SystemTags("run CYCLE:cycle >NIL: <NIL:",TAG_DONE);
Forbid();
g_msgport_p=FindPort(DESTINATION_PORT_NAME);
Permit();
if (!g_msgport_p) error_number=STARTUP_ERROR;
else {
       g_function=KillCycle;
       PushStack(g_resource_stack_p,g_function);
       Cycle(CYCLE_SETUP);
       }
return(error_number);
}
```

```
/* ------------------------------------------------ */
void KillCycle(void)
{
Cycle(CYCLE_EXIT);
}
/* ------------------------------------------------ */
```

The Colour Cycling Program Itself

The child process that performs the colour cycling is an independent program in its own right. From a logical viewpoint it works in much the same way as chapter 6's flash program and again has to have a message port available. Listing 12.5 shows how this is set up:

```
/* ------------------------------------------------ */
/*Listing 12.5: Port creation routines for the child process*/
UBYTE CreateCommandPort()
{
UBYTE error_number=NO_ERROR;
if((g_command_port_p=CreateMsgPort())==NULL)
     error_number=STARTUP_ERROR;
else {
     g_function=DeleteCommandPort;
     PushStack(g_resource_stack_p,g_function);
     }
     return(error_number);
}
/* ------------------------------------------------ */
void DeleteCommandPort(){DeleteMsgPort(g_command_port_p);}
/* ------------------------------------------------ */
```

The port needs to be added to Exec's *public ports* list and when the amiga.lib CreatePort() routine is used this is done automatically. With the Exec style functions it has to be done by the program itself using the Exec AddPort() function.

```
/* ------------------------------------------------ */
/*Listing 12.6: Making the command port of the child process public.*/
UBYTE MakeCommandPortPublic(void)
{
```

```
UBYTE error_number=NO_ERROR;
g_command_port_p->mp_Node.ln_Name=COMMAND_PORT_NAME;
AddPort(g_command_port_p);
g_function=RemovePublicCommandPort;
PushStack(g_resource_stack_p,g_function);
return(error_number);
}
/* -------------------------------------------------- */
void RemovePublicCommandPort(void)
{
RemPort(g_command_port_p);
}
/* -------------------------------------------------- */
```

These routines, like all allocator/deallocator function pairs, are controlled by a function pointer list and for the cycle program this looks like this:

```
UBYTE (*allocator_list[])() = {
    OpenGraphics,
    CreateTimerReplyPort,
    CreateTimerRequestBlock,
    OpenTimer,
    CreateCommandPort,
    MakeCommandPortPublic
};
```

The graphics library is needed because the LoadRGB4() is used to set up the colour register values. The timer entries are used to set up the Amiga's timer device, and the last two entries produce the command port that we've been discussing. Conceptually the program is straightforward. As soon as the program has completed its starting up operations it enters a wait loop based on the Exec WaitPort() function. As soon as a message wakes the program up the details are extracted like this:

```
command=((struct CycleMessage *)message_p)->command;
viewport_p=((struct CycleMessage *)message_p)->viewport;
frequency=((struct CycleMessage *)message_p)->frequency;
lower_reg=((struct CycleMessage *)message_p)->lower_reg;
upper_reg=((struct CycleMessage *)message_p)->upper_reg;
```

and the message is then replied to so that the main program knows that the command has been received and is being processed.

Because the CycleMessages hold a frequency value (our choice!) this needs to be converted into a real time delay for the timer device so immediately after collecting the message I carry out this frequency <-> time interval conversion:

```
secs=60/frequency;

microsecs=(60*1000000/frequency)%1000000;
```

Having done that a switch statement is used to distinguish between the various CycleMessage commands. Listing 12.7 shows the complete code for the colour cycling module:

```
/* -------------------------------------------------- */
/*Listing 12.7: The child process colour cycling routine.*/
/* amiga.c - child process code for colour cycling */
#include "general.h"
static UWORD g_cm[32],g_cm_copy[32];
static UBYTE g_count;
UBYTE AmigaProg(void)
{
UBYTE  lower_reg, upper_reg, command,
error_number=NO_ERROR;
ULONG  secs,microsecs,frequency;struct Message *message_p;
struct ViewPort *viewport_p;
do {
   WaitPort(g_command_port_p);
   while (message_p=GetMsg(g_command_port_p))
      {
      command=((struct CycleMessage *)message_p)->command;
      viewport_p=((struct CycleMessage *)message_p)->viewport;
      frequency=((struct CycleMessage *)message_p)->frequency;
      lower_reg=((struct CycleMessage *)message_p)->lower_reg;
      upper_reg=((struct CycleMessage *)message_p)->upper_reg;
      ReplyMsg(message_p);
      secs=60/frequency;
      microsecs=(60*1000000/frequency)%1000000;
      switch(command)
         {
```

```
                case CYCLE_ON:      CycleOn(viewport_p,lower_reg,
                                    upper_reg, secs, microsecs);
                                    break;
                case CYCLE_OFF:     CycleOff(viewport_p);
                                    break;
                                    error_number=PROGRAM_EXIT;
                                    break;
                default:            break;
                }
            }
        }while(error_number!=PROGRAM_EXIT);
    return(error_number);
}
/* -------------------------------------------------- */
void CycleOn(struct ViewPort *viewport_p,UBYTE
lower_reg,UBYTE upper_reg,ULONG secs,ULONG micros)
{
BOOL exit_flag=FALSE;
UWORD temp, *cm_p;COUNT i;
g_count=viewport_p->ColorMap->Count;
cm_p=viewport_p->ColorMap->ColorTable;
for (i=0;i<g_count;i++)
    { /* copy colour map details */
    g_cm_copy[i]=g_cm[i]=*cm_p++;
    }
while(!exit_flag)
    {
    if(!IsMsgPortEmpty(g_command_port_p)) exit_flag=TRUE;
    else {
        /* cycle colours around */
        temp=g_cm_copy[lower_reg];
        for (i=0;i<3;i++)
            {
            g_cm_copy[i]=g_cm_copy[i+1];
            }
        g_cm_copy[upper_reg]=temp;
        LoadRGB4(viewport_p,g_cm_copy,g_count);
        SetTimer(secs,micros);
```

```
            }
        }
    }
/* ------------------------------------------------- */
void CycleOff(struct ViewPort *viewport_p)
{
LoadRGB4(viewport_p,g_cm,g_count);
}
/* ------------------------------------------------- */
void __regargs SetTimer(ULONG seconds, ULONG microseconds)
{
g_timer_request_p->tr_time.tv_secs=seconds;
g_timer_request_p->tr_time.tv_micro=microseconds;
DoIO((struct IORequest *)g_timer_request_p);
}
/* ------------------------------------------------- */
```

Using the Cycle Utility

The thing to remember about the approach that we've adopted in this chapter is that the Cycle program, can now be regarded as a general utility. Any program that needs to cycle some or all of the colours of a screen can just set up a reply port, run the cycle program and then control the required effects by sending the program the appropriate CycleMessages. For the example associated with this chapter I've just used the routine to cycle the Workbench screen colours but it's not hard to envisage more interesting uses of this approach. Other enhancements, such as being able to alter the direction of the colour cycling, cycling whilst fading the intensity of the colours etc, could all be implemented by adding extra routines to the child *cycle* program and defining additional CycleMessage commands. The communications scheme would of course be exactly the same so such additions, once the message handling code is in place, would be likely to involve relatively little work.

13: Mixed Code Programming

This chapter deals with a topic that can initially be quite hard to get to grips with because it involves both C and assembler code. It's provided here so that the more advanced coders can get some appreciation of how assembler routines that can be used from C have to be written. Basically you need to know how to get from C to assembler code and back again! Whatever you do however – Don't Panic. This chapter provides details for 680x0 coders who wish to learn how to write their own mixed code. If you are not into assembler coding then please don't get disheartened – the mechanics of actually using suitably written assembler routines from C is *very* easy and if you concentrate on the overall ideas the details should fall into place relatively quickly.

Now you might at this stage be wondering why mixed coding is necessary anyway. It's because despite the fact that C is a very capable language for serious Amiga programming, there are still plenty of times when it pays to drop into assembler in order to gain some extra speed or flexibility. In suitable cases this fine tuning of important, or frequently used, areas of a program or routine can pay handsome dividends and the good news is that once you have seen it done once you will realise that it's not particularly difficult! All of the necessary mechanical details are invariably provided in the C compiler manuals but the explanations tend to be written in a way that only really makes sense once you know a little about what's going on. The purpose of this chapter then is to provide some tutorial help by doing three things: firstly, it should provide some background info so that the accounts you'll read about in your compiler manuals will (hopefully) make a little more sense. Secondly, I'll provide some details of the conventions used with two popular Amiga C compilers (Manx Aztec C and SAS/Lattice C). Thirdly I'll give you a couple of short, but runable, examples which will let you see how everything fits together.

Before we start I ought to mention that the techniques I'll be discussing are what you might call *conventional mixed code* C techniques, based on passing function arguments on the stack. Nowadays C compilers are clever beasts and some, the SAS Amiga C offering for example, can produce code which jams values directly into the 680x0 microprocessor registers in readiness for making a function call. With suitably written functions (ie functions written to expect arguments provided in such a way) this makes for faster parameter passing.

For our purposes however it's the stack-based ideas which are of interest so let's make a start by talking a bit about the magic which occurs when you place a call to a routine, say Encrypt(), into a C source program. The compiler uses such source code statements to generate a reference to the named routine and, under normal circumstances, both SAS/Lattice C, the Manx Aztec compiler, and many others tag on an initial underscore to the function name. The call to the function Encrypt() therefore has the linker searching for a routine called _Encrypt and it is this routine, if the linker is going to successfully resolve the reference, that must be provided in the assembly language module!

The code which various C compilers produce when they encounter a function call does vary but the conventions to be followed will always be detailed in the compiler manual. To start with all you really need to be aware of is that the end result is usually that any parameters present in the function call get pushed onto the stack prior to a call being made to the appropriate subroutine. I say usually because as just mentioned there are some qualifying conditions with compilers which allow register arguments to be used rather than the stack. SAS C for instance then uses an @ character, rather than an underscore, at the start of the function name.

Writing the appropriate C code is easy. It simply involves placing suitably named functions calls, with any required parameters, into the C source. This is done using normal C function conventions – you can even add your own ANSI C function prototypes to make sure that the compiler makes the appropriate usage and parameter type checks!

The next step involves writing suitable assembly language code and assembling it to produce linkable object code. A couple of assembler directives, called XDEF and XREF, have to be used to get things running smoothly.

XDEF and XREF

XDEF is an assembler directive used to define assembly language labels as being visible to other modules at link time. If you forget it the assembly stage will go OK but you'll get errors when linking because the linker will be unable to resolve the corresponding function reference in the C code module. XREF goes the other way, ie it tells the assembler that the information needed about the item in question will be imported when the assembly language module is linked. If you forget these then you'll get errors as soon as you try to assemble your code because the assembler will not realize that labels have been used whose values are unknown at assembly time.

Most assemblers, incidentally, place a limit on the number of characters within a label that will be regarded as significant. The ANSI C compiler standard also only requires that the compiler caters for six characters with external references, although most handle more. Either check first, or don't use long names for functions and variables whose references might need to be passed between modules. Manx's Aztec C offers #asm and #endasm statements to allow assembler code to be embedded within the C source. This can be useful on occasions but, in general, it is safer to always place assembler code into a separate module.

Specific SAS/Lattice C Conventions

Function Entry rules: upon entry to a function the stack, under conventional parameter passing conditions, contains the function arguments placed immediately above the long-word return address which register A7 (the stack pointer) points to. The arguments appear in left-to-right order with the leftmost item being the one immediately above the return address. Here's some standard function entry steps which need to be carried out:

1. Save register A5, which contains the previous function's stack frame pointer. The best idea is to push it onto the stack!
2. Copy the contents of A7 into A5, thereby establishing a frame pointer for the current function which allows you to access the arguments indirectly using the A5 base value.
3. Subtract any stack work area needed from A7.

These steps can, if the work area required is less than 32K, be achieved with the 68000's LINK instruction. Lattice/SAS expects registers D2-D7,A2-A4 and A6 to be intact on return so, if any of these registers are to be used, they must be preserved. Again it is common practice to place them on the stack. The above stack oriented procedure forms the basis of a powerful general parameter passing technique and it's well worth learning about. Lattice/SAS's register argument facilities, although good for speed, are less useful in general and for details of this approach the place to look is the Lattice/SAS C compiler reference manual. Function return values are passed back in one or more registers, depending on the data type declared for the function in question. Here are the return value details that must be adhered to:

Return Type	Size	Pass Back Details
char	8	low byte of D0
short	16	low word of D0
long	32	all of D0
float	32	all of D0
pointe	32	all of D0
double (IEEE)	64	passed in D0 and D1 with high bits in D0
double (FFP)	32	all of D0

Table 13.1. Function return values.

If, incidentally, the function returns an instance of a structure or union (as opposed to a pointer to the object) then it must define a static work area (*not* on the stack) to temporarily hold the returned object. In these cases the function should return in D0 a pointer to the temporary copy. Having set up the required return value the routine needs to reverse its entry steps (restoring the registers, advancing the A7 stack pointer past the work area, and restoring the previous frame pointer to A5 before exiting via an RTS instruction. Again the 68000 has an unlink (UNLK) instruction specifically intended to simplify these operations. (Note that it is the job of the calling function, and not the called function, to remove any arguments from the stack).

Aztec C Conventions

The Manx Aztec compiler exports the name of a function or variable by truncating the name to 31 characters and prepending the underscore character as mentioned earlier. The function entry rules, which are similar to Lattice/SAS, are as follows: upon entry to a function the stack again contains the function arguments placed immediately above the long-word return address (which register A7, the stack pointer, points to). The Aztec arguments appear in left-to-right order with the leftmost item being the one immediately above the return address.

The Aztec technical manual says that register usage is implemented according to the Amiga guidelines so all used registers except for

D0, D1, A0 and A1 must be stored and reinstated before the assembly language routine returns. However in the Assembler section it states that registers D0-D3, A0, A1 and A6 are available as *work registers* and follows this statement by saying that 'There is no need to preserve the values of work registers for other routines'. I've not had much time to experiment with Aztec C but I'd recommend sticking, the former, more restricted convention, unless you know otherwise – it works and it is definitely safe!

In-line, ie embedded, assembler code must also preserve the contents of the non-scratch registers (ie all except D0, D1, A0 and A1), and in addition should of course *not* make any assumptions about the contents of the processor registers – the code that the compiler currently generates for particular C statements might well change in later releases. The Manx Aztec function return conventions, incidentally, again use the D0 and D1 data registers.

A Couple Of Examples

If all the references and directives in the above stages are correct the rest is easy; the C source is compiled, the assembly language code assembled, and then the modules are linked together with the startup-code to produce a runable program.

Both of my Shell examples perform similar processes: each asks the user to type in a string, and then calls an assembly language routine called Encrypt(). The assembler routine performs an Exclusive-ORing (EOR) of all bytes in the string which are neither the NULL terminator nor equal to the mask value itself (thus protecting C's definition of a string by ensuring that we don't produce any NULL values within the body of the string). Having done that the program prints the modified string, repeats the Encrypt() process and prints it again. The second EORing process does of course result in the original input string being produced.

Where the coding differs is that in the first example the assembler routine is directly accessing the global variables g_input_string and g_EOR_mask present in the C source code. In the second example these variables are *not* global, and both the start of the string and the EOR mask value are given to the assembler routine as parameters, ie the values are provided as arguments during the Encrypt() call. This means that in the second example we have to get those arguments from the stack. Here's the run-down on what has happened just prior to entering our assembly language patch; the arguments will have been pushed, in left to right order, onto the stack. Then the return address will have been placed on the stack. My second assembler patch uses a LINK a5,#0 instruction which pushes the contents of a5 onto the stack as well. The result? To access the two arguments of the C function we've had to use positive offsets of 8 and 12 respectively.

Before you examine the source listings some points should be made: to start with you will notice in the pieces of assembler code provided that only the scratch registers A0 and D0 are used. This means that, for the examples, it is not necessary to preserve register contents on the stack. Despite this in the second of the assembler patches I have included some movem instructions to save and restore data registers d2-d7. Why? It's just so that you can see exactly whereabouts in the code those push/pop operations would be carried out had registers d2-d7 actually been in use.

Some 'Exclusive' Info

Exclusive-ORing, more commonly known as EOR, is a logical operation that is carried out on pairs of bits or bytes and works like this: The corresponding bits in each of the bit pattern are compared and if they are different then the result is a 0 value. If the bits are the same, ie either both bits are set to 0 or both are set to 1, the result is a 1 value. The truth table for the EOR operation therefore looks like this:

	BIT A	
	0	1
B 0	0	1
I		
T		
B 1	1	0

Exclusive OR Truth Table

For example: The result of exclusive-ORing 8F hex with 09 hex is 86 hex which is worked out like this:

Byte	1 0 0 0 1 1 1 1	8F hex
Byte	0 0 0 0 1 0 0 1	09 hex
Result after EOR	1 0 0 0 0 1 1 0	86 hex

Exclusive-ORing is an operation which when performed twice on a byte using the same EOR masking value produces the original byte back again (try it and see). This has led to the EOR operation being regularly used for simple encryption and decipher schemes. Take a piece of text, Exclusive-OR all the bytes with some mask value and the result will not be immediately obvious as a piece of text. Carry out the same process again with the same encryption key (ie the same EOR mask) and the original text will be produced. Get the key wrong and it won't!

This technique is, incidentally, the basis of a common simple encryption/decipher scheme and programmers are particularly fond of using it for encrypting graphics images, sound samples etc., since the encrypted forms are then not readable by conventional IFF based programs.

Figure 13.1. Exclusive OR.

```
/* -------------------------------------------------- */
/*Listing 13.1: Exclusive ORing via global variables*/
/* Example-CH13-1.c - uses Exclusive ORing patch via GLOB-
AL variables */
```

```c
#include <exec/types.h>
#include <stdio.h>
#define MESSAGE1 "Please enter a string\n"
#define MESSAGE2 "Encrypted string is..........."
#define MESSAGE3 "String after 2nd conversion..."
#define LINEFEED   10
#define MAX_CHARS  80
#define EOR_MASK   0x1FTEXT g_input_string[MAX_CHARS+1];
/* space for the user's string */
UBYTE g_EOR_mask=EOR_MASK;  /* Exclusive-ORing conversion mask */
main()
{
WORD  keyboard_character; UBYTE count=0;printf(MESSAGE1);
while ((keyboard_character=getchar())!=LINEFEED)
   {
   if (count<=MAX_CHARS) g_input_string[count++]=
   keyboard_character;
   };
g_input_string[count]=NULL;   /* add terminal NULL */
Encrypt();                    /* EOR the string */
printf("%s %s \n",MESSAGE2,g_input_string);
                              /* show user encrypted
                                 string */
Encrypt();                    /* 2nd EOR operation */
printf("%s %s \n",MESSAGE3, g_input_string);
                              /* show string again */
}
/* -------------------------------------------------- */


* ========================================================= *
/*Listing 13.2: The assembler patch without argument passing*/
* Example CH13-1.s - assembler patch without argument        *
   passing
* -------------------------------------------------------- *
* a0 is loaded with the starting address of the input
   string
        XDEF    _Encrypt
        XREF    _g_input_string
```

```
                XREF    _g_EOR_mask
*  ....................................................  *
      _Encrypt       move.l   #_g_input_string,a0  start of string
                     move.b   _g_EOR_mask,d0       get mask value
                     subq.l   #1,a0
*  ....................................................  *
      ENCRYPT_LOOP:  addq.l   #1,a0                move to next byte
                     tst.b    (a0)                 check it
                     beq      FINISH               quit if NULL terminator
                     cmp.b    (a0),d0              will it EOR to NULL ?
                     beq      ENCRYPT_LOOP         if YES don't EOR it
                     eor.b    d0,(a0)              safe to Encrypt
                     bra      ENCRYPT_LOOP         keep going
*  ....................................................  *
      FINISH         rts                           back to C
*  ====================================================  *
```

```c
/* .................................................... */
/*Listing 13.3: The function parameter based version of
the program*/
/* Example CH13-2.c - version which passes data as parame-
ters */
#include <exec/types.h>
#include <stdio.h>
#define MESSAGE1 "Please enter a string\n"
#define MESSAGE2 "Encrypted string is..........."
#define MESSAGE3 "String after 2nd conversion..."
#define LINEFEED   10
#define MAX_CHARS  80
#define EOR_MASK   0x1Fmain(){TEXT
input_string[MAX_CHARS+1]; /* space for the user's string*/
UBYTE EOR_mask=EOR_MASK;    /* Exclusive-ORing conversion
                               mask */
WORD  keyboard_character
UBYTE count=0;
printf(MESSAGE1);
while ((keyboard_character=getchar())!=LINEFEED)
   {
   if (count<=MAX_CHARS) input_string[count++]=
   keyboard_character;
```

```c
    };
    input_string[count]=NULL; /* add terminal NULL */
    Encrypt(input_string, EOR_mask);     /* EOR the string */
    printf("%s %s \n",MESSAGE2,input_string); /* show user
    encrypted string */
    Encrypt(input_string, EOR_mask);     /* 2nd EOR operation */
    printf("%s %s \n",MESSAGE3, input_string);  /* show string
                                                    again */
}
/* -------------------------------------------------------- */
```

```
* ========================================================= *
/*Listing 13.4: Assembler patch that uses data passed as
function parameters.*/
*Example CH13-2.s - assembler patch with argument passing*
* -------------------------------------------------------- *
XDEF        _Encrypt
* -------------------------------------------------------- *
_Encrypt        link a5,#0              don't need any work-
space
                movem.l d2-d7,-(sp)     normally where we save
                move.l  12(a5),d0       retrieve mask value
                move.l  8(a5),a0        retrieve string pointer
                subq.l  #1,a0
* -------------------------------------------------------- *
ENCRYPT_LOOP:addq.l #1,a0                move to next byte
                tst.b   (a0)             check it
                beq     FINISH           quit if NULL terminator
                cmp.b   (a0),d0          will it EOR to NULL ?
                beq     ENCRYPT_LOOP     if YES don't EOR it
                eor.b   d0,(a0)          safe to Encrypt
                bra     ENCRYPT_LOOP     keep going
* -------------------------------------------------------- *
FINISH          movem.l (sp)+,d2-d7     normally where we restore
                unlk    a5
                rts                     back to C
* ========================================================= *
```

14: Creating Static Tile Effects - Part One

The next two chapters deal with quite a simple topic, namely the drawing of a set of identical image tiles onto an Intuition screen but for a number of reasons (which will become apparent during the discussions, we take the ideas a little further than would normally be done).

The object of the exercise then is to produce a routine that takes a specified graphics object (defined as an Intuition image) and creates a tile/wallpaper effect within a window by drawing multiple copies of the image using this sort of caller-defined MxN grid.

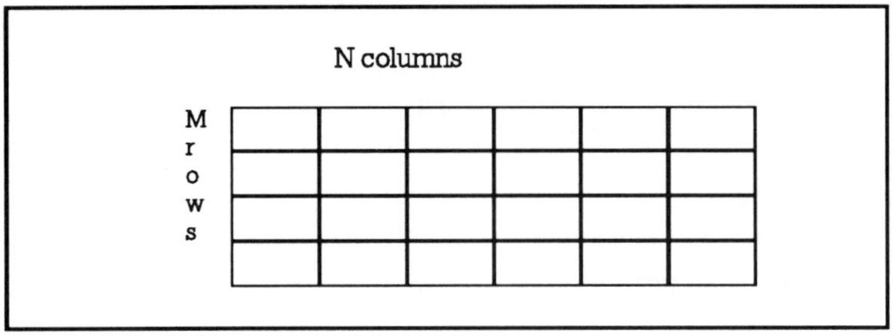

Figure 14.1. Grid of image tiles.

Our story starts with a typical C programmer's approach. The simplest way of creating a M x N grid of image tiles is to set up a twin loop that calculates the grid co-ordinates and uses them in conjunction with the Intuition library's DrawImage() routine. Perhaps the most obvious way to code such a routine would be like this:

```
/*Listing 14.1: An obvious C tiling routine*/
void DrawTiles(struct Image *image_p, struct RastPort
               *rastport_p, WORD rows, columns)
{
WORD width, height, left=0, top=0, i, j;
width=image_p->Width;
height=image_p->Height;
for (i=0;i<rows;i++)
   {
   for (j=0;j<columns;j++)
      {
      DrawImage(rastport_p,image_p,j*width, i*height);
      }
   }
}
```

In practice it is probably better to avoid the multiplication operations and track the new positions using addition operations like this:

```
/*Listing 14.2: These loop operations would be slightly
faster*/
void DrawTiles(struct Image *image_p, struct RastPort
               *rastport_p, WORD rows, WORD columns)
{
WORD width, height, left=0, top-0, i, j;
width=image_p->Width;
```

```
height=image_p->Height;
for (i=0;i<rows;i++)
   {
   for (j=0;j<columns;j++)
      {
      DrawImage(rastport_p,image_p,left, top);
      left+=width;
      }
   top+=height;
   left=0; /* reset for next row */
   }
}
```

As an extra refinement we could allow offset positions to be provided as function parameters so that we're able to position the graphics exactly where we want them. Here's the listing 14.2 example with the required offset modifications:

```
/*Listing 14.3:  A more flexible version of listing 14.2*/
void DrawTiles(struct Image *image_p, struct RastPort
*rastport_p, WORD rows, WORD columns, WORD left_offset,
WORD top_offset)
{
WORD width, height, left=0, top-0, i, j;
width=image_p->Width;
height=image_p->Height;
for (i=0;i<rows;i++)
   {
   for (j=0;j<columns;j++)
      {
DrawImage(rastport_p,image_p,left+left_offset,top+top_off-
set);
      left+=width;
      }
   top+=height;
   left=0; /* reset for next row */
   }
}
```

Perhaps the only other worthwhile modification might be to eliminate the width and height variables by referencing the image structure directly like this:

```c
/*Listing 14.4: Yet another tile creating routine possi-
bility*/
void DrawTiles(struct Image *image_p, struct RastPort
*rastport_p, WORD rows, WORD columns, WORD left_offset,
WORD top_offset)
{
WORD left=0, top-0, i, j;
for (i=0;i<rows;i++)
   {
   for (j=0;j<columns;j++)
      {
DrawImage(rastport_p,image_p,left+left_offset,top+top_off-
set);
      left+=image_p->Width;
      }
   top+=image_p->Height;
   left=0; /* reset for next row */
   }
}
```

Function Name:	**DrawImage()**
Description:	This is Intuition's high-level Image drawing routine
Call Format:	DrawImage(rastport_p, image_p, left_offset, top_offset);
C Prototype:	void DrawImage(struct Rastport *, struct Image *, WORD, WORD);
Registers:	a0 a1 d0 d1
Arguments:	rastport_p – pointer to a RastPort
	image_p – pointer to an Image structure
	left_offset – a general left offset which will be used with all of the linked Image structures of a particular DrawImage() call.
	top_offset – a general top offset which will be used with all of the linked Image structures of a particular DrawImage() call.
Return Value:	None
Notes:	It is convenient to have displacement offsets in the DrawImage() call itself because this allows a global offset to be applied to a whole chain of Image structures. You may have a group of a couple of dozen separate images on display but, if you so desire, will be able to reposition the whole group (keeping their relative positions the same) just by altering the global offsets.

Creating Static Tile Effects – Part One

A few experiments would soon tell which of the above C forms were the most efficient and coupled to some subsequent additional fine tuning (choice of variable sizes, passing parameters directly in registers and so on) you might be forgiven for thinking that these efforts would doubtless produce a reasonable tiling routine. As it happens, this particular task, over the next couple of chapters, is going to lead us to some interesting new ground but the point of interest at the present time concerns not the execution times of the routines, but the time it took to code them! The first DrawTiles() C routine that I've just discussed actually took me about one minute to sketch out and within five minutes I had thrown the code into a test program (along with a test image), and compiled and run it. Five minutes after that I had confirmed that the alternative modifications also worked without problem.

But how does this compare say with using 680x0 assembler code to do the job? Well, what I'm now going to do is develop an equivalent routine, again called DrawTiles(), using the low level approach. The reason I've chosen this simple tiling task as an example is that the equivalent C code will have been understandable to everyone and the idea now is to show you exactly how much more work is involved when you opt for the low – level approach. Along the way I'll also be able to illustrate both the advantages to be had and disadvantages encountered. I'll also spend rather more time discussing various coding issues so that those of you new to 680x0 coding get a chance to understand what's going on!

The Low-Level Approach

Quite a few parameters will need to be passed to the low-level DrawTiles() subroutine and, knowing (from the function description) that the Intuition DrawImage() library routine needs a rastport pointer in a0, an image pointer in a1, plus left and top offsets in d0 and d1, the following register arrangements were chosen:

```
a0 is to hold the window rastport pointer
a1 is to hold the image pointer
d0 is to hold the starting left offset value
d1 is to hold the starting top offset value
d2 is to hold the required horizontal block count,
   ie column count
d3 is to hold the required vertical block count,
   ie row count
```

The subroutine is going to draw each row of the grid by making DrawImage() library calls incrementing the function's left offset drawing position by the width of the image block each time. Once a row is complete the top offset value will be increased by the height of the image and the row drawing operations repeated. Rather unfortunately we must assume that the parameters present in a0,a1,d0 and d1 (the scratch registers) will be destroyed by each and every DrawImage() Intuition call, and so these values will need to be copied to other registers at the start of the routine so that they can be reloaded as required. Also, a copy has to be kept of the original left offset because one working value will need to be increased as the images in any given row are drawn but the original value will still be needed to reset the offset at the start of the second and subsequent row drawing operations.

Now all of these values could be placed on the 680x0's stack, or stored in ds.x defined memory locations but, for maximum execution speed, it is actually faster to keep as much data as possible within the 68000 registers themselves. I have therefore, somewhat arbitrarily, chosen to preserve the rastport pointer in register a2, the image pointer in register a3, the left offset in d7, the top offset in a4, the column block count in a5 and opted to collect and store the image width and height in d4 and d5 respectively. Additionally register d6 will be used to store the current left offset value at any given time. Why were address registers chosen for some data items? It's simply that almost all (data and address) registers were needed to store all of the various items. Here, for easy reference, are the parameters that need to be supplied:

```
a0    holds the window rastport pointer
a1    holds the image pointer
d0    holds the starting left offset value
d1    holds starting top offset value
d2    holds required horizontal block count,
      ie column count
d3    holds required vertical block count, ie row count
```

and here are the details of the additional registers to be used:

```
d4    used to store image width
d5    used to store image height
d6    used to hold an updated (current) left offset
d7    copy of original left offset
a2    copy of rastport pointer
a3    copy of image pointer
a4    copy of original top offset
a5    copy of original column count
```

It's worth remembering that 680x0 instructions which use smaller size operands do execute more quickly (plus of course memory space is saved) so graphics routines, such as the one we are developing, should make all reasonable efforts to take advantage of

Creating Static Tile Effects – Part One

such things. In our case a lot of the data, block counts, the DrawImage() offsets etc, can in fact be specified as word sized (two byte) data items.

As with the equivalent C routines, the image width and height values, which are also word sized fields, do not need to be explicitly provided because they're stored in the image structure itself and can be obtained using the word-based form of indirect addressing with displacement. In the case of the Intuition Image structure the displacements required to obtain the image width and height are given the standard ig_Width and ig_Height respectively. Prefined displacement values are available in the intuition.i include file but since they have absolute values of 4 and 6 it is easy enough to define identical EQUate values if necessary and so still write this type of 'conventional' Amiga code:

```
move.w   ig_Width(a1),d4     get image width in d4
move.w   ig_Height(a1),d5    get image height in d5
```

Coupled to the previously mentioned initial parameter copy operations, the subroutine entry code therefore ended up looking like this:

```
move.l   a0,a2               preserve rastport pointer
move.l   a1,a3               preserve image pointer
move.w   d0,d6               d6 = current left offset
move.w   d0,d7               preserve left offset for reuse
move.w   d1,a4               preserve top offset
move.w   d2,a5               preserve column count for reuse
move.w   ig_Width(a1),d4     get image width in d4
move.w   ig_Height(a1),d5    get image height in d5
```

Drawing A Row Of Images

Basically we draw the image structure, decrease the horizontal block count, and test to see whether the count is zero thus checking that all horizontal images in a row have been drawn. If the current row is complete we move onto the next row; otherwise we reset the top offset value in register d1 (which the library call might have destroyed), update the left offset value (by adding the image width to it), reset the d0, a0 and a1 parameters which may also have been destroyed by the library call, and continue looping back to the DrawImage() function:

```
draw_row  CALLSYS  DrawImage,_IntuitionBase
          subq     #1,d2         decrease count
          beq      next_row
          move.w   a4,d1         set top offset
          add.w    d4,d6         form new left offset
```

```
draw_row2   move.w   d6,d0        needed for library function
                                  call
            move.l   a2,a0        restore rastport pointer
            move.l   a3,a1        restore image pointer
            bra      draw_row     keep going
```

At the start of each new row we decrease the count value and check whether another row needs to be drawn. If it does the left offset value is reset to the start of the row, the column count (which represents the number of horizontal blocks to be drawn) is similarly reset, and the top offset value is increased by the height of the image. In the following code notice how branch on equal (beq) and branch always (bra) instructions are used to create program loops which finally exit when the count values (which are decreased by one each time a loop is executed) become zero:

```
next_row    subq     #1,d3        decrease count
            beq      draw_end
            move.w   d7,d6        reset start left offset for
                                  row
            move.w   a5,d2        reset column count
            move.w   a4,d1
            add.w    d5,d1
            move.w   d1,a4        top offset for next row
            bra      draw_row2
draw_end
```

The Completed Routine

By collecting all the things discussed so far we can piece together the reasonably efficient? DrawTiles() routine shown in listing 14.5. I have incidentally chosen to preserve and restore all registers used (including scratch registers d0, d1, a0 and a1) because this allows the routine to be quickly re-used without having to reload any unchanged scratch register based parameter values:

```
/*Listing 14.5: A nearly complete assembly language ver-
sion of DrawTiles()*/
DrawTiles:
    ;   Requires following parameters on entry:
    ;   a0 holds window rastport pointer
    ;   a1 holds image pointer
    ;   d0 holds starting left offset value
    ;   d1 holds starting top offset value
    ;   d2 holds required horizontal block count, ie column
        count
```

Creating Static Tile Effects – Part One

```
        ;       d3 holds required vertical block count, ie row count

                movem.l     d0-d7/a0-a5,-(sp)   preserve registers
                move.l      a0,a2               preserve rastport
                                                pointer
                move.l      a1,a3               preserve image pointer
                move.w      d0,d6               d6 = current left
                                                offset
                move.w      d0,d7               preserve left offset
                                                for reuse
                move.w      d1,a4               preserve top offset
                move.w      d2,a5               preserve column count
                                                for reuse
                move.w      ig_Width(a1),d4     get image width in d4
                move.w      ig_Height(a1),d5    get image height in d5
draw_row        CALLSYS     DrawImage,_IntuitionBase
                subq        #1,d2               decrease count
                beq         next_row
                move.w      a4,d1               set top offset
                add.w       d4,d6               form new left offset
draw_row2       move.w      d6,d0               needed for library
                                                function call
                move.l      a2,a0               restore rastport
                                                pointer
                move.l      a3,a1               restore image pointer
                bra         draw_row            keep going
next_row        subq        #1,d3               decrease count
                beq         draw_end
                move.w      d7,d6               reset start left off
                                                set for row
                move.w      a5,d2               reset column count
                move.w      a4,d1
                add.w       d5,d1
                move.w      d1,a4               top offset for next
                                                row
                bra         draw_row2
draw_end        movem.l     (sp)+,d0-d7/a0-a5   restore regsters
                rts
```

Are we finished? Not yet, because hidden in this routine is an inefficiency that is easily eliminated. The CALLSYS macro is pushing a6 ont o the stack and retrieving it after the DrawImage() routine returns. In this particular routine these actions are quite pointless because I've been a little crafty – register a6 has delberately *not* been used (except within CALLSYS). There is therefore no reason why, by just setting up a6 initially, we can't replace the CALLSYS generated code with the single equivalent indirect subroutine call, thus eliminating all of those a6 push/pull operations. This is typical of the sort of tricks an assembler coder will be able to spot and use and needless to say most C compilers, although they are extremely clever at optimising their code nowadays, will not always come up to the efficiency of a crafty 680x0er! Listing 14.6 shows the code after the modification that eliminated the register a6 inefficiencies:

/*Listing 14.6: This completed DrawTiles() routine works in much the same way as the C examples given at the start of the chapter*/

```
DrawTiles:
;       Requires following parameters on entry...
;       a0 holds window rastport pointer
;       a1 holds image pointer
;       d0 holds starting left offset value
;       d1 holds starting top offset value
;       d2 holds required horizontal block count, ie column
        count
;       d3 holds required vertical block count, ie row count

          movem.l   d0-d7/a0-a6,-(sp)   preserve registers
          move.l    _IntuitionBase,a6   set up library base
          move.l    a0,a2               preserve rastport
                                        pointer
          move.l    a1,a3               preserve image pointer
          move.w    d0,d6               d6 = current left
                                        offset
          move.w    d0,d7               preserve left offset
                                        for reuse
          move.w    d1,a4               preserve top offset
          move.w    d2,a5               preserve column count
                                        for reuse
          move.w    ig_Width(a1),d4     get image width in d4
          move.w    ig_Height(a1),d5    get image height in d5
draw_row  jsr       _LVODrawImage(a6)   a faster alternative
          subq      #1,d2               decrease count
```

Creating Static Tile Effects – Part One

```
              beq        next_row
              move.w     a4,d1                 set top offset
              add.w      d4,d6                 form new left offset
draw_row2     move.w     d6,d0                 needed for library
                                               function call
              move.l     a2,a0                 restore rastport pointer
              move.l     a3,a1                 restore image pointer
              bra        draw_row              keep going
next_row      subq       #1,d3                 decrease count
              beq        draw_end
              move.w     d7,d6                 reset start left off
                                               set for row
              move.w     a5,d2                 reset column count
              move.w     a4,d1
              add.w      d5,d1
              move.w     d1,a4                 top offset for next
row
              bra        draw_row2
draw_end      movem.l    (sp)+,d0-d7/a0-a6     restore regsters
              rts
```

Building A Test Framework

All we have to do now is put this subroutine into a runable example to check that it actually works. In order to do this we need some code which sets up some example parameters and then calls the DrawTiles() subroutine. Here is some code that will do for test purposes:

```
draw_images   move.l     d0,a1                 window address in a1
              move.l     wd_RPort(a1),a0       copy rastport pointer
                                               into a0
              lea        Image1,a1             pointer to image
              moveq      #20,d0                example left offset
              moveq      #15,d1                example top offset
              moveq      #20,d2                example columns count
              moveq      #10,d3                example rows count
              jsr        DrawTiles             our subroutine
```

The next program puts the above use of the DrawTiles() routine into a test framework that is suitable for a68k coders and others without the official includes. The program opens the dos and intuition libraries, locks the Workbench screen and opens a window using the (new from Release 2) OpenWindowTagList function. It then calls the DrawTiles() routine, waits a while, and shuts itself down. This version can, incidentally, be directly assembled by Charlie Gibb's A68k assembler:

```
/*Listing 14.7: DrawTiles() embedded in a runable test program*/
* Example CH14-1.s
LINKLIB     MACRO
            move.l      a6,-(a7)
            move.l      \2,a6
            jsr         \1(a6)
            move.l      (a7)+,a6
            ENDM
CALLSYS     MACRO
            LINKLIB     _LVO\1,\2
            ENDM


TRUE                    EQU     1
NULL                    EQU     0
DOS_VERSION             EQU     0

INTUITION_VERSION       EQU     36
SECONDS                 EQU     50
TIME_DELAY              EQU     10*SECONDS
TAG_DONE                EQU     0
WA_BASE                 EQU     $80000063
WA_Left                 EQU     WA_BASE+$01
WA_Top                  EQU     WA_BASE+$02
WA_Width                EQU     WA_BASE+$03
WA_Height               EQU     WA_BASE+$04
WA_Title                EQU     WA_BASE+$0B
WA_DragBar              EQU     WA_BASE+$1F
WA_PubScreen            EQU     WA_BASE+$16
wd_RPort                EQU     50
ig_Width                EQU     4
ig_Height               EQU     6
_AbsExecBase            EQU     4
_LVOOpenLibrary         EQU     -552
_LVOCloseLibrary        EQU     -414
```

```
            _LVOLockPubScreen           EQU    -510
            _LVOUnlockPubScreen         EQU    -516
            _LVOOpenWindowTagList       EQU    -606
            _LVOCloseWindow             EQU    -72
            _LVODelay                   EQU    -198
            _LVODrawImage               EQU    -114


start       lea         dos_name,a1         load pointer to
                                             library name
            moveq       #DOS_VERSION,d0 any version will do!
open_dos CALLSYS OpenLibrary,_AbsExecBase
            move.l      d0,_DOSBase         save returned pointer
            beq         exit                check open OK?
open_int lea            intuition_name,a1   load pointer to
                                             library name
            moveq       #INTUITION_VERSION,d0 specify mimimum lib
                                              version
            CALLSYS     OpenLibrary,_AbsExecBase
            move.l      d0,_IntuitionBase   save returned pointer
            beq         close_dos           check open OK?
lock_screen lea         workbench_name,a0   pointer to screen name
            CALLSYS     LockPubScreen,_IntuitionBase
            move.l      d0,workbench_p      save returned pointer
            beq         close_int           check  return value?
open_window move.l      #NULL,a0
            lea         tags,a1             our tag list
            CALLSYS     OpenWindowTagList,_IntuitionBase
            move.l      d0,window_p         pointer to our window
            beq         unlk_screen         draw_images
            move.l      d0,a1               window address in a1
            move.l      wd_RPort(a1),a0     copy rastport pointer
                                             into a0
            lea         Image1,a1           pointer to image
            moveq       #20,d0              example left offset
            moveq       #20,d1              example top offset
            move.w      #200,d2             example columns count
            move.w      #100,d3             example rows count
            jsr         DrawTiles           our subroutine
```

```
wait        move.l      #TIME_DELAY,d1
            CALLSYS     Delay,_DOSBase
            move.l      window_p,a0              window to close
            CALLSYS     CloseWindow,_IntuitionBase
unlk_screen move.l      #NULL,a0                 screen name not needed
            move.l      workbench_p,a1           screen to unlock
            CALLSYS     UnlockPubScreen,_IntuitionBase
close_int   move.l      _IntuitionBase,a1        library to close
            CALLSYS     CloseLibrary,_AbsExecBaseclose_dos
            move.l      _DOSBase,a1              library to close
            CALLSYS     CloseLibrary,_AbsExecBaseexit
            clr.l       d0
            rts                                  logical end of program


DrawTiles:
;       Requires following parameters on entry...
;       a0 holds window rastport pointer
;       a1 holds image pointer
;       d0 holds starting left offset value
;       d1 holds starting top offset value
;       d2 holds required horizontal block count, ie column
;       count
;       d3 holds required vertical block count, ie row count

            movem.l     d0-d7/a0-a6,-(sp)        preserve registers
            move.l      _IntuitionBase,a6        set up library base
            move.l      a0,a2                    preserve rastport pointer
            move.l      a1,a3                    preserve image pointer
            move.w      d0,d6                    d6 = current left offset
            move.w      d0,d7                    preserve left offset for
                                                 reuse
            move.w      d1,a4                    preserve top offset
            move.w      d2,a5                    preserve column count for
                                                 reuse
            move.w      ig_Width(a1),d4          get image width in d4
            move.w      ig_Height(a1),d5         get image height in d5
draw_row    jsr         _LVODrawImage(a6)        a faster alternative
            subq        #1,d2                    decrease count
```

Creating Static Tile Effects – Part One

```
            beq         next_row
            move.w      a4,d1               set top offset
            add.w       d4,d6               form new left offset
draw_row2   move.w      d6,d0               needed for library function
                                            call
            move.l      a2,a0               restore rastport pointer
            move.l      a3,a1               restore image pointer
            bra         draw_row            keep going
next_row    subq        #1,d3               decrease count
            beq         draw_end
            move.w      d7,d6               reset start left offset for
                                            row
            move.w      a5,d2               reset column count
            move.w      a4,d1
            add.w       d5,d1
            move.w      d1,a4               top offset for next row
            bra         draw_row2
draw_end    movem.l     (sp)+,d0-d7/a0-a6   restore regsters
            rts


_DOSBase            ds.l 1
_IntuitionBase      ds.l 1
window_p            ds.l 1
tags                dc.l WA_PubScreen
workbench_p         ds.l 1
                    dc.l WA_Left,50
                    dc.l WA_Top,20
                    dc.l WA_Width,640
                    dc.l WA_Height,250
                    dc.l WA_DragBar,TRUE
                    dc.l WA_Title,window_name
                    dc.l TAG_DONE,NULL
dos_name        dc.b    'dos.library',NULL
intuition_name  dc.b    'intuition.library',NULL
workbench_name  dc.b    'Workbench',NULL
window_name     dc.b    'DrawTiles() Subroutine Test',NULL


Image1:
```

```
            dc.w 0,0        ;XY origin relative to container TopLeft
            dc.w 2,2        ;Image width and height in pixels
            dc.w 0          ;number of bitplanes in Image
            dc.l NULL       ;pointer to ImageData
            dc.b $0000,$0001 ;PlanePick and PlaneOnOff
            dc.l NULL       ;next Image structure
            END
```

Normally anyone enthusiastic enough to get into 680x0 Amiga assembler coding will be enthusiastic enough to obtain the official Amiga include files. When these are available explicit definitions of many standard Amiga items can be avoided. Here for reference purposes is the equivalent version that gets its definitions via separate include files:

```
/*Listing 14.8 A version of the program that uses include
  files to provide the relevant definitions*/
* Example CH14-2.s
        INCLUDE intuition/intuition.i
        INCLUDE function_offsets.i
CALLSYS MACRO
        LINKLIB _LVO\1,\2
        ENDM


TRUE                    EQU     1
NULL                    EQU     0
DOS_VERSION             EQU     0
INTUITION_VERSION       EQU     36
SECONDS                 EQU     50
TIME_DELAY              EQU     10*SECONDS

start       lea      dos_name,a1          load pointer to
                                          library name
            moveq    #DOS_VERSION,d0      any version will do!
open_dos    CALLSYS  OpenLibrary,_AbsExecBase
            move.l   d0,_DOSBase          save returned pointer
            beq      exit                 check open OK?
open_int    lea      intuition_name,a1    load pointer to
                                          library name
            moveq    #INTUITION_VERSION,d0  specify mimimum
lib                                         version
```

Creating Static Tile Effects – Part One

```
                CALLSYS     OpenLibrary,_AbsExecBase
                move.l      d0,_IntuitionBase       save returned pointer
                beq         close_dos               check open OK?
lock_screen     lea         workbench_name,a0       pointer to screen name
                CALLSYS     LockPubScreen,_IntuitionBase
                move.l      d0,workbench_p          save returned pointer
                beq         close_int               check  return value?
open_window     move.l      #NULL,a0
                lea         tags,a1                 our tag list
                CALLSYS     OpenWindowTagList,_IntuitionBase
                move.l      d0,window_p             pointer to our window
                beq         unlk_screen
draw_images     move.l      d0,a1                   window address in a1
                move.l      wd_RPort(a1),a0         copy rastport pointer
                                                    into a0
                lea         Image1,a1               pointer to image
                moveq       #20,d0                  example left offset
                moveq       #15,d1                  example top offset
                move.w      #200,d2                 example columns count
                move.w      #100,d3                 example rows count
                jsr         DrawTiles               our subroutine
wait            move.l      #TIME_DELAY,d1
                CALLSYS     Delay,_DOSBase
                move.l      window_p,a0             window to close
                CALLSYS     CloseWindow,_IntuitionBase
unlk_screen     move.l      #NULL,a0                screen name not needed
                move.l      workbench_p,a1          screen to unlock
                CALLSYS     UnlockPubScreen,_IntuitionBase
close_int       move.l      _IntuitionBase,a1       library to close
                CALLSYS     CloseLibrary,_AbsExecBaseclose_dos
                move.l      _DOSBase,a1             library to close
                CALLSYS     CloseLibrary,_AbsExecBase
exit            clr.l       d0
                rts                                 logical end of program


DrawTiles:
;           Requires following parameters on entry...
```

```
;           a0 holds window rastport pointer
;           a1 holds image pointer
;           d0 holds starting left offset value
;           d1 holds starting top offset value
;           d2 holds required horizontal block count, ie column
;           count
;           d3 holds required vertical block count, ie row count

            movem.l   d0-d7/a0-a6,-(sp)   preserve registers
            move.l    _IntuitionBase,a6   set up library base
            move.l    a0,a2               preserve rastport
                                          pointer
            move.l    a1,a3               preserve image pointer
            move.w    d0,d6               d6 = current left
                                          offset
            move.w    d0,d7               preserve left offset
                                          for reuse
            move.w    d1,a4               preserve top offset
            move.w    d2,a5               preserve column count
                                          for reuse
            move.w    ig_Width(a1),d4     get image width in d4
            move.w    ig_Height(a1),d5    get image height in d5
draw_row    jsr       _LVODrawImage(a6)   a faster alternative
            subq      #1,d2               decrease count
            beq       next_row
            move.w    a4,d1               set top offset
            add.w     d4,d6               form new left offset
draw_row2   move.w    d6,d0               needed for library
                                          function call
            move.l    a2,a0               restore rastport
pointer
            move.l    a3,a1               restore image pointer
            bra       draw_row            keep going
next_row    subq      #1,d3               decrease count
            beq       draw_end
            move.w    d7,d6               reset start left off
                                          set for row
            move.w    a5,d2               reset column count
            move.w    a4,d1
            add.w     d5,d1
```

Creating Static Tile Effects – Part One

```
            move.w      d1,a4              top offset for next row
            bra         draw_row2
draw_end    movem.l     (sp)+,d0-d7/a0-a6  restore regsters
            rts


_DOSBase        ds.l    1
_IntuitionBase  ds.l    1
window_p        ds.l    1
tags            dc.l    WA_PubScreen
workbench_p     ds.l    1
                dc.l    WA_Left,50
                dc.l    WA_Top,20
                dc.l    WA_Width,640
                dc.l    WA_Height,250
                dc.l    WA_DragBar,TRUE
                dc.l    WA_Title,window_name
                dc.l    TAG_DONE,NULL
dos_name        dc.b    'dos.library',NULL
intuition_name  dc.b    'intuition.library',NULL
workbench_name  dc.b    'Workbench',NULL


window_name     dc.b    'DrawTiles() Subroutine Test',NULL


Image1:
        dc.w    0,0     ;XY origin relative to container TopLeft
        dc.w    2,2     ;Image width and height in pixels
        dc.w    0       ;number of bitplanes in Image
        dc.l    NULL    ;pointer to ImageData
        dc.b    $0000,$0001     ;PlanePick and PlaneOnOff
        dc.l    NULL    ;next Image structure
                END
```

The Bottom Line

By the time that the low-level DrawTiles() routine had been coded and tested the best part of a day had gone, and that was despite the fact that I knew very clearly what needed to be done code-wise. The big disadvantage with a 680x0 approach then is that it takes far longer before you get the routine up and running (especially since a few silly slips are inevitable at the 680x0 coding level).

The assembler routine, like the C routine, certainly works OK but this is not the end of the story by a long chalk. You'll notice that in both of the assembler examples I've defined a very small tile (2 pixel by 2 pixel) using an Image structure that, for simplicity, has no bitplane data. A grid of 100 rows and 200 columns were used so the tile ended up being *drawn* 20,000 times. I used a similar image definition when testing my C routines and this large duplication of a small tile definition did of course allow the speed of the drawing operations of the various routines to be compared.

The disturbing news here is that when you run the test programs you find the C version is as fast as the assembler version. Did we waste our time trying to improve our tile drawing operations by using assembler? Should we have stuck to our original C routine and thought no more about it? Or is there more to this seemingly simple problem than meets the eye? These are the type of questions that the next chapter is now going to answer.

15: Creating Static Tile Effects - Part Two

One of the purposes of the last chapter was to illustrate the time/effort differences between C and assembler level code development. Another reason that the comparison was made was to show you that moving to assembler is not always going to improve the execution time of a routine. In the case of the routines that we examined, the main *cost* of the routine lies in performing the DrawImage() function and with our current arrangements the routine is called as many times as there are tiles in the grid. This is the same for both the C and the assembler versions.

Compilers are able to generate perfectly efficient loop code and as the comparisons of the last chapter have now shown there is absolutely nothing to gained by converting the DrawTiles() routine to assembly language because speed-wise nothing at all is gained. So does this mean that we already have the best solution to our tiling problem? I'm afraid that the answer here is – most definitely not. The twin-loop approach we have so far adopted, though simple to code, is unfortunately totally inadequate.

We know that the main execution time cost of the routine is related to the image drawing function calls and because DrawImage() uses the blitter for its drawing operations my guess is that the bulk of the execution time penalty lies in setting up the required blitter operations rather than the *blit* operations themselves. In short I'm suggesting that the areas of graphics being drawn are less important than the number of function calls made and this means that if improvements are to be made to the DrawTiles() routine then we need to reduce the number of times DrawImage() or any equivalent drawing functions are used.

So what can be done? At the moment the drawing of an M rows x N columns grid requires M x N drawing function calls. One improvement could be to draw a row of M tiles and then use the blitter to copy that row N times down the screen. That would require M initial tile drawing operations followed by N copy operations. M+N is of course much less than MxN (eg for a 100 row x 200 column grid the original approach would need 20,000 function calls whereas the new approach would need only 100+200=300).

This quite obvious improvement enables us to produce some significant time savings and the following listing 15.1 code shows how the ideas can be implemented:

```
/*Listing 15.1: An improved DrawTiles() routine*/

void DrawTiles(struct Image *image_p,struct RastPort
*rastport_p,WORD rows,WORD columns, WORD left_offset, WORD
top_offset)
{
WORD left=0,top=0,row_width,width,height,i;
width=image_p->Width;
height=image_p->Height;
for (i=0;i<columns;i++)
   {
   DrawImage(rastport_p,image_p,left+left_offset,
   top+top_offset);
   left+=width;
   }
row_width=left;
for (i=1;i<rows;i++)
   {
   top+=height;
   ClipBlit(rastport_p,left_offset,top_offset,
            rastport_p,left_offset,top_offset+top,
            row_width,height,0xC0);
   }
}
```

Function Name:	**ClipBlit()**
Description:	This is a rastport-oriented blitter function that performs blitter operations in an Intuition compatible way
Call Format:	ClipBlit(source_rastport_p, sourceX_p, sourceY_p, dest_rastport_p, destX_p, destY_p, width, height, minterm);
C Prototype:	void ClipBlit(struct Rastport *, WORD, WORD struct Rastport *, WORD, WORD, WORD, WORD, UBYTE);
Registers:	a0 d0 d1 a1 d2 d3 d4 d5 d6
Arguments:	source_rastport_p - pointer to source RastPort dest_rastport_p - pointer to destination RastPort sourceX_p, sourceY_p - top left of area to blit destX_p, destY_p - top left of destination area width and height - width and height of area to be blitted minterm - blitter logic function for the operation
Return Value:	None
Notes:	Use 0xC0 as the minterm for a direct copy

Remember incidentally that when loops are performed a large number of times all the operations inside the loop take on a special significance. What may, in isolation, appear to be an almost trivial time penalty inside a loop can sometimes seriously affect the overall execution time if that loop were to be performed a large number of times. This incidentally is why I have chosen to copy the width and height values of the image being used to separate variables rather than have indirection operations inside the loops doing the ClipBlit() work.

This new routine makes a visible difference speed-wise but to see where further improvements can be made we now ought to think about how a row of tiles are drawn. A row of say 100 tiles needs 100 draw operations. Can we reduce this? Supposing we created a 2 tile block (which would require 2 drawing operations) and then copied that block 50 times (another 50 copy based draw operations). That would allow us to draw 100 tiles using only 52 draw/copy operations. If we created a 4 tile block (which would need four drawing operations) then only 25 copy operations would be needed making the total number of function calls 29! Table 15.1 shows some various possibilities:

Copy Operations	Blocksize	Left Over	Total Function Calls	
100	1	0	101	
50	2	0	52	
33	3	1	37	
25	4	0	29	
20	5	0	25	
16	6	4	26	
14	7	2	23	
12	8	4	24	
11 *	9	1	21	
10	10	0	20	
11	9	1	21	(* factors start repeating)

Table 15.1. The relationship between block size and the number of draw/copy function calls required.

It turns out that it isn't necessary to look at all possibilities – we only need look as far as the square root of the number concerned. It can be proved but a bit of experimenting with various test cases should convince you that the smallest amount of function calls will occur when the block size is the nearest integer to the square root of the number of tiles in the row. Once this is accepted it means that what we need is a routine that draws a single tile using the DrawImage() function and then blits that tile a sufficient number of times to make a tile block of optimum size. It must then blit the whole block until the first line of tiles is as near compete as possible before filling in any residual blocks with additional single tile copy operations. Setting up the block details is quite easy. We just find the largest integer smaller than the square root of the number of tiles in a row like this:

```
block_size=(WORD)floor(sqrt((double)columns));
```

and then calculate the number of blocks and residual tiles:

```
block_count=columns/block_size;
residual_tiles=columns-block_size*block_count;
```

Having done that we draw a tile, use a loop to copy it and produce a block of the required size, use another loop to copy the block the required number of times, and then use another loop that copies a single tile to fill in any gaps at the end of the row. Listing 15.2 is the code for the routine in its current state:

Creating Static Tile Effects – Part Two

```c
/*Listing 15.2: Further improvements to the DrawTiles()
routine*/

void DrawTiles(struct Image *image_p,struct RastPort
*rastport_p,WORD rows,WORD columns, WORD left_offset, WORD
top_offset)

{
WORD block_size,block_count,block_width,residual_tiles,
row_width,width,height,left=0,top=0,i;

width=image_p->Width;

height=image_p->Height;

block_size=(WORD)floor(sqrt((double)columns));

block_count=columns/block_size;

residual_tiles=columns-block_size*block_count;

DrawImage(rastport_p,image_p,left_offset,top_offset); /*
draw first tile */

left+=width; /* set left position of next tile */

/* and blit remaining tiles of first block... */

for (i=1;i<block_size;i++)

   {
   ClipBlit(rastport_p,left_offset,top_offset,
           rastport_p,left_offset+left,top_offset,
           width,height,0xC0);

   left+=width; /* set left position of next tile */

   }
block_width=left;

/* one complete block of tiles have been drawn so now blit
remaining    whole blocks of tiles into first row... */

for (i=1;i<block_count;i++)

   {
   ClipBlit(rastport_p,left_offset,top_offset,
           rastport_p,left_offset+left,top_offset,
           block_width,height,0xC0);

   left+=block_width;

   }
for (i=0;i<residual_tiles;i++)

   {
   ClipBlit(rastport_p,left_offset,top_offset,
           rastport_p,left_offset+left,top_offset,
           width,height,0xC0);

   left+=width;

   }
```

```
        row_width=left;
        for (i=1;i<rows;i++)
            {
            top+=height;
            ClipBlit(rastport_p,left_offset,top_offset,
                    rastport_p,left_offset,top_offset+top,
                    row_width,height,0xC0);
            }
        }
```

The routine has admittedly grown a bit in size and complexity, but the important thing is that it is much faster than our early efforts. Get clear in your mind how it works. We calculate the optimum block size, build the first row (now quite efficiently) and then copy that row down the screen.

A Crafty Twist Adds Another Dimension

Can you see where further improvements can be made? It's easy – we are *copying* rows one at a time – just like we were originally copying single tiles when producing the first row. Single row copying is unnecessary and what we now ought to do is calculate the optimum depth of a block and subsequently modify the routine to reduce the number of row copying operations that need to be performed.

What is the optimum depth? It's going to be the largest integer less than or equal to the square root of the number of rows and we already know how this can be calculated:

```
row_block_size=(WORD)floor(sqrt((double)rows));
row_block_count=rows/row_block_size; residual_rows=rows-
row_block_size*row_block_count;
```

With these values now available, and with the first row of tiles already drawn, we need only do three things. Firstly, copy a sufficient number of rows to produce an optimum depth block. Secondly, copy as many of those whole blocks as can be fitted into the specified row space. Thirdly, fill any remaining residual row space with tiles. Although the row co-ordinates are different the operations are of course very similar to those we've already dealt with and the result of incorporating these new ideas is the routine shown in listing 15.3 which follows:

```
/*Listing 15.3: The final iterative version of the
DrawTiles() function*/

void DrawTiles(struct Image *image_p,struct RastPort
*rastport_p,WORD rows,WORD columns, WORD left_offset, WORD
top_offset)
    {
```

Creating Static Tile Effects – Part Two

```
WORD block_size,block_count,block_width,residual_tiles,
     row_width,width,height,left=0,top=0,i;
WORD row_block_size,row_block_count,block_depth,
     residual_rows;
width=image_p->Width;
height=image_p->Height;
block_size=(WORD)floor(sqrt((double)columns));
block_count=columns/block_size;
residual_tiles=columns-block_size*block_count;
DrawImage(rastport_p,image_p,left_offset,top_offset); /*
draw first tile */
left+=width; /* set left position of next tile */
/* and blit remaining tiles of first block... */
for (i=1;i<block_size;i++)
   {
   ClipBlit(rastport_p,left_offset,top_offset,
            rastport_p,left_offset+left,top_offset,
            width,height,0xC0);
   left+=width; /* set left position of next tile */
   }
block_width=left;/* one complete block of tiles have been
drawn so now blit remaining    whole blocks of tiles into
first row... */
for (i=1;i<block_count;i++)
   {
   ClipBlit(rastport_p,left_offset,top_offset,
            rastport_p,left_offset+left,top_offset,
            block_width,height,0xC0);
   left+=block_width;
   }
for (i=0;i<residual_tiles;i++)
   {
   ClipBlit(rastport_p,left_offset,top_offset,
            rastport_p,left_offset+left,top_offset,
            width,height,0xC0);
   left+=width;
   }
row_width=left;
row_block_size=(WORD)floor(sqrt((double)rows));
row_block_count=rows/row_block_size;
residual_rows=rows-row_block_size*row_block_count;
```

```
            top=height; /* starting row position */
            for (i=1;i<row_block_size;i++)
               {
               ClipBlit(rastport_p,left_offset,top_offset,
                        rastport_p,left_offset,top+top_offset,
                        row_width,height,0xC0);
               top+=height;
               }
            block_depth=top;
            /* two-dimensional block has been drawn so now blit
            required    number of whole blocks down the screen... */
            for (i=1;i<row_block_count;i++)
               {
               ClipBlit(rastport_p,left_offset,top_offset,
                        rastport_p,left_offset,top_offset+top,
                        row_width,block_depth,0xC0);
               top+=block_depth;
               }
            for (i=0;i<residual_rows;i++)
               {
               ClipBlit(rastport_p,left_offset,top_offset,
                        rastport_p,left_offset,top_offset+top,
                        row_width,height,0xC0);
               top+=height;
               }
         }
```

The DrawTiles() Routine - Advanced Approach

Up until now the various stages in the development of our tile drawing routine should have be quite easy to understand. The improvements which follow however are not because they involve recursion, ie the use of routines which, during their operation, make further calls to themselves! Imagine that you are drawing a grid of 100 rows by 200 columns. The first job is to draw a row of 200 tiles and we know that this should be done using 14 blocks of 14 tile copy operations plus four additional copies for the residual tiles needed to complete the row.

At the moment our tile drawer would draw the first tile and then create the first block of 14 tiles by using a loop that makes 14-1=13 iterations. But we now know that a block of 14 tiles can be drawn with less than 14 operations – the square root of 14 is 3.74 and so we really ought to be drawing this first block by initially creating a block of three tiles, copying this block four times, and then copying

Creating Static Tile Effects – Part Two

the two residual tiles needed. With larger numbers the nesting goes further and the way to get the ultimate minimum as far as the number of function calls is concerned is to devise a DrawRow() routine that recursively calls itself to generate its tile blocks as efficiently as possible.

Recursive routines must have a limiting condition which stops further calls being made and the limiting condition in our case is trying to create a one tile block of tiles. In short if a block size is not greater than one no further recursive calls will be made and instead we draw the first tile using Intuition's DrawImage() function:

```
if(block_size>1)
left=DrawRow(image_p,rastport_p,block_size,left_offset,top
_offset);
   else {
        DrawImage(rastport_p,image_p,left_offset+left,
        top_offset);
        left+=width; /* set left position of next tile to
        be drawn */
}
```

In order for the row drawing routine to place tiles into the right positions a simple rule is adopted. Whenever a tile is drawn or copied, a variable, called left, is incremented by a value equal to the width of the image being drawn. With recursion now being used *all* instances of the recursively-called routine need to know the current left position for drawing and this means that a DrawRow() call must return an appropriate value to routine that called it. Listing 15.4 shows the code arrangements that I chose to adopt:

```
/*Listing 15.4: A recursive DrawRow() routine*/
WORD DrawRow(struct Image *image_p,struct RastPort *rast-
port_p,WORD columns, WORD left_offset, WORD top_offset)
{
static WORD left; /* initialized to zero for first use */
WORD block_size,block_count,block_width,residual_tiles,
     width,height,i;
width=image_p->Width;
height=image_p->Height;
block_size=(WORD)floor(sqrt((double)columns));
block_count=columns/block_size;
residual_tiles=columns-block_size*block_count;
if(block_size>1) left=DrawRow(image_p,rastport_p,
   block_size, left_offset,top_offset);
```

```
        else {
             DrawImage(rastport_p,image_p,left_offset+left,
                       top_offset);
             left+=width; /* set left position of next tile to be
                             drawn */
        }
   /* one complete block of tiles have been drawn so now blit
   remaining   whole blocks of tiles into first row... */
   block_width=left;
   for (i=1;i<block_count;i++)
      {
      ClipBlit(rastport_p,left_offset+left-block_width,
               top_offset,rastport_p,left_offset+left,top_off
               set, block_width,height,0xC0);
      left+=block_width;
      }
   for (i=0;i<residual_tiles;i++)
      {
      ClipBlit(rastport_p,left_offset+left-width,top_offset,
               rastport_p,left_offset+left,top_offset,
               width,height,0xC0);
      left+=width;
      }
   return(left);
   }
```

At the highest recursion level the left value returned by DrawRow() will be the pixel width of the row and by coding the column drawing operations in the same recursive style we can get a situation whereby both row creation and row copying operations are minimised. The row copy operations need to know the width of the row and so an extra parameter is needed resulting in the highest level of the new recursive form of our DrawTiles() routine looking like this:

```
row_width=DrawRow(image_p,rastport_p,columns,left_offset,
                  top_offset);
CopyRows(image_p,rastport_p,rows,row_width,left_offset,
         top_offset);
```

Recursion is a difficult topic to understand and recursive routines are difficult to test. One good idea is to study the code and trace

Creating Static Tile Effects – Part Two

out its potential actions with pen and paper. The following example, listing 15.5, includes a variable called n whose job is simply to count the number of draw/copy operations performed:

```
/* -------------------------------------------------- */
/*Listing 15.5: A trace version of the new DrawTiles()
routine*/
void DrawTiles(struct Image *image_p,struct RastPort
*rastport_p,WORD rows,WORD columns, WORD left_offset, WORD
top_offset)
{
WORD row_width;
row_width=DrawRow(image_p,rastport_p,columns,left_offset,t
op_offset);
CopyRows(image_p,rastport_p,rows,row_width,left_offset,top
_offset);
}
/* -------------------------------------------------- */
WORD DrawRow(struct Image *image_p,struct RastPort *rast-
port_p,WORD columns, WORD left_offset, WORD top_offset)
{
static WORD left; /* initialized to zero for first use
*/WORD block_size,block_count,block_width,residual_tiles,
width,height,i,n=0;
width=image_p->Width;
height=image_p->Height;
block_size=(WORD)floor(sqrt((double)columns));
block_count=columns/block_size;
residual_tiles=columns-block_size*block_count;
if(block_size>1)
left=DrawRow(image_p,rastport_p,block_size,left_offset,top
_offset);
else {
   DrawImage(rastport_p,image_p,left_offset+left,
             top_offset);
   left+=width; /* set left position of next tile to be
                   drawn */
   n++;
   }
/* one complete block of tiles have been drawn so now blit
remaining    whole blocks of tiles into first row... */
block_width=left;
for (i=1;i<block_count;i++)
```

```
    {
    ClipBlit(rastport_p,left_offset+left-block_width,
            top_offset,rastport_p,left_offset+left,
            top_offset,block_width,height,0xC0);
    left+=block_width;
    n++;
    }
for (i=0;i<residual_tiles;i++)
    {
    ClipBlit(rastport_p,left_offset+left-width,top_offset,
            rastport_p,left_offset+left,top_offset,
            width,height,0xC0);
    left+=width;
    n++;
    }
printf("%d\n",n);
return(left);
}
/* ------------------------------------------------- */
WORD CopyRows(struct Image *image_p, struct RastPort
*rastport_p,WORD rows, WORD row_width, WORD left_offset,
WORD top_offset)
{
static WORD top; /* initialized to zero for first use */
WORD block_size,block_count,block_depth,residual_rows,
height,i,n=0;height=image_p->Height;
block_size=(WORD)floor(sqrt((double)rows));
block_count=rows/block_size;residual_rows=rows-
block_size*block_count;
if(block_size>1)
top=CopyRows(image_p,rastport_p,block_size,row_width,left_
offset,top_offset);
else {
    top+=height;
    }
/* two-dimensional block has been drawn so now blit
required    number of whole blocks down the screen... */
block_depth=top;
for (i=1;i<block_count;i++)
    {
```

Creating Static Tile Effects – Part Two

```
        ClipBlit(rastport_p,left_offset,top_offset,
                rastport_p,left_offset,top_offset+top,
                row_width,block_depth,0xC0);

        top+=block_depth;

        n++;

        }
    for (i=0;i<residual_rows;i++)
        {
        ClipBlit(rastport_p,left_offset,top_offset,
                rastport_p,left_offset,top_offset+top,
                row_width,height,0xC0);

        top+=height;

        n++;

        }
    printf("%d\n",n);
    return(top);
    }
/* ------------------------------------------------- */
```

When the routine shown in listing 15.5 was placed into a test program that created a 100 row by 200 column tile grid, the values of n returned were 3, 5, 17, 2, 3, and 9. These represented three recursive calls to DrawRow() and three recursive calls to CopyRows(). This is where the numbers come from:

For the 200 columns		
14 blocks of 14 tiles + 4 residual tiles =	18-1 = 17	draw/copy operations
4 blocks of 3 tiles + 2 residual tiles =	6-1 = 5	draw/copy operations
3 tiles to create first block	3	draw/copy operations
For the 100 rows		
10 blocks of 10 rows + 0 residual rows	10-1 = 9	draw/copy operations
3 blocks of 3 rows + 1 residual row	4-1 = 3	draw/copy operations
2 rows to create first block	2	draw/copy operations

Table 15.2. Test values.

What this means, in this particular test case, is that only 39 draw/copy operations were needed in order to create a tile arrangement of 200 x 100, ie 20,000 tiles. In this case our recursive routine is only doing about 0.2% of the drawing/copying function setting up work that our first routine of the previous chapter was doing. In other words it is about 500 times more efficient!

Listing 15.6 shows the final version of the routine (without the trace statements):

```
/* -------------------------------------------------- */
/*Listing 15.6: The final recursive DrawTiles() routine
and the end of our tile drawing road!*/
void DrawTiles(struct Image *image_p,struct RastPort
*rastport_p,WORD rows,WORD columns, WORD left_offset, WORD
top_offset)
{
WORD
row_width;row_width=DrawRow(image_p,rastport_p,columns,lef
t_offset,top_offset);
CopyRows(image_p,rastport_p,rows,row_width,left_offset,top
_offset);
}
/* -------------------------------------------------- */
WORD DrawRow(struct Image *image_p,struct RastPort *rast-
port_p,WORD columns, WORD left_offset, WORD top_offset)
{
static WORD left; /* initialized to zero for first use */
WORD block_size,block_count,block_width,residual_tiles,
width,height,i;
width=image_p->Width; height=image_p->Height;
block_size=(WORD)floor(sqrt((double)columns))
;block_count=columns/block_size;
residual_tiles=columns-block_size*block_count;
if(block_size>1)
left=DrawRow(image_p,rastport_p,block_size,left_offset,top
_offset);
else {
    DrawImage(rastport_p,image_p,left_offset+left,
    top_offset);
    left+=width; /* set left position of next tile to be
    drawn */
    }
/* one complete block of tiles have been drawn so now blit
remaining    whole blocks of tiles into first row... */
block_width=left;
for (i=1;i<block_count;i++)
   {
```

```c
        ClipBlit(rastport_p,left_offset+left-
                block_width,top_offset,rastport_p,
                left_offset+left, top_offset,block_width,
                height,OxCO);
        left+=block_width;
    }
for (i=0;i<residual_tiles;i++)
    {
    ClipBlit(rastport_p,left_offset+left-width,top_offset,
            rastport_p,left_offset+left,top_offset,
            width,height,OxCO);
    left+=width;
    }
return(left);
}
/* -------------------------------------------------- */
WORD CopyRows(struct Image *image_p, struct RastPort
*rastport_p,WORD rows, WORD row_width, WORD left_offset,
WORD top_offset)
{
static WORD top; /* initialized to zero for first use */
WORD block_size,block_count,block_depth,residual_rows,
     height,i,n=0;
height=image_p->Height;
block_size=(WORD)floor(sqrt((double)rows));
block_count=rows/block_size;
residual_rows=rows-block_size*block_count;
if(block_size>1) top=CopyRows(image_p,rastport_p,
block_size,row_width,left_offset,top_offset);
else {
    top+=height;
    }
/* two-dimensional block has been drawn so now blit
required    number of whole blocks down the screen... */
block_depth=top;
for (i=1;i<block_count;i++)
    {
    ClipBlit(rastport_p,left_offset,top_offset,
            rastport_p,left_offset,top_offset+top,
            row_width,block_depth,OxCO);
    top+=block_depth;
```

```
            }
       for (i=0;i<residual_rows;i++)
          {
          ClipBlit(rastport_p,left_offset,top_offset,
                   rastport_p,left_offset,top_offset+top,
                   row_width,height,0xC0);
          top+=height;
          }
       return(top);
       }
       /* ---------------------------------------------- */
```

Some Important Ideas

It should now be apparent that if you want a routine to be as fast as possible then you *must* think about its underlying basis, ask yourself where the main execution time penalties are occurring, and ask also what you can do about them. When the simple twin-loop C tile drawing approach of the last chapter was being used to create a tile drawing routine things were fine as long as only small numbers of rows and columns were involved. When the numbers of rows and columns became large however the number of function calls required increased dramatically and it was to see the effect of this that I chose very small tile sizes in the example programs.

The re-coding using assembly language during the previous chapter did nothing to improve matters and there's an important lesson to be learnt here – the attempted *speed up* failed quite simply because we were not addressing the root cause of the problem. The moral of this chapter? It is probably that if you need dramatic speed increases in a routine then the chances are that what you really need is a better algorithm for whatever you are doing. This therefore is often where the bulk of your design and coding efforts should be concentrated.

We've been doing just this in this chapter and the improvements made to the DrawTiles() routine are dramatic and become increasingly so as the numbers of rows and columns increase. A similar routine could now be developed in low-level 680x0 code although it would be no faster that the one we've developed in C because the function calls overhead that remain would be the same in both cases. If you don't believe me – write a 680x0 version and see!

One last thing needs to be said concerning the arrangements finally adopted for the tile drawing operations. Developing algorithms which tackle problems in efficient, but often less *intuitively obvious*, ways is something that comes naturally to very few people and most people (myself included) have to work hard to achieve good results. There's no doubt that the more practice you get *problem solving* the better your chances of success in general and this means that, within reason, you make a point of jumping at each and every opportunity that presents itself. I say 'within reason' because I've found one particular criteria to be absolutely crucial to success – you *must* be interested in the problem either because you need to make practical use of the solution you discover, or because you find the problem itself interesting from an *academic* viewpoint. Either way your interest will usually prove to be a valuable ally!

16: Creating Mosaic Effects

This chapter deals with another problem that involves finding a better solution than that which is most obvious. A few years ago I was playing around with some ideas involving the encryption of two-dimensional picture data using a two-key based, two-dimensional rearrangement method. The idea was to imagine that a picture was composed of an arbitrary number of squares or *tiles* and then use selected horizontal and vertical encryption keys to *apparently randomly* rearrange the ordering of the tiles. In doing this the picture became unrecognisable yet, given the right encryption keys, the picture could be rapidly restored to its original form.

During the course of these, essentially theoretical, studies I was interested to see the visual effect of the various rearrangements and so the routines were tested in a way that showed the step-by-step changes as they *occurred*. When I saw the results I realised that somewhere here was a method for producing mosaic rearrangements (such as those you see on TV where the picture breaks into hundreds of small squares which are then randomly disintegrated, faded or otherwise modified). Plenty of other uses came to mind including games effects, screen wipes, jigsaw puzzles etc.

As with the previous chapter tile size is irrelevant. We may be shifting 1 pixel by 1 pixel blocks around, or the blocks may consist of 4 x 4 pixels, 20 x 100 pixels and so on. Let's suppose then that we consider a rectangular *source* area of the screen as being broken into an unspecified number of smaller rectangular blocks. It seems reasonable to identify these blocks by some co-ordinate scheme and I've opted for using the top left co-ordinates in all cases. If we do this it becomes possible to create a nice simple model whereby identified screen blocks such as:

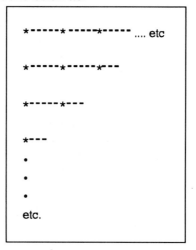

Figure 16.1. Screen blocks.

are represented just by their virtual top-left co-ordinates:

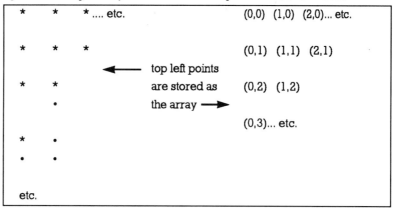

Figure 16.2. Co-ordinate positions.

In other words we could describe the locations of all of the tiles in a mosaic pattern using an array containing the (x,y) block number co-ordinates. To divide up, randomly rearrange, and copy a picture it stands to reason that all blocks must be used and the obvious way to do this is to generate all possible co-ordinate pairs for the tile area in question and randomly rearrange them. If however you have a 200 x 100 block rearrangement to do you would need to create a randomly rearranged list of 20,000 co-ordinate pairs. As the numbers of blocks involved increases so too does both the amount of memory needed for this list, and the amount of time needed to randomly rearrange it.

Making A Start

The task then is to find a better (quicker and more memory efficient) approach and essentially the problems we are solving are these: firstly, we want to find a way of generating a random, or apparently random, set of block (x,y) co-ordinates without eating into too much memory (ie without building lists of every possible co-ordinate pair). Secondly we want a way of accessing these co-ordinates using a mechanism which ensures that, after the operations have been completed, tiles corresponding to every co-ordinate pair will have been used.

Now rather than use a two dimensional array I will, in the following discussion, be using separate one dimensional arays. There's no real difference as far as coding complexity goes, but the one dimensional (vector) approach does make the explanations a little easier to understand.

One obvious way to ensure that every mosaic block would be used is to use a twin loop like this:

```
for (x=0; x<XMAX; x++)
   {
   for (y=0; y<YMAX; y++)
     {
     do something with block (x,y)
     eg copy block (x,y) to location (x+offset_x,
                                     y+offset_y)
     }
   }
```

This certainly moves all of the blocks but it does so in a uniform way. What we want is some way of making the effect look *random* so to start with let's assume that we have a mosaic block *vertical_block_count* blocks high and *horizontal_block_count* blocks wide. Our first step is to create a complete, but randomised, list of vertical co-ordinates by initializing and rearranging the values like this:

```
for (n=0; n<vertical_block_count; n++) { yvector[n]=n; }
for (n=0; n<vertical_block_count; n++)
   {
   r=rand() % vertical_block_count;   /* identify an r
                                         value */
   d=yvector[n]; /* swap r'th and n'th array elements */
   yvector[n]=yvector[r];
```

```
        yvector[r]=d;
     }
```

We obtain the horizontal co-ordinate set in a rather different fashion. Instead of calculating a full co-ordinate set we just, for reasons that will become apparent, calculate a set of random offset values like this:

```
for (n=0; n<horizontal_block_count; n++)
{
offset[n] = rand() % horizontal_block_count;
}
```

Although there are horizontal_block_count items in this set and they all lie in the range 0 to (horizontal_block_count-1) you should note that, because rand() can return the same number more than once, the set of values is unlikely to be the complete set of x co-ordinate values. In other words duplicates may occur and so some numbers of the co-ordinate set are likely to be missing. Perhaps surprisingly this will not matter!

The Co-ordinate Generation Scheme

This is where the tricky stuff begins. Take a look at the program shown in listing 16.1 and think about the code in relation to the ideas just mentioned:

```
/*Listing 16.1:  Generation of the x/y co-ordinate values.*/
/* Example CH16-1.c */
#include <stdio.h>
#include <stdlib.h>
#define X_MAXSIZE 150
#define Y_MAXSIZE 150
main()
{
int n,m,r,d,
    vertical_block_count,horizontal_block_count,
    offset[X_MAXSIZE], yvector[Y_MAXSIZE],
    x,ty;
/* some constant values for the copy (example specific)... */
vertical_block_count=5;         /* alter as required */
horizontal_block_count=6; /* for other block sizes */
/* randomizes the vertical (y) co-ordinates... */
for (n=0; n<vertical_block_count; n++) { yvector[n]=n;
}for (n=0; n<vertical_block_count; n++)
```

```
        {
        r=rand() % vertical_block_count;
        d=yvector[n];
        yvector[n]=yvector[r];
        yvector[r]=d;
        }
    /* create the offset values... */
    for (n=0; n<horizontal_block_count; n++)
        {
        offset[n] = rand() % horizontal_block_count;
        }
    /* now compute x/y tile co-ordinates and print results... */
    for (m=0; m<vertical_block_count; m++)
        {
        printf("m=%d\n\n",m);
        for (n=0; n<horizontal_block_count; n++)
          {
          /* calculate the block co-ordinates... */
          x = n;
          y = ((yvector[m] + offset[n]) % vertical_block_count);
          printf("yvector=%d\toffset= %d\t\t",yvector[m],
           offset[n]);
          printf("x=%d\ty=%d\n\n",x,y);
          }
        }
    }
```

It is not too difficult to see from listing 16.1 that the x co-ordinates generated within the double loop always take the current value of the inner loop variable n (we can incidentally therefore eliminate x from the loop and use n directly). Note also that this means the values of n generated will cover every x co-ordinate position for each value of m used in the outer loop.

The calculation of a set of y values is more awkward and best explained by imagining first what would happen if y was calculated using the expression:

    y=yvector[m];

Each value of m in the outer loop would produce a given y value and we know yvector[] contains *all* possible y co-ordinates (because we generated them and then just swapped them around). So, the outer loop covers all the y values whilst the inner loop generates all x values for each y value generated. This of course means that the whole set of (x,y) co-ordinate values are generated. By adding the offset value and using the modulus function (%) to keep the y position within the range of allowed values, ie using this expression:

```
y = ((yvector[m] + offset[n]) % vertical_block_count);
```

we are able to break up the order in which the y values are generated and it is this which generates the randomising effect. To get an idea of the values produced look at table 16.1 which shows the results that the listing 16.1 program produces:

```
m=0
    yvector=1    offset= 1    x=0    y=2
    yvector=1    offset= 2    x=1    y=3
    yvector=1    offset= 3    x=2    y=4
    yvector=1    offset= 4    x=3    y=0
    yvector=1    offset= 3    x=4    y=4
    yvector=1    offset= 2    x=5    y=3
m=1
    yvector=3    offset= 1    x=0    y=4
    yvector=3    offset= 2    x=1    y=0
    yvector=3    offset= 3    x=2    y=1
    yvector=3    offset= 4    x=3    y=2
    yvector=3    offset= 3    x=4    y=1
    yvector=3    offset= 2    x=5    y=0
m=2
    yvector=0    offset= 1    x=0    y=1
    yvector=0    offset= 2    x=1    y=2
    yvector=0    offset= 3    x=2    y=3
    yvector=0    offset= 4    x=3    y=4
    yvector=0    offset= 3    x=4    y=3
    yvector=0    offset= 2    x=5    y=2
m=3
    yvector=4    offset= 1    x=0    y=0
    yvector=4    offset= 2    x=1    y=1
    yvector=4    offset= 3    x=2    y=2
    yvector=4    offset= 4    x=3    y=3
    yvector=4    offset= 3    x=4    y=2
    yvector=4    offset= 2    x=5    y=1
m=4
    yvector=2    offset= 1    x=0    y=3
    yvector=2    offset= 2    x=1    y=4
    yvector=2    offset= 3    x=2    y=0
    yvector=2    offset= 4    x=3    y=1
    yvector=2    offset= 3    x=4    y=0
    yvector=2    offset= 2    x=5    y=4
```

Table 16.1. The output obtained from program 16.1.

Every (x,y) co-ordinate position has been covered and this is quite general – it'll work for any tile arrangement. This gives us a way of generating (apparently randomly) each and every tile location so what we need to do now is convert these tile co-ordinates to real screen locations. As well as converting the tile co-ordinates to pixel co-ordinates I've also added base addresses of source and target screen areas for a little extra flexibility. ClipBlt() is being used to move the data but obviously how you use the generated co-ordinates depends on what you are wanting to do. Normally some of the operations shown in the listing 16.2 code would be coded together but, for clarity, I've kept the individual stages distinguishable:

```
/*Listing 16.2: The guts of the mosaic transfer routine*/
for (m=0; m<vertical_block_count; m++)
   {
   for (n=0; n<horizontal_block_count; n++)
      {
      /* calculate the block co-ordinates... */
      y=source_y = ((yvector[m] + offset[n]) %
            vertical_block_count);
      x=n*pixel_block_width; /* now translate to real
                        screen co-ordinates... */
      y*=pixel_block_height;
      dest_x=dest_x_base+x; /* add the base addresses and
                        move the data... */
      dest_y=dest_y_base+y;
      x+=x_source_base;
      y+=y_source_base;
      /* and use the blitter to do the hard work... */
      ClipBlit(source_rastport_p, x, y,
            dest_rastport_p, dest_x, dest_y,
            pixel_block_width, pixel_block_height,
            minterm);
      }
   }
```

A Complete Mosaic Copy Routine

If we put both the co-ordinate generation and co-ordinate use ideas together we can now build a call-able routine, shown in listing 16.3 that can perform these mosaic transfer operations automatically:

```
/*Listing 16.3: The completed mosaic copy routine!*/
void MosaicCopy(WORD vertical_block_count,
         WORD horizon    tal_block_count, struct
         RastPort *source_rastport_p, struct
         RastPort *dest_rastport_p,
         WORD pixel_block_height, WORD
         pixel_block_width,
         WORD source_x_base, WORD source_y_base,
```

Creating Mosaic Effects

```c
                WORD dest_x_base, WORD dest_y_base,
                UBYTE minterm)
{
WORD d,m,n,r,x,y;yvector[MAXSIZE],offset[MAXSIZE],dest_x,
dest_y;
for (n=0; n<vertical_block_count; n++) { yvector[n]=n; }
for (n=0; n<vertical_block_count; n++)
   {
   r=rand() % vertical_block_count;
   d=yvector[n];
   yvector[n]=yvector[r];
   yvector[r]=d;
   }
for (n=0; n<horizontal_block_count; n++)
   {
   offset[n] = rand() % horizontal_block_count;
   }
/* now compute (x,y) tile co-ordinates and move them... */
for (m=0; m<vertical_block_count; m++)
   {
   for (n=0; n<horizontal_block_count; n++)
     {
     y = ((yvector[m] + offset[n]) %
          vertical_block_count);
     /* now translate (x,y) position to real screen
        co-ordinates... */
     x=n*pixel_block_width;
     y*=pixel_block_height;
     dest_x=dest_x_base+x; /* add the base addresses and
                              move the data */
     dest_y=dest_y_base+y;
     x+=source_x_base;
     y+=source_y_base;
     ClipBlit(source_rastport_p, x, y,
              dest_rastport_p, dest_x, dest_y,
              pixel_block_width, pixel_block_height,
              minterm);
```

The Blitter Minterm Byte

In the listing 16.3 routine the minterm byte is the logic function that tells the blitter how to perform its copy operations when reading from any or all of its three source dma channels (A,B, and C) and writing to its destination channel D. ClipBlit() associates channel B with the source rastport and channel C with the destination rastport, so to make a direct copy from the source rastport the minterm value should be set to 0xC0. Table 16.2 lists some common equation/minterm values involving blitter channels B and C (further information can be found in the Addison Wesley RKM Hardware manual).

Equation	Minterm	
D=B	0xCC	(Direct Copy)
D=B'	0x33	(Inverted copy)
D=C'	0x55	(Inverted destination)
D=B'+C	0xBB	
D=BC	0x88	
D=BC'	0x44	
D=B'C	0x22	
D=B+C'	0xDD	
D=B'C'	0x77	

Table 16.2. Common ClipBlit() related logic equations and blitter minterm equvalents.

Mosaic Disintegration

Now that we've got a copy routine available, disintegrating a picture whilst re-building elsewhere is easy. We just make an additional ClipBlit() call to clear each tile after it has been copied so that as the source area disintegrates the destination graphic will be built up. Here's the modification needed:

```
/*Listing 16.4: Code modification needed to produce 'mosa-
ic disintegration'*/

void MosaicDisintegration(WORD vertical_block_count, WORD
                          horizontal_block_count,struct
                          RastPort *source_rastport_p,
                          struct RastPort *dest_rastport_p,
                          WORD pixel_block_height,
                          WORD pixel_block_width,
                          WORD source_x_base, WORD
                          source_y_base,
                          WORD dest_x_base, WORD
                          dest_y_base,
                          UBYTE minterm)
```

```
{
WORD d,m,n,r,x,y;yvector[MAXSIZE],offset[MAXSIZE],dest_x,
dest_y;
for (n=0; n<vertical_block_count; n++) { yvector[n]=n; }
for (n=0; n<vertical_block_count; n++)
   {
   r=rand() % vertical_block_count;
   d=yvector[n];
   yvector[n]=yvector[r];
   yvector[r]=d;
   }
for (n=0; n<horizontal_block_count; n++)
   {
   offset[n] = rand() % horizontal_block_count;
   }
/* now compute (x,y) tile co-ordinates and move them... */
for (m=0; m<vertical_block_count; m++)
   {
   for (n=0; n<horizontal_block_count; n++)
   {
   y = ((yvector[m] + offset[n]) % vertical_block_count);
   /* now translate (x,y) position to real screen
   co-ordinates... */
   x=n*pixel_block_width;
   y*=pixel_block_height;
   dest_x=dest_x_base+x; /* add the base addresses and
                            move the data */
   dest_y=dest_y_base+y;
   x+=source_x_base;
   y+=source_y_base;
   ClipBlit(source_rastport_p, x, y,
            dest_rastport_p, dest_x, dest_y,
            pixel_block_width, pixel_block_height, minterm);
            ClipBlit(source_rastport_p, x, y,
            dest_rastport_p, x, y,
            pixel_block_width, pixel_block_height, 0);
      }
   }
```

}

There are of course a whole range of related effects that can be produced using the same basic randomisation framework. Random mosaic wipes for instance can be achieved by just filling in background colour tiles on top of the original graphic. If, incidentally, variable timing is required for these types of effects all you have to do is insert a time delay after the blit operations. Once you've got the hang of coding the randomisation process all manner of uses will doubtless suggest themselves!

17:
Scrolling and Intuition

This chapter is going to deal with one of those 'not strictly legal' grey areas that nice programmers are not supposed to mention. The subject is the smooth vertical scrolling of Intuition screens from within the Intuition programming environment. I've chosen this subject because it is something which does not seem to get much coverage. Cynics will tell you that the reason is because such things should not be done in the first place but I disagree – in fact I think that experiments such as the ones we'll be doing are, at the very least, a good way to learn more about the Amiga.

An Amiga display, as you'll doubtless know, is made up of areas of chip memory called *bitplanes* such that each bit in a bitplane represents a pixel position on the display. By taking the appropriate pixel bit from each bitplane the Amiga's display hardware generates a value which represents a colour register number and it is the contents of that register that determines the on-screen colour of the pixel (this is the colour indirection scheme that was mentioned in chapter 12).

The structure used to tell the system where to find the bitplanes is called a BitMap and if you look in the graphics/gfx.h header file you will see that it has the following arrangement:

```
struct BitMap
{
UWORD      BytesPerRow;
UWORD      Rows;
UWORD      Flags;
UBYTE      Depth;
UBYTE      pad;
PLANEPTR   Planes[8]; /* pointers to the bitplanes */
};
```

Now there is a system routine in the graphics library called ScrollVPort() which can be used to create scroll effects but a better course of action in this case is to take a lower level approach especially since vertical playfield scrolling, as most Amiga hackers and demo writers know, is relatively straightforward. The trick is to arrange for the display's bitplane pointers to be increased (or decreased) by an amount which corresponds to the pixel-width of the screen. If you do this at the right time then the result is a flicker-free smooth scroll! With a full screen display there's a minor snag – as you increase (or decrease) the bitplane pointers you bring new memory into the screen display area. The result, in most cases, is that you get rubbish displayed on the screen as the scroll proceeds. The secret is of course to set up an oversized display-memory area so that you only scroll within the bounds of valid graphics data.

This subject domain, which leads into the realms of do-it-yourself copper lists and so forth, is quite well documented even though it may not be particularly easy to get to grips with on first reading. For detailed explanations a good place to start, incidentally, is the Addison Wesley Amiga Hardware manual. The situation I want to concentrate on is a little different from the norm because it concerns the manipulation of an existing display and not the creation of a new one: let's imagine that we're working within an Intuition environment, ie we have in use screens, windows, menus etc. In opening a screen Intuition will have done a lot of work for us. Amongst its many jobs it will have built a View structure together with the Copper list necessary to describe the display. It may even have set up a BitMap and allocated the necessary bitplane memory (if we have chosen not to supply our own). Under these conditions we don't need to create our own Copper lists... we just need to find out how to dynamically modify those which Intuition has created. In short we need to find and adjust the Copper list instructions which jam the bitplane pointers into the Copperhardware registers.

All that's necessary then, once Intuition has prepared its display, is a bit of Copperlist searching and remember here that it is the real hardware list, the one which the Copper itself reads, that we are searching in this case: There is a pointer to this in the View structure that Intuition sets up and so the first thing we need to do is get the address of this structure (there is a ViewAddress() intuition library call available for this) and then use a loop to locate the appropriate bitplane instructions. After that, we just replace the original bitplane pointer values with new values. This, in case you've wondered, is what is meant by that delightful expression: *poking* a Copperlist.

Searching The Copper List

The Copper instruction to be found is the first of a series which put data into the bitplane pointer registers and it looks like this:

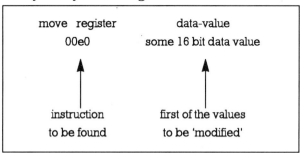

Figure 17.1.Finding a Copper instruction.

We've already seen that Copper instructions consist of two 16 bit words. What we need now is a loop which can skip through a hardware Copperlist until it finds the appropriate instruction. This sort of beloved hacker's loop does the trick perfectly well:

```
view_p=ViewAddress();

copperlist_reference_p=view_p->LOFCprList->start;

while ((*copperlist_reference_p)!=0x00e0) copperlist_reference_p+=2;

copperlist_reference_p++; /* move to second word in that
first 0x00e0 instruction */
```

The terminal increment takes us to the second word of the first bitplane oriented Copperlist instruction. Don't worry if it all seems like magic at the moment... the code will make more sense when you examine it in the context of the demo. The important thing is the effect – this loop enables us to find out whereabouts in the Copperlist Intuition has placed those bitplane address values. Knowing this makes the scrolling problem much easier to tackle:

The Scroll Routine

Once the Copper instructions to be modified have been found the rest of the vertical scroll routine is actually quite straightforward although there are one or two details that have to be taken into account. Poking the View structure's hardware Copperlists can, display-wise, be a bit dangerous because these lists are used both by Intuition and by the display hardware (ie the Copper). Worse than that each 32 bit bitplane pointer is stored as separate high and low words and if Copperlists are poked during the time that bitplane pointer values are being read display glitches can occur.

So, when do these bitplane pointers get used? Well, during the vertical blanking interrupt interval the Amiga is doing a lot of housekeeping work. This includes setting up the Copper registers ready to display the next frame. This happens at the start of the vertical blanking gap and the result, most of the time, is that the Copper is re-executing a list that already exists. If however you alter the display, by say pulling down one screen to expose another, then Intuition has to remake the Copperlists of the viewports associated with those screens (to produce an updated view). If incidentally we were scrolling one of the screens this list remaking and installation would play havoc with that display because our poked Copperlist would be re-written by Intuition. Needless to say this is something to watch for and it is just because of such limitations that Commodore do not actively encourage such tricks in an Intuition environment.

Now as far as glitches during bitplane pointer poking is concerned it might be thought then that, if we disabled the interrupt system by making a call to the Exec Disable() routine before making the changes that we could prevent the system from installing a modified list before the relevant changes had been made. Listing 17.1 shows some first attempt pseudo-code that attempts to describe this sort of technique:

```
/*Listing 17.1: First attempt vertical scrolling pseudo-
code */

scroll:
INITIALISE COPY OF BIT PLANE POINTERS
FOR EACH SCREEN LINE
make a copy of the Copperlist pointer
FOR EACH PLANE
    calculate new bitplane address
    split address into high and low parts
NEXT PLANE
disable() - safety precaution whilst playing with Copperlist?
FOR EACH PLANE
```

Scrolling and Intuition

```
        poke high and low values into Copperlist
        increment Copperlist pointer for next plane
NEXT PLANE
enable()
include a time delay to 'slow things down' to required
speed?
NEXT SCREEN LINE
return
```

With the Listing 17.1 approach there's an inherent flaw present – because although the Disable() call would prevent pointers to any new list from being installed it does not stop the Copper reading the existing Copperlist and, since we are modifying an existing list not creating a new one Disable() actually has no effect at all. What we need to do is make sure that any *poking* operations are done *after* the current bitplane pointers have been used and *before* they are read again.

The trick is to realise two things: firstly, that the bitplane pointer instructions occur near the start of the Copperlist. Secondly, that the system interrupt code that re-starts the Copper for the current frame occurs early on in the vertical blanking interrupt interval. In fact by the time the vertical blank interrupt jobs have been carried out the Copper will already have read and used the bitplane pointers in the Copperlist! It is therefore quite safe to make pointer changes whenever the video beam is moving down the screen or is near the bottom of the display (just prior to the next vertical blanking period). Since there is a graphics library call, WaitBOVP(), that allows a program to wait until the display beam is at the bottom of a viewport I've opted for the scroll routine arrangement shown in listing 17.2:

```
/*Listing 17.2: The final vertical scrolling pseudo-code
*/
scroll:
INITIALISE COPY OF BIT PLANE POINTERS
FOR EACH SCREEN LINE
make a copy of the Copperlist pointer
FOR EACH PLANE
    calculate new bitplane address
    split address into high and low parts
NEXT PLANE
wait till beam is near bottom of screen and then...
FOR EACH PLANE
    poke high and low values into Copperlist
```

```
        increment Copperlist pointer for next plane
NEXT PLANE
include a time delay to 'slow things down' to required speed
NEXT SCREEN LINE
return
```

Some Example Code

What do these scroll routines look like in C? Well, let's look at the main components of a ScrollUpwards() routine. Having searched the Intuition View's hardware Copperlist and located the bitplane pointers we need to make a copy of the values. Rather than do this from the Copperlist though – it is easier to copy the duplicate set of values stored in the screen's BitMap structure like this:

```
for (j=0;j<bitmap_p->Depth;j++)
    bitplanes_copy[j]=(ULONG)(*bitmap_p).Planes[j];
```

During the updating operations we have to split these bitplane pointers into their respective high and low words because that's how they are stored in the Copperlist. I use a couple of arrays called low[] and high[] to store the separated values coupled with this sort of masking and shifting code:

```
low[j]=((ULONG)bitplanes_copy[j])&0xFFFF;
high[j]=((ULONG)bitplanes_copy[j])>>16;
```

The Bitmap structure tells us how many screenlines are involved and the width of the screen in bytes so, having copied the bitplane pointers, we use a twin loop to perform a bitplane pointer addition for each visible line of the screen (so scrolling it completely out of the display). Note that we need to keep a copy of the first word being changed because this will be incremented as each bitplane is dealt with:

```
/*Listing 17.3: A twin loop for adjusting the bitplane
pointers in a Copperlist*/
for(k=0;k<bitmap_p->Rows;k++)
  {
  copperlist_p=copperlist_reference_p;
  for (j=0;j<bitmap_p->Depth;j++)
    {
    bitplanes_copy[j]+=bitmap_p->BytesPerRow;
    low[j]=((ULONG)bitplanes_copy[j])&0xFFFF;
    high[j]=((ULONG)bitplanes_copy[j])>>16;
    }
  WaitBOVP(&screen_p->ViewPort);
  for (j=0;j<bitmap_p->Depth;j++)
```

```
        {
        *copperlist_p=high[j];copperlist_p+=2;
        *copperlist_p=low[j]; copperlist_p+=2;
        }
    }
```

It's quite easy to package these ideas up in easy to use fashion by writing a ScrollUpwards() routine that just takes a screen pointer as a parameter. Inside the routine we search the Intuition View hardware Copperlist as previously explained. The location of the screen's BitMap structure is also needed but this is easily obtained like this:

```
bitmap_p=&screen_p->BitMap;
```

By adding the various sections of code discussed together we end up with the routine shown in listing 17.4. I've not incidentally included any time delays in these examples routines but this could be easily added as part of the end of the outer k loop:

```
/*Listing 17.4: The completed ScrollUpwards() scrolling routine*/

void ScrollUpwards(struct Screen *screen_p)

{
ULONG bitplanes_copy[8];
UWORD low[8], high[8], *copperlist_reference_p, *copperlist_p;
WORD j, k;
struct View *view_p;
struct BitMap *bitmap_p;
view_p=ViewAddress();
bitmap_p=&screen_p->BitMap;
copperlist_reference_p=view_p->LOFCprList->start;
while ((*copperlist_reference_p)!=0x00e0) copperlist_reference_p+=2;
copperlist_reference_p++;
for (j=0;j<bitmap_p->Depth;j++)
        bitplanes_copy[j]=(ULONG)(*bitmap_p).Planes[j];
for(k=0;k<bitmap_p->Rows;k++)
    {
    copperlist_p=copperlist_reference_p;
    for (j=0;j<bitmap_p->Depth;j++)
        {
        bitplanes_copy[j]+=bitmap_p->BytesPerRow;
```

```
                low[j]=((ULONG)bitplanes_copy[j])&0xFFFF;
                high[j]=((ULONG)bitplanes_copy[j])>>16;
                }
        WaitBOVP(&screen_p->ViewPort);
        for (j=0;j<bitmap_p->Depth;j++)
                {
                *copperlist_p=high[j];copperlist_p+=2;
                *copperlist_p=low[j]; copperlist_p+=2;
                }
        }
}
```

The Downward Scroll

Downward scrolling is done in an almost identical fashion except that we set the bitplane pointers to their topmost values and then successively reduce them as the scroll proceeds. That said all that remains to finish this chapter is the code for getting a screen back to its starting position and this follows in listing 17.5:

```
/*Listing 17.5: An equivalent downward scrolling routine*?
void ScrollDownwards(struct Screen *screen_p)
{
ULONG bitplanes_copy[8];
UWORD low[8], high[8], *copperlist_reference_p, *copperlist_p;
WORD j, k;
struct View *view_p;
struct BitMap *bitmap_p;
view_p=ViewAddress();
bitmap_p=&screen_p->BitMap;
copperlist_reference_p=view_p->LOFCprList->start;
while ((*copperlist_reference_p)!=0x00e0) copperlist_reference_p+=2;
copperlist_reference_p++;
for (j=0;j<bitmap_p->Depth;j++)
        bitplanes_copy[j]=(ULONG)
        (*bitmap_p).Planes[j]+bitmap_p->BytesPerRow*bitmap_p->Rows;
for(k=0;k<bitmap_p->Rows;k++)
        {
   copperlist_p=copperlist_reference_p;
```

```
      for (j=0;j<bitmap_p->Depth;j++)
        {
        bitplanes_copy[j]-=bitmap_p->BytesPerRow;
        low[j]=((ULONG)bitplanes_copy[j])&0xFFFF;
        high[j]=((ULONG)bitplanes_copy[j])>>16;
        }
      WaitBOVP(&screen_p->ViewPort);
      for (j=0;j<bitmap_p->Depth;j++)
        {
        *copperlist_p=high[j];copperlist_p+=2;
        *copperlist_p=low[j]; copperlist_p+=2;
        }
    }
}
```

18: Boot Code and the TrackDisk Device

This chapter is going to deal with a subject dear to the hearts of all self respecting hackers – boot block code! To understand the discussions which follow you do of course need to know a little about the way data is stored on disks so this is where our story will start.

With a conventional floppy, AmigaDOS provides a physical basis for storing data by formatting each side of a floppy disk into 80 tracks which, if you could see them, would appear as concentric circles radiating from the centre of the disk. Tracks are, by convention, labelled from zero and since each pair of upper and lower tracks is called a cylinder, the top track 0 plus bottom track 0 constitutes cylinder 0, top track 1 plus bottom track 1 constitutes cylinder 1, and so on.

Each track is divided into sections called sectors and these can hold 512 bytes (ie 0.5K) of data. The original Amiga filing system, now called the Old Filing System or OFS, used an 11 sector arrangement and this therefore provided an overall disk capacity of 880k since:

2	x	80	x	11	x	512	=	880k
sides		tracks		sectors		bytes		disk capacity

Not all of this space is actually available to the user – some areas of the disk are reserved for storing boot code and holding root directory information. New Amigas fitted with high density drives can divide tracks into 22 sectors (which again can each hold 512 bytes of data). This increases the potential disk capacity to 1.76 megabytes and the new Amiga filing systems take advantage of this when high density disks are being used.

From Release 2 of the operating system there has been a trackdisk command, called TD_GETGEOMETRY, that allows a program to determine the characteristics of a given drive. The data is returned in a structure called DriveGeometry that has this sort of layout:

```
struct DriveGeometry
{
ULONG   dg_Sector_Size;    /* in bytes */
ULONG   dg_TotalSectors;
ULONG   dg_Cylinders;
ULONG   dg_CylSectors;     /* sectors per cylinder */
ULONG   dg_Heads;
ULONG   dg_TrackSectors;   /* sectors per track */
ULONG   dg_BufMemType;     /* preferred buffer memory type */
UBYTE   dg_DeviceType;     /* SCSI-2 spec */
UBYTE   dg_Flags;
UWORD   dg_Reserved;
};
```

For our current purposes collecting this data would allow us to determine the number of sectors on a track and therefore distinguish between the normal and high density floppies. Although this would guarantee that we got the correct buffer size for track reads and writes it is not actually necessary to make this call when just writing boot sectors.

The Boot Sectors

The space corresponding to disk blocks 0 and 1 (cylinder 0 sector 0, head 0, and cylinder 0 sector 1, head 0) on a floppy is reserved by the operating system for bootstrap code. This is the *boot program* that gets your Amiga up and running when booting from a floppy. When you use the AmigaDOS Install command this writes the code into the first block (block 0) on the disk. Relative to the 2 x 512, ie 1024 bytes, available in the two boot sectors the bootstrap code itself is tiny and even though with the current Amigas the

Boot Code and the Trackdisk Device

code has grown a bit in size it still occupies less that 24 long words (actually 94 bytes). If you look at the sector data of block 0 you'll see that the sector starts with these 24 long words:

444F5300 E33D0E73 00000370 43FA003E 70254EAE FDD84A80 670C2240 08E90006

00224EAE FE6243FA 00184EAE FFA04A80 670A2040 20680016 70004E75 70FF4E75

646F732E 6C696272 61727900 65787061 6E73696F 6E2E6C69 62726172 79000000

What do they mean? Well, by taking the above numbers and seeing what 680x0 microprocessor instructions or ASCII data they represent it is possible to sketch out a general plan that, written in assembly language, looks like the code shown in listing 18.1:

/*Listing 18.1: A partial Amiga Boot Code Disassembly- Exec library base already in a6*/

FFFFFFA0	_LVOFindResident	EQU	-$0060
FFFFFDD8	_LVOOpenLibrary	EQU	-$0228
FFFFFE62	_LVOCloseLibrary	EQU	-$019E
444F5300	dc.l	$444F5300	DOS
E3390E73	dc.l	$E33D0E73	checksum
00000370	dc.l	$00000370	root block of disk
43FA003E	lea	expname(pc),a1	expansion library name
7025	moveq	#37,d0	minimum version
4EAEFDD8	jsr	_LVOOpenLibrary(a6)	
4A80	tst.l	d0	
670C	beq.s	no_exp	
2240	movea.l	d0,a1	
08E900060022	bset	#6,$22(a1)	sets some flag value
4EAEFE62	jsr	_LVOCloseLibrary(a6)	
43FA0018 no_exp	lea	dosname(pc),a1	dos library name
4EAEFFA0	jsr	_LVOFindResident(a6)	
4A80	tst.l	d0	
670A	beq.s	set_error	
2040	movea.l	d0,a0	dos resident tag
20680016	movea.l	$16(a0),a0	loads some value into a0
7000	moveq	#$00,d0	success
4E75		rts	
70FF set_error	moveq	#$ff,d0	failed - sign extended
4E75		rts	

```
        646F732E6C69627261727900
                    dosname     dc.b      'dos.library',0
        657870616E73696F6E2EEE6C696272617279000000
                    expname     dc.b      'expansion.library',0
```

What the code does is not particularly important for our purposes. The key thing is that normally the rest of the data present in sector 0, and the complete block of data in sector 1 are normally set to all zero values. What this chapter is going to do is tell you a little about how you modify the code to create so called *custom* boot blocks.

Opening The Trackdisk Device

The Amiga's trackdisk device provides the easiest way to write bootblock data to a disk and like other Amiga devices there's a certain amount of setting up operations to do before the device can be used. Three steps are needed: firstly, you need to create a message port by calling CreatePort() or the equivalent Exec function. Secondly, you need to create an I/O request structure (note here that because some trackdisk commands need an IOExtTD sized request rather than a standard one most programmers set up an IOExtTD for all trackdisk device communications). Lastly, you do an OpenDevice() call to open the trackdisk device. As you should expect by now I'll be using my stack based allocation method for the setting up operations and will be setting the flags field to zero when opening the device which is right for 3.5" drives (it's unit 0, the internal 3.5" drive that we shall be interested in). The system calls being used were outlined in chapter 10 when the serial device was discussed so please refer to that chapter for details of the various functions.

With only three things needing to be done the allocation action list is very straightforward:

```
            UBYTE (*action_list[])() = {
                CreateTDReplyPort,
                CreateTDRequestBlock,
                OpenTDDevice,
            };
```

and resource allocation follows the usual approach of either returning an error value to the main setting up loop or pushing a pointer to the successfully opened resource onto the deallocation stack as in listing 18.2 below:

Boot Code and the Trackdisk Device

```
/*Listing 18.2: These sort of allocation arrangements
should be very familiar by now!*/
if((g_td_reply_port_p=CreatePort(TD_NAME,0))==NULL)
        error_number=STARTUP_ERROR;
else {
    g_function=DeleteTDReplyPort;
    PushStack(g_resource_stack_p,g_function);
    }
```

Listing 18.3 is the source for a preliminary program that does nothing other than opening the required resources and closing them down again. If you compare the operations to those in chapter 10 you'll see that there is a lot of common ground between the various device setting up steps in the two chapters. Some labels change and so on but the basic steps, and the code needed, remains essentially the same.

```
/* ========================================================= */
/*Listing 18.3: Code for setting up the trackdisk device,
request block and reply port */
/* Module name: writeboot.c - preliminary WriteBoot pro-
gram code
/* ————————————————————————————————— */
#define ALLOCATE_GLOBALS
#include "general.h"
#define ACTION_COUNT 3
UBYTE (*action_list[])() = {
        CreateTDReplyPort,
        CreateTDRequestBlock,
        OpenTDDevice,
        };
main(int argc, char *argv[])
{
UBYTE error_number=NO_ERROR;
printf(SIGN_ON);
if(!(g_resource_stack_p=CreateStack(void *))) error_num-
ber=NO_STACK;
else {
        /* attempt to allocate resources... */
        if(!AllocateResource(ACTION_COUNT,action_list))
                {
                /* DO SOMETHING */
```

```
                    }
            while(!PopStack(g_resource_stack_p,g_function))
                    g_function();
            KillStack(g_resource_stack_p);
        }
    return(0);
    } /* Logical end of program */
    /* ——————————————————————————————————————————— */
    UBYTE AllocateResource(UBYTE count,UBYTE (*list[])())
    {
    UBYTE i, error_number;
    for (i=0;i<count;i++)
            {
             if(error_number=list[i]())
               {
                 printf("%s %d\n",CANNOT_ALLOCATE,i);
                 i=count; /* force exit from loop */
               }
            }
    return(error_number);
    }
    /* ——————————————————————————————————————————— */
    UBYTE CreateTDReplyPort(void)
    {
    UBYTE error_number=NO_ERROR;
    if((g_td_reply_port_p=CreatePort(TD_NAME,0))==NULL)
            error_number=STARTUP_ERROR;
    else {
        g_function=DeleteTDReplyPort;
        PushStack(g_resource_stack_p,g_function);
        }
    return(error_number);
    }
    /* ——————————————————————————————————————————— */
    void DeleteTDReplyPort(void)
    {
    DeletePort(g_td_reply_port_p);
```

```c
}
/* ─────────────────────────────────────────── */
UBYTE CreateTDRequestBlock()
{
UBYTE error_number=NO_ERROR;
g_td_request_p=(struct IOExtTD *)
CreateExtIO(g_td_reply_port_p,sizeof(struct IOExtTD));
if (g_td_request_p==NULL) error_number=STARTUP_ERROR;
else {
      g_function=DeleteTDRequestBlock;
      PushStack(g_resource_stack_p,g_function);
     }
return(error_number);
}
/* ─────────────────────────────────────────── */
void DeleteTDRequestBlock()
{
DeleteExtIO((struct IORequest *)g_td_request_p);
}
/* ─────────────────────────────────────────── */
UBYTE OpenTDDevice()
{
UBYTE error_number=NO_ERROR;
if((OpenDevice(TD_NAME,0,(struct IORequest
*)g_td_request_p,0))!=NULL) error_number=STARTUP_ERROR;
else {
      g_function=CloseTDDevice;
      PushStack(g_resource_stack_p,g_function);
     }
return(error_number);
}
/* ─────────────────────────────────────────── */
void CloseTDDevice()
{
CloseDevice((struct IORequest *)g_td_request_p);
}
/* ─────────────────────────────────────────── */
```

Reading From The Trackdisk Device

You read from the trackdisk device using a CMD_READ command with the number of bytes to be read in io_Length, the address of the read buffer in io_Data, and the track you want to read specified as the io_Offset field. You don't provide track numbers – the offset is calculated by multiplying the number of the track you wish to read by the number of bytes in a track (nowadays usually obtained by asking the trackdisk device to supply the appropriate drive geometry info).

Writing To The Trackdisk Device

Same approach as before – you write to the device using a CMD_WRITE command with the number of bytes to be written in io_Length, the address of the write buffer in io_Data, and the track you want to write specified as the io_Offset field. Again you don't provide track numbers but calculate the offset by multiplying the number of the track you wish to read by the number of bytes in a track.

Getting the Drive Geometry Data

It's easy! First, we set up some space for the DriveGeometry structrure like this:

```
struct DriveGeometry drive_geometry={0};
```

then we place the address of the structure into the data field of the I/O request and set the command field to TD_GETGEOMETRY:

```
g_td_request_p->iotd_Req.io_Data=&drive_geometry;

g_td_request_p->iotd_Req.io_Command=TD_GETGEOMETRY;
```

and then we perform a device DoIO() function call:

```
DoIO((struct IORequest *)g_td_request_p);
```

The trackdisk device fills in all the fields and all we have to do is read them. The fragment shown in listing 18.4 would, if inserted into the previous program, calculate the size of a track:

```
/*Listing 18.4: Fragment showing the modifications needed
to deduce the track size*/

main(int argc, char *argv[])

{
UBYTE error_number=NO_ERROR;

ULONG sector_size,sector_count, buffer_size;

printf(SIGN_ON);

if(!(g_resource_stack_p=CreateStack(void *))) error_num-
ber=NO_STACK;

else  {

        /* attempt to allocate resources... */
```

```
            if(!AllocateResource(ACTION_COUNT,action_list))
                {
                g_td_request_p-
                        >iotd_Req.io_Data=&drive_geometry;
                g_td_request_p-
                        >iotd_Req.io_Command=TD_GETGEOMETRY;
                DoIO((struct IORequest *)g_td_request_p);
                sector_size=drive_geometry.dg_SectorSize;
                sector_count=drive_geometry.dg_TrackSectors;
                buffer_size=sector_size*sector_count;
                printf("Track size %d\n",buffer_size);
                }
        while(!PopStack(g_resource_stack_p,g_function))
                g_function();
        KillStack(g_resource_stack_p);
        }
    return(0);
    } /* Logical end of program */
```

Custom Boot Code

The first twelve bytes in the bootblock are important for a number of reasons, mainly though that if you get them wrong your boot sectors will not be recognised. Floppy disks have a *header* that consist of a *DOS* string, a checksum (that I'll discuss later), and a value which identifies the disk's root block:

```
        dc.l    $444F5300           DOS
        dc.l    $00000000           checksum space
        dc.l    $000000370          root block location
```

Following this comes the boot code that performs a variety of system magic that will not concern us. The bootblock code has changed with recent releases of the Amiga's O/S but the bit we are interested in is the section I've marked in listing 18.5:

```
        /*Listing 18.5: This shows the code area related to the
        end of a successful boot!*/
        43FA0018   no_exp    lea      dosname(pc),a1    dos library name
        4EAEFFA0             jsr      _LVOFindResident(a6)
        4A80                 tst.l    d0
        670A                 beq.s    set_error
            <control passes through here if the boot process is
        successful>
        2040                 movea.l  d0,a0                        dos resident tag
```

```
20680016    movea.l    $16(a0),a0        loads some value into
                                         a0
7000                   moveq     #$00,d0           success
   <control passes through here if the boot process is
successful>
4E75                   rts

70FF        set_error  moveq     #$ff,d0    failed - sign
                                            extended
4E75                   rts
```

To modify the bootblock code all we have to do is tack on some additional code in the area shown. Actually it's not that easy for two reasons: firstly, the code has to be written so that it is truly relocatable (this is because of the way the code is placed in memory during the booting process). Secondly, if you modify the code you have to calculate a new checksum because the O/S boot routines check to see that this is valid before executing the code.

The checksum is called a *longword additive carry wraparound of $ffffffff*. Sounds good but all this means is that you start with the first longword of the two sectors and add it to the next longword. You then look at the sum produced and if the result has overflowed (ie produced a *carry*) then you add an extra one to the result. You then continue to loop through the boot sector contents making exactly the same additions, overflow tests, and adjustment until you've examined all 256 longwords (256 words = 1024 bytes = 2 sectors). Having done that you just invert all the bits in the final sum to produce a checksum for storing in the bootblock. Listing 18.6 shows the sort of C code loop needed to calculate a bootblock checksum for bootcode held in a ULONG array:

```
/*Listing 18.6 Bootblock checksums the easy way!*/
for(i=0;i<256;i++)
   {
   if (sum+bootcode[i]>=sum)
      sum+=bootcode[i];
   else sum=sum+bootcode[i]+1;
   }
bootcode[1]=~sum;
```

Producing the Code

Like many other coders I initially disassembled the standard boot code more for fun than anything else but, once an assembly language framework was available, it was not too difficult to see how additions could be made. Not knowing which registers were important as the boot code exits I've always made a point of how additions could be made. Not knowing which registers were important as the boot code exits I've always made a point of preserving and restoring all registers and in fact, for simplicity, I just push all registers except a7 onto the stack like this:

```
        movem.l     d0-d7/a0-a6,-(a7)      preserve registers
```

I've opted for a very simple piece of additional code a loop that holds up the completion of the boot process until the user presses the ESCape key. This code, shown in listing 18.7, is similar to that used in the Chapter Seven examples and if we put all the fragments previously discussed together the result is the *assembly language program* shown in listing 18.8:

```
/*Listing 18.7 Waiting for the ESCape key to be pressed*/
        lea         CUSTOM,a5
loop:   move.b      vhposr(a5),d0          get scanline
        cmp.b       #$ff,d0                line $ff?
        bne.s       loop
;  Could do something here until ESCape key is pressed!
        move.b      $bfec01,d0             read keyboard
        eor.b       #$ff,d0                decode byte
        ror.b       #1,d0
        cmp.b       #$45,d0                ESCape key?
        bne.s       loop                   keep going
        movem.l     (a7)+,d0-d7/a0-a6      restore registers


/*Listing 18.8: The finished bootblock code*/
; Custom Bootcode example
CUSTOM       EQU  $DFF000
NULL         EQU  0
vhposr       EQU  $6
_LVOFindResident     EQU  -96
_LVOOpenLibrary EQU  -552
_LVOCloseLibrary     EQU  -414
        dc.l        $444F5300              DOS
        dc.l        $00000000              checksum space
        dc.l        $000000370             root block location
        lea         expname(pc),a1         expansion library
                                           name
        moveq       #37,d0                 minimum version
        jsr         _LVOOpenLibrary(a6)
```

```
            tst.l       d0
            beq.s       no_exp
            movea.l     d0,a1
            bset        #6,$22(a1)           sets some flag value
            jsr         _LVOCloseLibrary(a6)
no_exp      lea         dosname(pc),a1       dos library name
            jsr         _LVOFindResident(a6)
            tst.l       d0
            beq.s       set_error
            movea.l     d0,a0
; this is where our new code goes:
            movem.l     d0-d7/a0-a6,-(a7)    preserve registers
            lea         CUSTOM,a5
loop:       move.b      vhposr(a5),d0        get scanline
            cmp.b       #$ff,d0              line $ff?
            bne.s       loop
;   Could do something here until ESCape key is pressed!
            move.b      $bfec01,d0           read keyboard
            eor.b       #$ff,d0              decode byte
            ror.b       #1,d0
            cmp.b       #$45,d0              ESCape key?
            bne.s       loop                 keep going
            movem.l     (a7)+,d0-d7/a0-a6    restore registers
; ... end of new code section!
            movea.l     $16(a0),a0           loads rt_Init into a0
            moveq       #$00,d0
            rts
set_error   moveq       #$ff,d0              sign extends
            rts
dosname     dc.b        'dos'
            dc.b        '.library',NULL
expname     dc.b        'expansion'
            dc.b        '.library',NULL
```

Now we can assemble this, but you are probably wondering how we get the code into the bootblock sectors after that. Well there are a variety of hacker tools available for these types of jobs and diassemblers like the Puzzle Factory's ReSource package are absolutely brilliant for this type of work. The standard approach listing to produce an array of numbers representing the instructions. Listing 18.9 shows the listing obtained with HiSoft's Devpac package and listing 18.10 shows the C array that I built using copy/paste editing operations along with an array that represents the original bootblock code:

/*Listing 18.10 - Original and modified bootblock code in C-style hex format*/

HiSoft GenAm 680x0 Macro Assembler v3.04   Jul 1 1994   Page 1

Bootcode.s

```
     1 00.00000000                  ;Custom Bootcode example
     2 00.00000000
     3    =00DFF000        CUSTOM       EQU           $DFF000
     4 00.00000000
     5    =00000000        NULL         EQU           0
     6 00.00000000
     7    =00000006        vhposr       EQU           $6
     8 00.00000000
     9    =FFFFFFA0        _LVOFindResident  EQU      -96
    10 00.00000000
    11    =FFFFFDD8        _LVOOpenLibrary   EQU      -552
    12 00.00000000
    13    =FFFFFE62        _LVOCloseLibrary  EQU      -414
    14 00.00000000
    15 00.00000000
    16 00.00000000 444F5300           dc.l          $444F5300
DOS
    17 00.00000004
    18 00.00000004 00000000           dc.l          $00000000
checksum space
    19 00.00000008
    20 00.00000008 00000370           dc.l          $000000370
root block location
    21 00.0000000C
    22 00.0000000C 43FA0068           lea           expname(pc),a1
expansion library name
    23 00.00000010
    24 00.00000010 7025               moveq         #37,d0
minimum version
    25 00.00000012
```

```
26 00.00000012  4EAEFDD8                        jsr
27 00.00000016
28 00.00000016  4A80                            tst.l                   d0
29 00.00000018
30 00.00000018  670C                            beq.s
31 00.0000001A
32 00.0000001A  2240                            movea.l d0,a1
33 00.0000001C
34 00.0000001C  08E900060022                    bset            #6,$22(a1)
sets some flag value
35 00.00000022
36 00.00000022  4EAEFE62                        jsr_LVOCloseLibrary(a6)
37 00.00000026
38 00.00000026  43FA0042        no_exp          lea             dosname(pc),a1
dos library name
39 00.0000002A
40 00.0000002A  4EAEFFA0                        jsr
_LVOFindResident(a6)
41 00.0000002E
42 00.0000002E  4A80                            tst.l                   d0
43 00.00000030
44 00.00000030  6734                            beq.s           set_error
45 00.00000032
46 00.00000032  2040                            movea.l d0,a0
47 00.00000034
48 00.00000034
49 00.00000034                  ; this is where our new code goes...
50 00.00000034
51 00.00000034  48E7FFFE                        movem.l d0-d7/a0-a6,-(a7)
preserve registers
52 00.00000038
53 00.00000038  4BF900DFF000                    lea             CUSTOM,a5
54 0000000003E
55 0000000003E  102D0006        loop:           move.b  vhposr(a5),d0
get scanline
56 00.00000042
57 00.00000042  B03C00FF                        cmp.b           #$ff,d0
line $ff?
```

Boot Code and the Trackdisk Device

HiSoft GenAm 680x0 Macro Assembler v3.04   Jul 1 1994   Page 2
Bootcode.s

```
    58 00.00000046
    59 00.00000046 66F6                bne.s         loop
    60 00.00000048
    61 00.00000048              ;      Could do something here
until ESCape key is pressed!
    62 00.00000048
    63 00.00000048 103900BFEC01        move.b        $bfec01,d0
read keyboard
    64 00.0000004E
    65 00.0000004E 0A0000FF            eor.b         #$ff,d0
decode byte
    66 00.00000052
    67 00.00000052 E218                ror.b         #1,d0
    68 00.00000054
    69 00.00000054 B03C0045            cmp.b         #$45,d0
ESCape key?
    70 00.00000058
    71 00.00000058 66E4                bne.s         loop
keep going
    72 00.0000005A
    73 00.0000005A
    74 00.0000005A
    75 00.0000005A 4CDF7FFF            movem.l       (a7)+,d0-d7/a0-a6
restore registers
    76 00.0000005E
    77 00.0000005E              ;      end of new code section!
    78 00.0000005E
    79 00.0000005E
    80 00.0000005E 20680016            movea.l       $16(a0),a0
loads rt_Init into a0
    81 00.00000062
    82 00.00000062 7000                moveq         #$00,d0
    83 00.00000064
    84 00.00000064 4E75                rts
    85 00.00000066
Warning: sign extended operand at line 86 in file Bootcode.s
```

```
         85 00.00000066
Warning: sign extended operand at line 86 in file Bootcode.s
         86 00.00000066 70FF              set_error    moveq           #$ff,d0
sign extends
         87 00.00000068
         88 00.00000068 4E75                           rts
         89 00.0000006A
         90 00.0000006A 646F73            dosname      dc.b                   'dos'
         91 00.0000006D 2E6C69627261727900              dc.b      '.library',NULL
         92 00.00000076
         93 00.00000076 657870616E73696F6E   expname   dc.b
'expansion'
         94 00.0000007F 2E6C69627261727900              dc.b      '.library',NULL


              GLOBAL SYMBOLS
00DFF000      A   CUSTOM
00000000      A   NULL
FFFFFE62      A   _LVOCloseLibrary
FFFFFFA0      A   _LVOFindResident
FFFFFDD8      A   _LVOOpenLibrary
00000006      A   vhposr


              MODULE BOOTCODE.S
0000006A     00.R  dosname
00000076     00.R  expname
0000003E     00.R  loop
00000026     00.R  no_exp
00000066     00.R  set_error
```

Listing 18.9 Devpac listing showing object code details:
ULONG orig_bootcode[256] = {
0x444F5300,0x00000000,0x00000370,0x43FA003E,
0x70254EAE,0xFDD84A80,0x670C2240,0x08E90006,
0x00224EAE,0xFE6243FA,0x00184EAE,0xFFA04A80,
0x670A2040,0x20680016,0x70004E75,0x70FF4E75,
0x646F732E,0x6C696272,0x61727900,0x65787061,
0x6E73696F,0x6E2E6C69,0x62726172,0x79000000
};

```
0x444F5300,0x00000000,0x00000370,0x43FA0068,
0x70254EAE,0xFDD84A80,0x670C2240,0x08E90006,
0x00224EAE,0xFE6243FA,0x00424EAE,0xFFA04A80,
0x67342040,0x48E7FFFE,0x4BF900DF,0xF000102D,
0x0006B03C,0x00FF66F6,0x103900BF,0xEC010A00,
0x00FFE218,0xB03C0045,0x66E44CDF,0x7FFF2068,
0x00167000,0x4E7570FF,0x4E75646F,0x732E6C69,
0x62726172,0x79006578,0x70616E73,0x696F6E2E,
0x6C696272,0x61727900
};
```

Putting It All Together

All that remains is to take the bootcode array and couple it to a program that opens the trackdisk device and writes the data into the first two sectors of track zero. Listing 18.11 is just such a program and is typical of the type that *hackers* will knock up to store bootblock code (I've left both the original and modified bootblock code arrays in the source just for comparison purposes). Most of the program will be familiar from the preliminary code given in listing 18.3 and all that has been added is the checksum fragment mentioned earlier and functions to perform trackdisk CMD_WRITE and TD_MOTOR commands both of which are easy to understand from the code. (The latter command is used with a zero length value to turn the motor off – and it is the programmers responsibility to do this).

The modified code doesn't actually do a lot – if you boot up with a disk that's had its boot sectors re-written by this program you find that the screen stays blank, and the drive light stays on, *until* you press the ESCape key (at which point the boot process continues normally). It will incidentally work on machines running Workbench 1.3 and upwards. Not exactly stunning effects-wise but it is the simplest example that I could come up with that dealt with all the main issues. If incidentally you use the original bootblock array then you'll write a normal bootblock – in other words the program becomes equivalent to the Amiga system Install command!

main issues. If incidentally you use the original bootblock array then you'll write a normal bootblock – in other words the program becomes equivalent to the Amiga system Install command!

```c
/* ======================================================== */
/*Listing 18.11 The final version of the bootblock re-writing program*/
/* Module name: writeboot.c - contains the WriteBoot program code
/* ---------------------------------------------- */
#define ALLOCATE_GLOBALS
#include "general.h"
struct DriveGeometry drive_geometry={0};
#define ACTION_COUNT 3
UBYTE (*action_list[])() = {
        CreateTDReplyPort,
        CreateTDRequestBlock,
        OpenTDDevice
        };
ULONG orig_bootcode[256] = {
0x444F5300,0x00000000,0x00000370,0x43FA003E,
0x70254EAE,0xFDD84A80,0x670C2240,0x08E90006,
0x00224EAE,0xFE6243FA,0x00184EAE,0xFFA04A80,
0x670A2040,0x20680016,0x70004E75,0x70FF4E75,
0x646F732E,0x6C696272,0x61727900,0x65787061,
0x6E73696F,0x6E2E6C69,0x62726172,0x79000000
};
ULONG bootcode[256] = {
0x444F5300,0x00000000,0x00000370,0x43FA0068,
0x70254EAE,0xFDD84A80,0x670C2240,0x08E90006,
0x00224EAE,0xFE6243FA,0x00424EAE,0xFFA04A80,
0x67342040,0x48E7FFFE,0x4BF900DF,0xF000102D,
0x0006B03C,0x00FF66F6,0x103900BF,0xEC010A00,
0x00FFE218,0xB03C0045,0x66E44CDF,0x7FFF2068,
0x00167000,0x4E7570FF,0x4E75646F,0x732E6C69,
0x62726172,0x79006578,0x70616E73,0x696F6E2E,
0x6C696272,0x61727900
};
main(int argc, char *argv[])
```

Boot Code and the Trackdisk Device

```c
    ULONG sum=0;
    printf(SIGN_ON);
    if(!(g_resource_stack_p=CreateStack(void *))) error_number=NO_STACK;
    else   {
          /* attempt to allocate resources... */
             if(!AllocateResource(ACTION_COUNT,action_list))
                {
                for(i=0;i<256;i++)
                   {
                   if (sum+bootcode[i]>=sum)
                        sum+=bootcode[i];
                        else sum=sum+bootcode[i]+1;
                   }
                bootcode[1]=~sum;
                printf("checksum = %x\n",bootcode[1]);
                if(!(error_number=WriteBootSectors()))
                     printf(FUNCTION_COMPLETE);
                 else printf(ERROR_MESSAGE);
                 }
          while(!PopStack(g_resource_stack_p,g_function)) g_function();
          KillStack(g_resource_stack_p);
       }
    return(0);
    }  /* Logical end of program */
    /* ─────────────────────────────────────── */
    UBYTE WriteBootSectors(void)
    {
    UBYTE error_number=NO_ERROR;
    g_td_request_p->iotd_Req.io_Length=1024;
    g_td_request_p->iotd_Req.io_Data=&bootcode;
    g_td_request_p->iotd_Req.io_Offset=0;
    g_td_request_p->iotd_Req.io_Command=CMD_WRITE;
    if(DoIO((struct IORequest *)g_td_request_p)) error_number=TRACKDISK_ERROR;
       else {
             g_td_request_p->iotd_Req.io_Command=CMD_UPDATE;
```

```c
            if(DoIO((struct IORequest *)g_td_request_p))
                error_number=TRACKDISK_ERROR;
            }
MotorOff();
return(error_number);
}
/* ————————————————————————————————— */
void MotorOff(void)
{
g_td_request_p->iotd_Req.io_Length=0;
g_td_request_p->iotd_Req.io_Command=TD_MOTOR;
DoIO((struct IORequest *)g_td_request_p);
}
/* ————————————————————————————————— */
UBYTE AllocateResource(UBYTE count,UBYTE (*list[])())
{
UBYTE i, error_number;
for (i=0;i<count;i++)
    {
     if(error_number=list[i]())
       {
        i=count; /* force exit from loop */
       }

    }
return(error_number);
}
/* ————————————————————————————————— */
UBYTE CreateTDReplyPort(void)
{
UBYTE error_number=NO_ERROR;
if((g_td_reply_port_p=CreatePort(TD_NAME,0))==NULL)
        error_number=STARTUP_ERROR;
else {
     g_function=DeleteTDReplyPort;
     PushStack(g_resource_stack_p,g_function);
     }
```

```
return(error_number);
}
/* ————————————————————————— */
void DeleteTDReplyPort(void)
{
DeletePort(g_td_reply_port_p);
}
/* ————————————————————————— */
UBYTE CreateTDRequestBlock()
{
UBYTE error_number=NO_ERROR;
g_td_request_p=(struct IOExtTD *)
CreateExtIO(g_td_reply_port_p,sizeof(struct IOExtTD));
if (g_td_request_p==NULL) error_number=STARTUP_ERROR;
else {
      g_function=DeleteTDRequestBlock;
      PushStack(g_resource_stack_p,g_function);
    }
return(error_number);
}
/* ————————————————————————— */
void DeleteTDRequestBlock()
{
DeleteExtIO((struct IORequest *)g_td_request_p);
}
/* ————————————————————————— */
UBYTE OpenTDDevice()
{
UBYTE error_number=NO_ERROR;
if((OpenDevice(TD_NAME,0,(struct IORequest
*)g_td_request_p,0))!=NULL) error_number=STARTUP_ERROR;
else {
      g_function=CloseTDDevice;
      PushStack(g_resource_stack_p,g_function);
    }
return(error_number);
}
```

```c
/* ———————————————————————————————————————— */
void CloseTDDevice()
{
CloseDevice((struct IORequest *)g_td_request_p);
}
/* ———————————————————————————————————————— */
```

19: Some Extra Programming Tips and Tricks

Programming is, to some extent, still just as much an art as a science but nowadays there are plenty of guidelines to help. Over the years I've written many thousands of lines of code, on many different machines and operating systems and with all manner of languages. Needless to say I have, during this time, learnt quite a bit about what to do if a piece of newly written code fails to behave as expected. In this last chapter I want to both share some of the tricks I've learnt and pass on a little of the *coding philosophy* I've acquired along the way.

Before getting into the nitty-gritty stuff however there are a few preliminary issues to get out of the way. To start with it's worth remembering that program development involves planning, coding, testing and debugging and since the latter two areas can be the most time consuming stages of software development it's worth trying to minimise this potential overhead right from the start. You do this by properly planning your program before starting to bash out code at the keyboard. Now in theory a decent plan, coupled with careful coding, ought to eliminate program bugs completely but, as you doubtless know, it doesn't. This does not mean that these pre-coding design stages are a waste of effort, far from it – by reducing the chances of errors in the logic of the program, those plans will still greatly reduce both development troublespots and the number of debug/test problems you encounter. What it cannot possibly do however is eliminate all of the problems and the fact of the matter is that, no matter how conscientious a programmer you are, mistakes are bound to be made.

One of the seemingly less troublesome coding errors that can occur are syntax errors, ie errors due to the fact that you've written something which does not conform to the rules of the language. Such mistakes can be caused by misconceptions about the language, by dyslexic slips, or by a multitude of other silly things – such as inserting a semi-colon when you meant to write a colon (because you didn't hit the shift key at the right time). You might even make mistakes due to the programmer's equivalent of *jet lag*. C, for instance, expects array subscripts to be enclosed in square brackets. If therefore you write array[2] as array(2), as you might well inadvertently do if you'd spent the last few months programming in Basic, the compiler would rightly complain.

A lot of programmers regard syntax errors as trivial and qualify that by suggesting that they are trivial because they are easily found and corrected. One point which ought to be made loudly and clearly is that these types of mistakes are not however inherently harmless! Despite the fact that these slips usually have trivial origins... finding them could, especially with large programs, be very time consuming. Programmers rely heavily on their assemblers, compilers and interpreters to catch such errors and from experience we know that the well supported software development tools really will catch 99+% of such errors. In short – with good commercial development tools a program is unlikely to get to a *runable stage* until it is syntactically correct.

Once you are past the syntax error correction stage, and your program assembles, compiles or otherwise seems to run in some fashion then you should be home and dry. Unfortunately this isn't always so... a program may run to a point and then for no obvious reason fail to behave as expected, crash or do other unspeakable things to your system. Although it is at this stage of course that we enter the realm of debugging proper, careful programmers will have sought to minimise potential snags well before a program is first run and the number one rule is this: never get yourself into a position where it is necessary to check through large amounts of code!

There are two key elements to follow: firstly, build your programs using small self contained subroutines or functions that do specific jobs. If a task looks to be complex then break it up into more manageable pieces. Secondly, opt for a development approach that is based on *incremental testing*. This involves starting with a very simple version of a program and then developing it by adding small sections of additional code, assembling, compiling and running the

Some Extra Programming Tips And Tricks

new versions as each new part is added. The idea is of course that any errors and faults which appear will almost certainly be related to the most recently added section. How do you run an incomplete program? One useful idea is to incorporate dummy subroutines/calls for the parts of the program which are not yet written. With C *do-nothing* type function calls can be written:

```
void DoNothing(void) { /* temporary dummy call */ }
```

With Basic and ARexx you can use the equivalent of this type of routine:

```
DoNothing: RETURN
```

and with 68000 assembler you might use:

```
DoNothing:RTS       dummy call for development purposes
```

In practice it is of course usually best if such routines are given names which correspond to the final routines they're supposed to correspond to (this enables the skeleton structure of the program to be created early on). Remember that these ideas can be applied to all languages – the ARexx fragment in listing 19.1 for example shows calls to a variety of unwritten functions whilst listing 19.2 shows the contents of two such routines at an early development stage:

```
/*Listing 19.1: Calls to unwritten routines are a big help
during development.*/

do until g_exit_flag
    select
            when item$='B' then call BuildNewDatabase()
    when item$='O' then call OpenExistingDatabase()
    when item$='A' then call AddRecord()
    when item$='E' then call EditRecord()
    when item$='F' then call FindRecord()
    when item$='C' then call CloseDatabase()
    when item$='Q' then call QuitProgram()
    otherwise call Writech(raw_window, INVALID_OPTION)
end
/* ───────────────────────────── */

/*Listing 19.2: Begin coding the easy stuff and use dummy
calls for more involved routines.*/

CloseDatabase:
/* needs code for closing the database */
return
/* ───────────────────────────── */
```

```
QuitProgram:g_exit_flag=TRUE
return
/* ————————————————————————— */
```

Calls like these keep the interpreters, compilers and assemblers happy and allow us to concentrate on the testing (in runable form) of those sections of the program which have actually been written to-date. Bear in mind that all of these ideas need to be dictated by circumstances. It may for instance be necessary for a dummy routine to return a piece of data in order for the existing part of a program to work correctly. Similarly it may be necessary to force a variable to a fixed value (so that you can be sure of the value it takes). At one stage, whilst coding support routines for a Midi utility, the routine which extracted delta times from a Midi file had not been written. Since it was necessary to have some time delay in order to check the MidiHandler() routine that had been written I simply inserted a temporary constant value and marked the source accordingly:

```
/* do delta-time pause and then transmit... */
SetTimer(0,1000);
/* TEMPORARY DEVELOPMENT MEASURE */
current_status=MidiHandler(current_byte, current_status,
                           source_p, dest_p);
```

Sometimes you can't just invent or ignore data items quite so easily. Your program may, for example, have to scan through a sequential data file. This does not mean however that your coding must have progressed to the point where you are able to use *every* piece of file data before you start program testing. A useful trick is to create routines, such as that shown in listing 19.3, that let a program read but discard any specified amount of file data. You'll see a similar routine used to discard unused Midi file events in my MidiPlayer program.

```
/*Listing 19.3: Routines that safely throw away file data
are extremely useful at times.*/
UBYTE DiscardBytes(ULONG count, FILE *source_p)
{
UBYTE error_number=NO_ERROR;
while(count-)
   {
   if (fgetc(source_p)==EOF){error_number=BAD_CHUNK_DATA;
                             count=0;} /* force exit */
   }
return(error_number);
}
```

When It All Goes Wrong

All the things I've discussed so far are aimed at minimising potential problems so that written code, when tested, works OK. Needless to say you occasionally get to a point where a particular piece of code *bombs out* or fails.

I've found that with all slips that are not immediately obvious, working solely from a VDU display is usually a mistake. The best idea is to print out a copy of the routine and then get right away from your computer – it doesn't matter whether you go to another room, the garden, or even the pub (as long as it's quiet)! Don't guess, just take some time to quietly look through the code, and go over the basic ideas about what the routine should and should not do, and check the overall structure of the routine looking carefully at loops, decisions, initialisation of important variables, use of system calls, pointer use etc. Most programmers at this stage tend to convince themselves that their code is OK. The plain fact of the matter is that if a routine isn't working properly then there *is* a logical reason why and although you can convince yourself that your code is fine unfortunately the odds are extremely high that it is not.

It is a well known fact that programmers find it all too easy to miss their own mistakes – they seem to have psychological blind spots regarding such errors. Don't dwell on this too much – just accept that if you've looked through the appropriate code and decided it's OK... then you have hit just such a blind spot.

With incremental development you will normally already have a very good idea of where the problem lies and at this stage it is most useful, having assumed that there is an error, to simply look for a ways of proving that certain sections of code are error free. Often you'll need to look at particular variable values that are either being passed to, or used within, the code in question and that means you need facilities for tracing those values at run time. Languages like Basic and ARexx offer inbuilt dynamic trace facilities. C compilers, and even assemblers, nowadays also often provide highly sophisticated source-level debugging tools which allow programmers to trace through a program looking at variables and statements. These tools are fine if you have them but they are not essential and the well established older trick of adding additional print statements to the code to display important values, or bring particular conditions to the attention of the programmer, is usually just as effective.

C coders might dump values using printf() statements. Assembler programmers similarly might make temporary use of the printf() routine available in the amiga.lib library. The idea in all such cases is that the extra code allows the programmer to systematically trace program execution through an area of interest.

Helping Yourself

Obviously debugging is made easier if your code is easily readable. Descriptive variable names help here, as do the use of conventions which make it easy to identify particular types of variables. One useful convention is that of naming pointer variables using a _p suffix. Quite simply it serves as a useful reminder that a pointer variable is being dealt with and thus helps reduce the likelihood of inadvertent misuse. A common, and usually fatal, pointer error on the Amiga involves initialisation, or rather the lack of it. With many system calls (such as memory allocation functions) the system tells you that an operation has been unsuccessful by returning a NULL (zero) pointer. If you do not religiously check such return values the chances are that your program under particular load or system conditions will be unreliable. Bear this in mind when someone tells you that a piece of code, which seems to work fine on your system, falls over on someone else's machine.

On the Amiga there are plenty of system variables (eg message blocks and other system structure pointers) which have to be used in many different places within a program. Large numbers of graphics calls require users to identify target rasterports and viewports using pointer variables. The time taken to pass local copies of these pointers down though nested function calls is the last thing you want for graphics work and in such cases globals are a realistic solution. In short use globals on such occasions – but use them with caution. Write code which makes it obvious which variables are global. A useful convention is to prefix all such variables with the letter g, for example:

```
struct Screen *g_screen_p;
```

Now these tricks and conventions certainly help minimise potential trouble spots in all languages but, as you can imagine, some languages are inherently easier to work with than others. The ability to interrupt Basic and ARexx programs, coupled with these languages inbuilt debugging facilities, is a big help. Other languages help in other ways and of late C programmers have been given some major assistance in the form of ANSI C. In the 'old days', ie prior to the development of the ANSI standard, many C problems were caused by inadvertently misusing function return values and supplying parameters of an incorrect type. The new style function declarations and function prototypes have eliminated this problem. ANSI C's function prototypes are important because they allow the compiler to check for correct function use. Your compiler is unlikely to force you to use them (at least yet), but the benefits are very real so it is best to get into the habit of using them. Unfortunately, although prototypes may protect you against function and pointer misuse, plenty of other pitfalls still remain. A well established C slip, which turns an equality test into a variable assignment is that of accidentally typing = instead of ==. Such

Some Extra Programming Tips And Tricks

mistakes can cause loops which should terminate at some stage: to execute forever!

68000 assembler coders have a relatively rougher time when it comes to testing and debugging than anyone else. Listings are both larger and more detailed, and major errors can be caused by slips that are far harder to see at first glance. Even obvious errors, like getting the boundary and exit conditions of loops wrong, can slip through the net. This loop, for example, executes eleven times:

```
        MOVE.B     #10, d0
Loop:JSR  DoSomething
        DBRA Loop
```

It's the DBcc which causes the problem – DBRA quits the loop when the counter register hits -1 so the count should really have been loaded with one less than the required iteration value. You may think that slips related to these types of loops should be easy to find but such errors are easily missed as also are addressing mode errors. For example writing:

```
        MOVE.B     10, d0
```

which loads d0 with the contents of memory location 10 when you really meant to load d0 with the value 10 like this:

```
        MOVE.B     #10, d0
```

Often such trivial slips will cause a program to completely crash and in such circumstances it must be said that debugging tools do help make life easier. By tracing through the appropriate code area the instructions producing the crash can be directly identified and by working backwards from this point the cause can usually be found. If, for instance, a function call is to blame then its arguments can be examined for NULL pointers or otherwise incorrect values. If the program crashes with an addressing error (ie a Guru 03) then it's the addresses of the data items that have to be examined. Utilities like Devpac's Monam debugger make all such investigations a piece of cake.

There are a million and one things to watch out for and even if I gave you a list of every slip that had ever been made... you, like everyone else, would find your own variations. General guidelines? Well, for my money these are the ones that will protect you from major trauma. Design and plan carefully *before* writing any code. Then, write understandable code and document your programs well enough for both yourself and others to understand. Build your program out of small code units that do well defined jobs and use an incremental development approach. This will not only minimise potential problems but will ensure that, if and when a trouble spot does arise, you will be able to quickly identify the area of code and the problem related to it.

Oh, and by the way, there's one other thing that's worth doing when you hit a coding snag. Make up your mind to enjoy the challenge and have a little laugh about it along the way!

20: Parting Advice

No matter how many years of coding experience you have, coming to terms with a different computer system always means another *learning curve* to contend with. To be honest the Amiga's system documentation, both in physical size and complexity, has stopped many would-be Amiga programmers dead in their tracks and the fact is that complexity-wise the Amiga presents a whole new ball game. One look at the contents of the official Addison Wesley Amiga reference manuals is more than enough to convince anyone that things have changed considerably from the good old *eight bit* days.

Coping with thousands of pages of documentation, especially since they are coupled to complex hardware and very sophisticated O/S ideas, is quite a daunting prospect even to the pros. The important point to bear in mind is, of course, that you do not have to learn about everything at once!

The best idea is to adopt the same principles as the programmers who work with mainframes – they don't memorise everything... they just develop an understanding of (some would say a sympathy with) the system they use. Having said that, most will still spend as much time as they can reading the manuals, but what they are primarily trying to do is build up an overview, ie a general picture, of the system as a whole. It is this familiarity with both the general working of the system as a whole, and with the documentation, that makes it easy for them to get hold of information as and when they need it.

If, you ask the average professional Amiga programmer what an Exec Task structure looks like, or what numerical value is assigned to Intuition's WLFG_BACKDROP flag... they are unlikely to know (or particularly care in the latter case). But one thing is certain... they *will* know where to find out! Many programmers will specialize graphics, sound, comms etc, and again if you ask a graphics specialist how you set up the Amiga's serial port for high-speed MIDI transmission the chances are again odds on that they won't be able to tell you. Given some time and the necessary documentation however they will come across with the goods.

Experience with the machine is important but all professional Amiga programmers will tell you the same thing... access to decent technical info comes extremely high on the list of priorities. The first piece of parting advice is simply this: do not even think about trying to enter the world of serious Amiga programming without getting the official documentation – it really is worth its weight in gold. What you may also need, because the official manuals are written primarily for professional programmers, are other books (such as this one) which attempt to explain some of the issues using a softer, tutorial style, approach.

I've had the chance to see a lot of Amiga code that has been written by programmers in their 'early Amiga system days' (and of course I also have walked into many *technical snags* as I became Amiga system literate). As far as common pitfalls are concerned however, a number of things have stuck in my mind:

Firstly, a lot of programmers who have come up via the route which involved hacking the eight bit Commodore 64, Sinclair ZX81 and the like and tried to adopt the same *suck it and see whilst you type* approach on the Amiga. Basically it's just not possible to just sit down at the keyboard and start writing Amiga programs because they tend to be too large and too complex to tackle in that way. You have to decide what you want to do, plan, design, code and then test your program carefully. You also have to implement your ideas in a way which follows the rules which the multi-tasking Exec imposes on all Amiga programs (except those which take over the machine completely). This means you will need to take an interest in program design as an integral part of code preparation. For the Amiga programmer such ideas are not useful extras – a systematic approach is a necessity. This book was not the place to deal with program design issues but underneath all of the examples I've given there has been a solid, and carefully planned, design framework.

Secondly I've noticed that many programmers who are new to C come to grief because of silly mistakes with pointers and use of the

Parting Advice

address-of (&) operator (especially when passing parameters to library functions). The use of ANSI C's prototypes can, if used properly, almost eliminate these types of errors so if you are using an ANSI C compiler get used to making the most of this new facility.

Thirdly, I've noticed a lot of code which has had either poor, or totally non-existent, error handling and pointer-validity checking schemes. If there is one thing that the Amiga programmer should not be... it's an optimist in these areas. I've offered, and used throughout the book, an ADT based resource allocation/deallocation scheme that has proved its worth time and time again. Don't feel obliged to use my scheme but do make sure that you implement some equivalent procedure.

The fourth area that needs to be mentioned concerns the assembler coder. The hardest thing about learning assembly language on the Amiga is not learning about the 680x0 instructions – it's coming to terms with the Amiga's operating system. To do that you need to be able to use both the system documentation and the large number of tutorial style books that are available and the bad news is that most of the system explanations are written with the C programmer in mind. The solution is simple – all aspiring assembly language programmers MUST learn C – if only to be able to understand the system documentation! In coming to terms with C and with the Amiga's O/S and its documentation – most of the problems normally associated with low-level 680x0 coding on the Amiga will disappear!

Now all these complexity issues, as always, are relative not absolute: if you have studied computer science at school or college, or have worked with a multi-tasking computer system before, then you will have less to learn because many concepts will already be familiar. Similarly, if you've used languages like Pascal (which uses records in much the same sort of way that C uses structures) some language transition problems will be less troublesome. If, because of prior experience, the Amiga road seems relatively straightforward then be thankful. If you are still struggling then be patient and don't worry – almost everyone who has ever sat down to learn about the Amiga system will have had, at some time or other, to cope with exactly the same difficulties.

With a system as complex as the Amiga we are getting to the point where even the professionals will admit that they'll never learn all there is to know about the Amiga. My advice? Don't worry about the amount of material that needs to be understood – at any one time concentrate only on those aspects related to the project which you are currently involved with (in other words adopt a 'need to know' policy to guide your path through the system documentation). Above all, as I've said before, you should enjoy the challenge because it is undoubtedly good for the soul!

Appendix A: The Warnier Diagram

On a few occasions within this book I have provided program design sketches called Warnier diagrams. Most of you will not have heard of these so here are a few notes about how to interpret them. First however an important point: Warnier diagrams are a general tool and, as such, aim to obtain solutions to problems that are completely independent of both the computers and the languages which might eventually be used to implement the chosen design. These latter factors may well affect the final coding stages, but they should not usually influence the logical solution to a design problem. It is therefore a design method which is equally applicable whether programs end up being coded in high level languages such as Basic, C, C++, Pascal or Cobol, or coded in low level languages such as 680x0 assembly language.

It's fair to ask why you should need to use something like the Warnier diagram in the first place especially when many high-level languages are *self documenting* to some extent anyway. With a high level language it is frequently possible to write short programs without any explicit design stage and this is especially true if you know exactly what you want to do. With more complex programming tasks, or when programming with say assembly language, trust me – the design stage does not only become far more important – it becomes vital. It provides a means of separating the logical problems of design from the practical problems of coding and by so doing enables you to tackle your programming in coherent stages. This separation is especially important with machines such as the Amiga because Intuition based programs tend to be both large and relatively complicated.

A Warnier diagram is essentially a set of curly brackets, that define both particular groups of operations and the order in which they should be performed. The easiest way to show you about these diagrams is to take an example. In this appendix I'm going to use a simple example just to enable the general notational ideas to be understood.

Let's imagine then that we wish to produce a report, consisting of details held on a computer file on disk. The Warnier diagram of the basic problem is shown in figure A1.1.

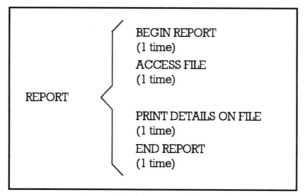

Figure A1.1. Essential characteristics of the simple report generator.

The bracket is read from top to bottom and describes a procedure or group of operations that has, arbitrarily, been called REPORT. The numbers which you see written underneath the various statements identify how many times the item is to be performed and, with just those two conventions, our first diagram is already illustrating some essential features. Do we know anything more about the problem? Can we think of any information that could be relevant? Well, we know that: computer files need to be opened before reading and closed once the read operation is complete. These details could therefore also be added to the diagram. To enable us to explain some further conventions used with Warnier diagrams let us first add a minor complication to the problem – let us suppose: the user wishes to access a file of his (or her) own choosing and to obtain a printed report of the details on the file. The specified file may not exist, and, if this is the case the user should be informed.

Appendix A: The Warnier Diagram

These changed or altered requirements can be represented by a more detailed Warnier diagram:

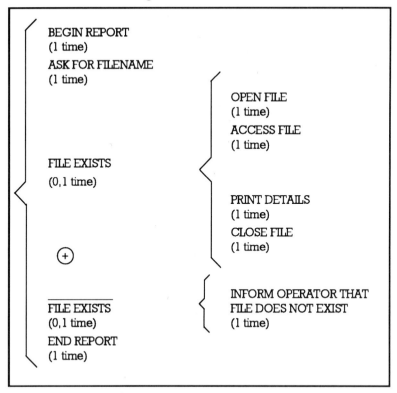

Figure A1.2. Some new restrictions added to Figure A1.1.

Figure A1.2 shows, in Warnier diagram form, the requirements of the problem as it is at the moment. We are using the convention that the logical opposite of a statement is written by placing a bar over it.:

$\overline{\text{FILE EXISTS}}$ means   FILE DOES NOT EXIST

I'm also using a ⊕ sign to separate mutually exclusive operations (sets of operations which will not occur together). In the present example the file will either exist or it will not exist — so only one of these two operations would be performed at any one time and (0,1 time) is written underneath the statements involved. At other times the operations shown within a bracket may need to be repeated and in these cases an expression such as (1,N times) would be used.

The conventions used so far are in fact the only ones you will need for the majority of problems that you are likely to encounter. Here they are collected together for convenience:

- Brackets are used to define sets of operations.
- Brackets are read, and performed, downwards within any

one *level*. The item at the top of the bracket is performed first, the item at the bottom performed last

- The logical opposite of a statement can be written as the original statement with a bar drawn over it.

- Brackets written to the right of a statement indicate the operations to be performed IF that statement is performed.

- Underneath each item or statement we indicate the number of time the operations should be performed.

- Mutually exclusive statements are written separated by a (+) sign.

Using these conventions we can express in English exactly what figure A1.2 tells us: we are dealing with a certain procedure, called REPORT that starts by asking for the name of a file. If the file exists then it is opened, accessed, the details printed, and then the file is closed. If it does not exist then the operator is informed of the fact. Remember that if the file does exist then it is the group of actions (subset) shown to the right of the label FILE EXISTS that are performed.

It's important to realise that these diagrams are not just useful for describing the *static logic* of a finished program, they're a visual aid that are used to sketch out the characteristics of a problem or a piece of code during the time that it is being created. Usually the ideas on what needs to be done changes, sometimes drastically, as your initial ideas are examined in more detail and to appreciate the elegance and speed with which these diagrams can accommodate all manner of changing requirements let's now place some further restrictions on this problem: within this hypothetical computer system are files containing sensitive data (perhaps personnel data, wages or medical records). Such data must be protected from unauthorised access and users are therefore issued with access code numbers, so that examination of sensitive files is restricted to those users with the proper authority. If unauthorised attempts to access this data are made the computer should record the fact, perhaps by making an entry into a special *security* file.

Let's first consider the new constraints in isolation. We need to check whether the file specified by the user is a restricted file, if it is we must ask for the user's code number. If the code is correct then we allow access, if not we write a *security record* indicating an attempted illegal access.

Appendix A: The Warnier Diagram

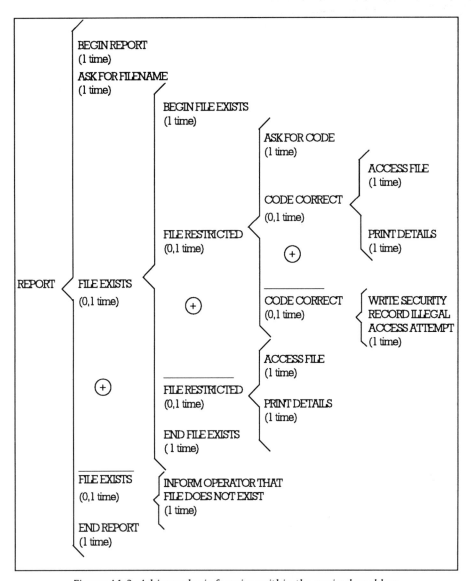

Figure A1.3. A hierarchy is forming within the revised problem.

The diagram in Figure A1.3 shows the Warnier form that describes our new requirements. Notice that although I've redefined the problem and added more detailed restrictions it has not been necessary to restructure the complete diagram – all I've had to do is superimpose the new details and restrictions on to the existing diagram structure. The diagram is therefore actually growing as we successively modify and redefine the known details of the problem. It's actually doing a lot more than this because, as well as documenting and expressing the logical requirements of the problem, it is providing a description that makes the conversion to a computer language equivalent form remarkably simple. The secret of converting a Warnier diagram into a finished program lies in regarding each bracket involving more than one operation as a subroutine. There are exceptions to this general statement but they occur only when the statements involved are obviously simple to code. Here's a simple pseudocode Basic sketch to illustrate what I mean...

```
* ===========================================================

         P S E U D O - B A S I C - R E P O R T - M O D U L E
*  _____

INPUT NAME OF FILE

IF FILE EXISTS THEN GOSUB `FILE EXISTS' ELSE PRINT `FILE DOES NOT EXIST'

RETURN TO CALLING PROGRAM
*  _____

REM SUBROUTINE..........FILE EXISTS

IF FILE IS RESTRICTED THE GOSUB `RESTRICTED FILE' ELSE GOSUB `ACCESS'

RETURN
*  _____

REM SUBROUTINE..........RESTRICTED FILE

INPUT SECURITY CODE

IF SECURITY CODE=CORRECT CODE THEN GOSUB `ACCESS' ELSE GOSUB `ILLEGAL ACCESS'

RETURN
*  _____

REM SUBROUTINE..........ILLEGAL ACCESS

WRITE TO I/A LOG FILE THE TIME OF ATTEMPT AND THE ACCESS CODEPRINT `THIS IS A RESTRICTED FILE - PLEASE MAKE NO FURTHER ATTEMPTS'

RETURN
*  _____

REM SUBROUTINE..........ACCESS

THIS WOULD BE A ROUTINE TO ACCESS THE DATA IN THE FILE AND DISPLAYON TERMINAL OR PRINTER ETC.

RETURN
* ===========================================================
```

Figure A1.4. Pseudo-BASIC code for the example.

Appendix A: The Warnier Diagram

The Warnier diagram can be used to develop a *picture* of individual routines, of programs and individual modules, and of complete systems. One technique, one set of rules... but a great many applications! All such descriptions do however share a common bond – the descriptions are logical plans! The problem itself may be related to, and therefore dependent to some extent on, a particular machine, but the diagrams themselves offer essentially general solutions, isolated completely from specific computer languages.

Basically then the idea is to tackle the problem of designing a program by looking at the logical characteristics. The only effect of a final choice of language has during these stages is that you need to keep in mind the fact that all of your diagram statements will eventually need to be turned into real code. You must therefore continue to expand your diagram statements until you reach a point where it is possible to say 'Yes, the operations we are describing in the lower levels of the diagrams (the right-most levels) are easily capable of being coded directly in the language I have chosen to use!'

In practice we reach this point far sooner with high-level languages than with assembly languages because more complex operations are supported. The relevant point to make here is that the general design principles are always the same – the only difference is that when you analyse problems that will be coded in assembly language you will need to carry the analysis further.

Appendix B: More Program Design Notes

Having provided the basics of the Warnier diagram notation I thought one C-style example of how they are used would be of interest. The following problem involves some very common file handling operations and although it is a simple design task I've dealt with the issues in some depth in order to give you an idea of how I tackle code design. The idea is to write a program which opens specified source and destination disk files, and then transfers data on a byte-by-byte basis from the source to the destination doing some (as yet unspecified) processing. The first step is to tackle the general aspects of the problem without worrying about what will be done to each byte as it is transferred. This will provide a framework for the program into which we'll then be able to slot in suitable code to carry out whatever processing is needed.

It is very tempting, since the above description both tells us and implies a lot about what needs be done, to sketch a suitable C framework program directly. Now I know that this is what most experienced C programmers would do anyway but that is only because they'll be completely aware of what needs to be done. I want to show you how such code can be crafted from the ground up using these Warnier techniques because the ideas are generally applicable to the design of all complex code modules (where direct coding usually leads to all sorts of difficulties).

The first step is to try and identify what the program has to do. In other words we shall try and sketch the output set. The benefits of this are two-fold: firstly, this analysis helps us understand more about the problem itself Secondly, since any vagueness which might be present in the original description can be eliminated, we'll usually be able to build a better framework for the program than might otherwise have been possible.

Describing the Output Set

What do we regard as the output set? The best idea is to opt for including *anything* that can be recognized as being something which the program does – either in the way of internal processing or external output. Thus printed output, graphics/text displayed on the screen, files being opened, files being closed etc, are all *output* in our sense of the word. Perhaps the most important observation at this point in time is that we want to describe everything the program does, not just the things it does when everything is going smoothly. For instance – the problem description suggests that the first thing the program should do is open the source file but what we need to recognize is that this operation might fail. Bearing this in mind I decide to start the output description as shown in figure A2.1:

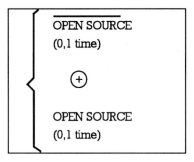

Figure A2.1. Making a start.

What should the program do if the specified source file cannot be opened? Let's assume it should print an error message:

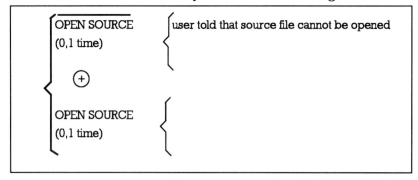

Figure A2.2. adding an error message note.

Another thing the program must do is open a destination file. Since it only needs to do this if the source file has been successfully opened we place these new open details within the OPEN SOURCE subset:

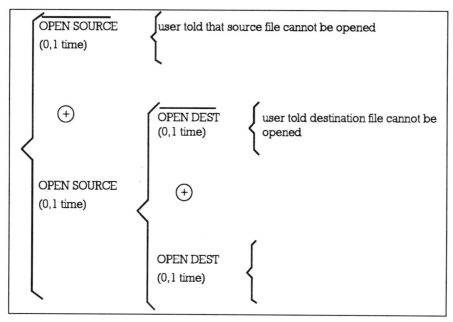

Figure A2.3. More details are added.

If the files open OK the program is going to do some processing. It will read bytes from the source, modify them and write them back to the destination file. These are repetitive actions which will occur as many times as there are bytes in the file so we extend the diagram as shown in Figure A2.4:

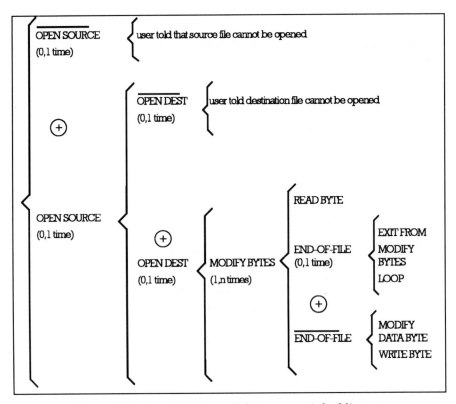

Figure A2.4. A useful picture of the program is building up.

We also know that files which are opened have to be closed. Where do these details go? Again it's not too hard to fathom out: files can only be closed if they have been sucessfully opened. Furthermore we'll only want to close the files after all read/write operations have been completed. The obvious place for the file close operations is near the end of the brackets which indicate successful opening – that way every file that is ever successfully opened will be closed. If we adopt this plan the output description will grow accordingly:

More Program Design Notes

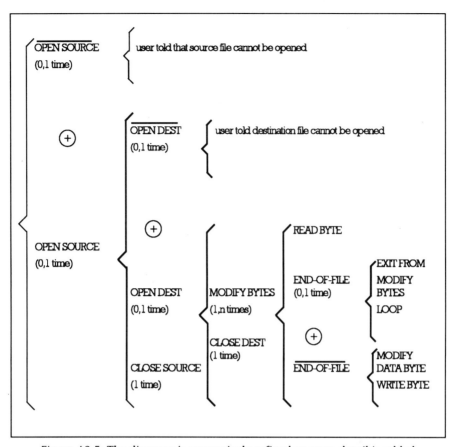

Figure A2.5: The diagram is successively refined as more detail is added.

The thing to recognize here that the WRITE BYTE operation might well fail – the disk could be full. I'll assume that if a write is unsuccessful the program will display an error message, close the (perhaps partially written) file, and then remove it. Figure A2.6 shows how these thoughts are incorporated into the design:

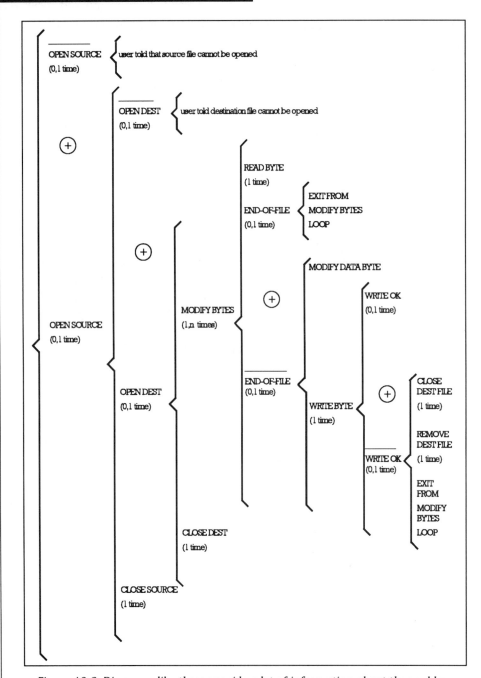

Figure A2.6. Diagrams like these provide a lot of information about the problem.

Now we have a slight problem: according to the diagram the program always closes destination files at the end of the OPEN DEST bracket but we have decided that, in the event of a bad write, the destination file is going to be closed prematurely and removed. We cannot therefore leave the original CLOSE DEST operation where

More Program Design Notes

it is because we have decided that, where a write error has occured, the destination file will no longer exist.

We have got to move the original CLOSE DEST operation to a more suitable position and here's how we do it: Firstly, we note that destination files fall into one of two mutually exclusive categories - those where a write error occured, and those where no write error occured! The secret now is to recognize that, out of all the file read and write operations which take place, only ONE normal read EOF will occur and at that time all of the necessary destination data would have been sent to the destination file. That subset therefore has both the right position and right frequency correspondence to hold our CLOSE DEST operation for closing destination files under non-error conditions.

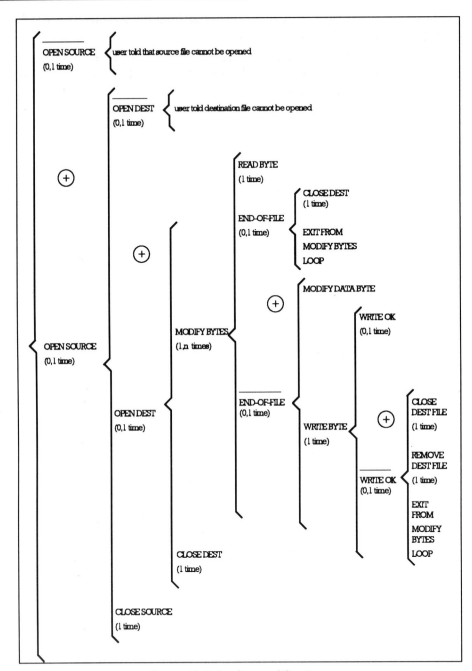

Figure A2.7. Further modifications.

Now, the details present in the output set have been growing but there are still a few things missing, such as how the program knows which files are being dealt with! We should also recognize that the program will not just attempt to open files that are *open-able* – it must of necessity try and open all files. The point to bear in mind here is that, although some file opening operations will succeed and others will fail, the actual attempted open operations will be made on each and every filename.

With these details added the *output set*, the description of what the program should do shown in Figure A2.8, is beginning to look reasonably complete:

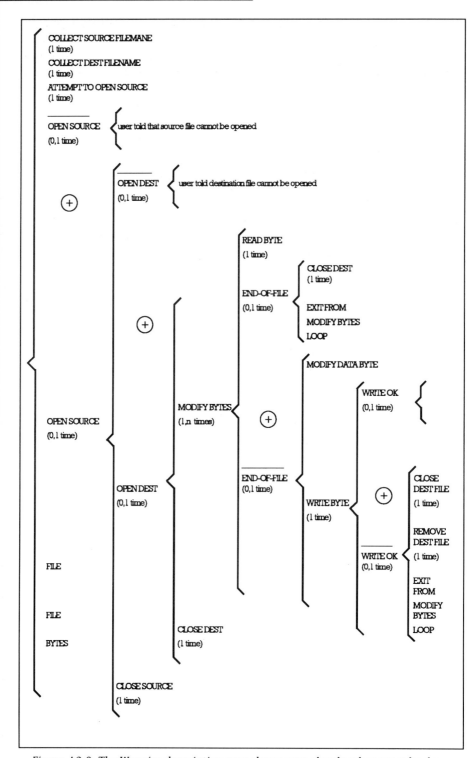

Figure A2.8. The Warnier description now shows very clearly what must be done.

More Program Design Notes

I think you'll agree that we now have a much better idea of what the program has to do, and have a clear idea of the various assumptions which have been made along the way. The thing to bear in mind at this point is that this output set should be a description of the actions that are to be carried out by the program. If we've thought carefully enough it *will* be, and in this sense it is a statement of output requirements which are invariant – in other words it is a description of the things which we now recognize the program *must* do!

It is of course quite possible that, as our understanding of the problem we are tackling grows, we may discover that we have forgotten to include something of importance but, notwithstanding such omissions, this output set description can be considered complete in the sense that it now appears to represent all of the actions which we feel the program should carry out.

The Input Set

On the face of it there is very little in the way of input data. Two obvious input items are the two filenames supplied:

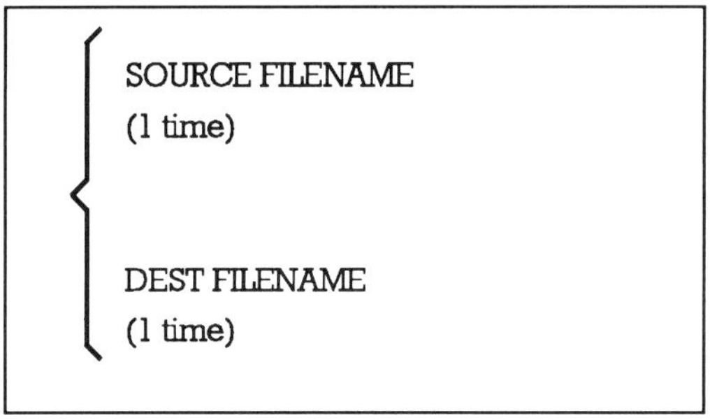

```
{  SOURCE FILENAME
   (1 time)


   DEST FILENAME
   (1 time)
```

Figure A2.9. Attempt to decribe the programs input.

The other inputs to the program is the source file, but here this may or may not exist depending on whether the source filename corresponds to a real file. This being so, we can expand the input set definition to this:

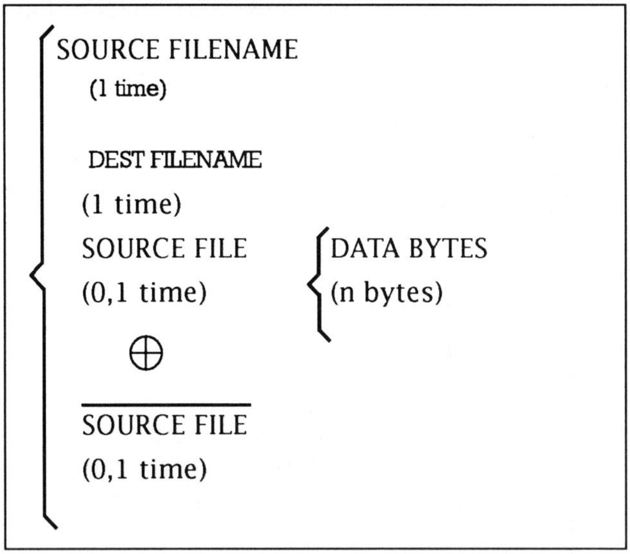

```
       ⎧ SOURCE FILENAME
       ⎪    (1 time)
       ⎪
       ⎪   DEST FILENAME
       ⎪   (1 time)
       ⎨   SOURCE FILE      ⎧ DATA BYTES
       ⎪   (0,1 time)       ⎨ (n bytes)
       ⎪       ⊕            ⎩
       ⎪   ─────────
       ⎪   SOURCE FILE
       ⎩   (0,1 time)
```

Figure A2.9. Input set description after a few additions.

We now need to build a program description based on any extension of this input set which is compatible with both the existence of the data items shown in the input set and their frequencies. Given the trivial nature of the abovementioned input set I'm going to create the program description simply by duplicating the hierarchy of output set using the diagram shown in Figure A2.10:

More Program Design Notes

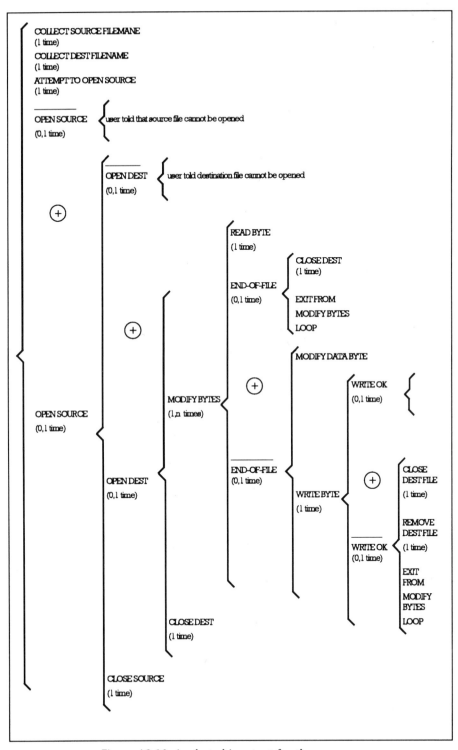

Figure A2.10. A selected input set for the program.

What were the frequency correspondences which had to be present when I mixed these descriptions? Here they are paired together:

Input Set Items (these things exist as input to the program)	Output Set Actions (these are things which the program has to do)
SOURCE FILENAME (1 time)	COLLECT SOURCE FILENAME (1 time)
DEST FILENAME (1 time)	COLLECT DEST FILENAME (1 time)
SOURCE FILE (0,1 time)	OPEN SOURCE (a successful open) (0,1 times)
──────── SOURCE FILE (0,1 time)	──────── OPEN SOURCE (unsuccessful open) (0,1 time)
SOURCE DATA BYTES (n bytes)	MODIFY BYTES (processes n bytes) (1, n times)

Figure A2.11. Some input/output set frequency correspondences.

Diagram to Code Conversion

Having produced a reasonably detailed Warnier diagram of the program my thoughts would be yes it is now time to start coding. How do I know that the diagram is complete? To be honest I don't, but: I am happy that all of the operations OPEN SOURCE, OPEN DEST, WRITE BYTE etc, shown on the diagram are things which (in my opinion) are very easily coded.

The idea then is to code the main bracket levels as function calls and only deviate from this when the code at a particular level is simple enough to code directly in-line. Obviously as we get into the code translation we have a certain amount of syntactic detail to show. ANSII C requires that you define prototypes for function calls so that the compiler can check that argument types and return values are correctly typed. It is possible to add this sort of detail to the Warnier diagram, ie include details such as those shown in Figure A2.12:

More Program Design Notes

SPECIFY INCLUDE FILES (1 time)	stdio.h types.h
DEFINE FUNCTION PROTOTYPES (1 time)	void OpenSource(void); void OpenDest(void);
DEFINE GLOBALS (1 time)	FILE *g_source_p; FILE *g_dest_p;

Figure A2.12. These sort of additions are normally unneccessary.

I didn't do this and in fact, in my opinion, the addition of this type of syntactic detail is unnecessary. The Warnier diagram should provide a language-independent description of what needs to be done – it seems quite absurd to clutter such diagrams with details that are going to be present in the code in almost the same form. My advice then is to keep the language-specific coding details well away from the Warnier diagram representation. Having said that you ought to try to document the program in a way which makes it easy for someone reading the source to see the layout. A simple scheme is all that's needed. Here's one that I commonly use:

title

includes

defines

prototypes

globals

main() function

nested level() functions

support functions

For clarity I divide the various sections using /* —— */ lines and for non-function sections I'll include a title and, if I think it will help, perhaps some additional notes.

My translation of our example program is going to be a straightforward 'vanilla C' version that will run on anything from an ST or an Amiga to a UNIX system. Some notes are in order:

> • I've chosen to collect filenames via command line argc/argv[] parameters. source and destination filename pointers are declared and these are initialized to point to the original command line arguments.

> • I'm not checking for the correct number of parameters, so if the user doesn't supply one or other filenames that name pointer will be NULL and the corresponding fopen() call will fail – experience tells me it should fail harmlessly!

- This first translation, after all I've said about minimizing the use of global variables, does in fact use global variables for the filenames and the FILE pointers. Why? Initial simplicity in the first runable version. It also allows me to defer thinking about what parameters are needed until I've got a C sketch available which shows clearly what information each routine will need access to.

- ANSII C's buffered file operations can be used to handle the file opening and closing with statements like fopen(g_name_p,"rb") being used to open the specified files for binary mode reading. I've opted for binary file mode because we haven't yet decided what processing is to be done.

- I've layered the open close operations as nested function calls but the do/while loop used to represent the MODIFY BYTES operations I've kept within a single routine by using if { } else { } statements.

- In this example my error message routines are just simple printf() statements. I have however deliberately kept them away from the bulk of the code by writing a short function ErrorMessage().

Here then is the first version:

```
/* ———————————————————— */
/* Example: A2-1: skeleton framework
*/
/* ———————————————————— */
/* some includes: */
#include <stdio.h>
#include <exec/types.h>
/* ———————————————————— */
/* some defines... */
#define NO_SOURCE "cannot open source file\n"
#define NO_DEST   "cannot open destination file\n"
/* ———————————————————— */
/* some prototypes...*/
void OpenSourceOK(void);
void OpenDestOK(void);
void ErrorMessage(TEXT *error_message);
/* ———————————————————— */
/* some globals... */
FILE *g_source_p, *g_dest_p;
TEXT *g_source_name_p, *g_dest_name_p;
```

```
/* ——————————————————————— */
main(int argc, char *argv[])
{
g_source_name_p=argv[1]; g_dest_name_p=argv[2];
   if(g_source_p=fopen(g_source_name_p,"rb"))
      OpenSourceOK();
         else ErrorMessage(NO_SOURCE);
}
/* ——————————————————————— */
void OpenSourceOK(void)
{
   if (g_dest_p=fopen(g_dest_name_p,"wb"))
      OpenDestOK();
         else ErrorMessage(NO_DEST);
      fclose(g_source_p);
}
/* ——————————————————————— */
void OpenDestOK(void)
{
   BOOL exit_flag; int c;
   do {
     if((c=fgetc(g_source_p))==EOF)
        {
        fclose(g_dest_p); exit_flag=TRUE;
        }
        else
        {
        /* DO SOMETHING WITH DATA BYTE */
        if((fputc(c, g_dest_p))==EOF)
           {
           fclose(g_dest_p);
           remove(g_dest_name_p);
           exit_flag=TRUE;
           }
        }
   }while(!exit_flag);
}
```

```
/* ─────────────────────────────── */
void ErrorMessage(TEXT *error_message) {printf(error_mes-
sage);}
/* ─────────────────────────────── */
```

One thing you might notice is that we've forgotten to include error message for bad write cases. It is obviously not a major omission and these details are easily imposed onto the Warnier description:

More Program Design Notes

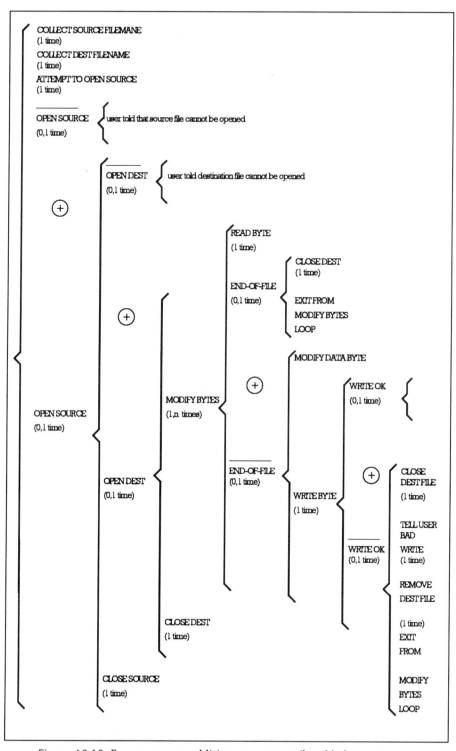

Figure A2.13. Error message additions etc, are easily added at any stage.

What you will no doubt notice is that there was absolutely no difficulty in deciding where on the diagram this extra message would need to be placed. Similarly the section of C code in the program is also easily identified. and the changes simply involve adding a new #define message and changing the fragment which reads:

```
fclose(g_dest_p);
remove(g_dest_name_p);
exit_flag=TRUE;
```

to:

```
fclose(g_dest_p);
ErrorMessage(BAD_WRITE);
remove(g_dest_name_p);
exit_flag=TRUE;
```

The result of these changes is shown below:

```
/* ------------------------------------------------ */
/* Example: A2-2... modified skeleton framework     */
/* ------------------------------------------------ */
/* some includes... */
#include <stdio.h>
#include <exec/types.h>
/* ------------------------------------------------ */
/* some defines... */
#define NO_SOURCE "cannot open source file\n"
#define NO_DEST   "cannot open destination file\n"
#define BAD_WRITE "error whilst writing - removing desti-
nation file\n"
/* ------------------------------------------------ */
/* some prototypes...*/
void OpenSourceOK(void);
void OpenDestOK(void);
void ErrorMessage(TEXT *error_message);
/* ------------------------------------------------ */
/* some globals... */
FILE *g_source_p, *g_dest_p;
TEXT *g_source_name_p, *g_dest_name_p;
/* ------------------------------------------------ */
main(int argc, char *argv[])
```

More Program Design Notes

```c
{
g_source_name_p=argv[1]; g_dest_name_p=argv[2];
   if(g_source_p=fopen(g_source_name_p,"rb"))
      OpenSourceOK();
         else ErrorMessage(NO_SOURCE);
}
/* ——————————————— */
void OpenSourceOK(void)
{
   if (g_dest_p=fopen(g_dest_name_p,"wb"))
      OpenDestOK();
         else ErrorMessage(NO_DEST);
   fclose(g_source_p);
}
/* ——————————————— */
void OpenDestOK(void)
{
   BOOL exit_flag; int c;
   do {
      if((c=fgetc(g_source_p))==EOF)
         {
          fclose(g_dest_p); exit_flag=TRUE;
         }
         else
         {
         /* DO SOMETHING WITH DATA BYTE */
         if((fputc(c, g_dest_p))==EOF)
            {
             fclose(g_dest_p);
             ErrorMessage(BAD_WRITE);
             remove(g_dest_name_p);
             exit_flag=TRUE;
            }
         }
   }while(!exit_flag);
}
/* ——————————————— */
```

```
void ErrorMessage(TEXT *error_message) {printf(error_mes-
sage);}
/* ——————————————————————————— */
```

A More Sophisticated Translation

Let us now create a more useful 'black box' version which, when given source and destination filenames, will carry out the file modification process returning a success failure indicator to the calling program.

We've already got the basic shell of the program complete so we don't need to go back and change anything design wise. What we must do however is firstly eliminate those globals and secondly remove our error message routine and replace it with code which returns an error number to the calling program.

It's an easy translation to do but in case you're new to such things here are the exact stages I used: first of all I removed globals and altered the function calls so that filename and file pointers are passed between the various levels, modifying the prototypes accordingly.

Other than the easy task of re-defining the error messages as error numbers I did *not* want to tackle the function parameter code changes and the success/failure error code changes at the same time. Consequently I removed the ErrorMessage() routine and commented out corresponding error calls – this enabled me to compile and check most of this partly complete version without getting any compiler errors:

```
/* ——————————————————————————— */
/* Example: A2-3... partly complete version without glob-
als          */
/* ——————————————————————————— */
/* some includes... */
#include <stdio.h>
#include <exec/types.h>
/* ——————————————————————————— */
/* some defines... */
#define NO_ERROR    0
#define NO_SOURCE   1
#define NO_DEST     2
#define BAD_WRITE   3
/* ——————————————————————————— */
/* some prototypes...*/
void OpenSourceOK(FILE *g_source_p, TEXT *g_dest_name_p);
```

Disk Order Form

Please rush me my copies of the two Mastering Amiga Programming Secrets disks.

I enclose a Cheque/Postal Order* for £4.00.

Name. ....

Address. ....

....

.... Post Code ....

Contact phone number. ....

*Cheques payable to *Bruce Smith Books Ltd.*

Send your order to:

Programming Secrets Disks, Bruce Smith Books Ltd,

PO Box 382, St. Albans, Herts, AL2 3JD

Please note that unless otherwise requested we will add you to our mailing list. This mailing list is currently only used to mail out to our readers details of new and forthcoming books. This includes our catalogue *Mastering Amiga News.*

Please take the time to answer the following questions:

How did you find out about Mastering AmigaDOS Secrets?

Where did you purchase your copy?

What other titles would you like to see in the Mastering Amiga range of books?

Book Order Form

Please rush me the following:
- ☐ Mastering AmigaDos 3 Volume One - Tutorial £21.95
- ☐ Mastering AmigaDOS 3 Volume Two - Reference £19.95
- ☐ Mastering AmigaDOS Scripts £19.95
- ☐ Workbench 3 A to Z Guide £14.95
- ☐ Amiga 1200 Insider Guide £14.95
- ☐ Amiga 1200 Next Steps £14.95
- ☐ Amiga assembler Insider Guide 14.95
- ☐ Amiga Disks and Drives £14.95
- ☐ A1200 Beginners Pack .... £39.95+£3 P&P
- ☐ Amiga Workbench 3 Booster Pack .... £39.95+£3 P&P
- ☐ Introduction to the A1200 video - Basic Tutorial £14.99
- ☐ Introduction to the A1200 video - A Deeper Look £14.99
- ☐ Mastering Amiga System - Advanced C £29.95
- ☐ Mastering Amiga Printers £19.95
- ☐ Mastering Amiga C £19.95
- ☐ Mastering Amiga ARexx £21.95
- ☐ Amiga BASIC – A Dabhand Guide £17.95
- ☐ Secrets of Frontier Elite £9.95
- ☐ Secrets of Sim City 2000 .... £9.95

I enclose a cheque/postal order for £   .   p

I wish to pay by Access/Visa/Mastercard

Card Number: ☐☐☐☐☐☐☐☐☐☐☐☐☐☐☐☐

Expiry Date: ☐☐☐☐

Name: ....

Address: ....

.... Post Code ....

Contact Phone Number: ....

Signed: ....

Please send your cheques, made payable to Bruce Smith Books Ltd to:

**Bruce Smith Books Ltd, FREEPOST 282, PO Box 382
St Albans, Herts, AL2 3BR
Telephone: (01923) 894355 - Fax (01923) 894366**

E&OE.

```c
void OpenDestOK(FILE *g_source_p, FILE *g_dest_p, TEXT
*dest_name_p);
/* ——————————————————— */
UBYTE ConvertFile(TEXT *g_source_name_p, TEXT
*g_dest_name_p)
{
FILE *g_source_p;
   if(g_source_p=fopen(g_source_name_p,"rb"))
      OpenSourceOK(g_source_p, g_dest_name_p);
/*         else ErrorMessage(NO_SOURCE);
*/
return(NO_ERROR);
}
/* ——————————————————— */
void OpenSourceOK(FILE *g_source_p, TEXT *g_dest_name_p)
{
FILE *g_dest_p;
   if (g_dest_p=fopen(g_dest_name_p,"wb"))
      OpenDestOK(g_source_p, g_dest_p, g_dest_name_p);
/*         else ErrorMessage(NO_DEST);
*/
   fclose(g_source_p);
}
/* ——————————————————— */
void OpenDestOK(FILE *g_source_p, FILE *g_dest_p, TEXT
*g_dest_name_p)
{
   BOOL exit_flag; int c;
   do {
      if((c=fgetc(g_source_p))==EOF)
         {
         fclose(g_dest_p); exit_flag=TRUE;
         }
         else
         {
          /* DO SOMETHING WITH DATA BYTE */
          if((fputc(c, g_dest_p))==EOF)
             {
```

```
                    fclose(g_dest_p);
/*                   ErrorMessage(BAD_WRITE);
*/
                    remove(g_dest_name_p);
                     exit_flag=TRUE;
                    }
               }
        }while(!exit_flag);
    }
/* ─────────────────────────────────────── */
```

After a quick compile check confirming that no silly slips had been made it was time to decide how to get success/failure information back up to the calling program. I chose to use local error number variables passing the error status back via return(). Notice incidentally, that the error variables are initialized to a NO_ERROR state and reassigned only if an error occurs. Again this sort of translation seemed relatively trivial and, since the structure of the program is still essentially unchanged, I saw little need to describe the initialization of the error numbers and so forth on the Warnier diagram.

What I'm trying to do of course is show you how I use these diagram and coding techniques in practice. I am not trying to kid either you (or myself) that trivial coding changes are best solved by going back and working in diagram form. I was quite happy making the global variable to parameter variable changes, and equally happy to revamp the error message code so that we dealt with error numbers. What I did not do however is make any significant changes to the overall program structure which the design diagrams led us to adopt!

Enough of the lecture, here's the final code without globals:

```
/* ─────────────────────────────────────── */
/* Example: A2-4... complete parameter driven version
   without globals    */
/* ─────────────────────────────────────── */
/* some includes... */
#include <stdio.h>
#include <exec/types.h>
/* ─────────────────────────────────────── */
/* some defines... */
#define NO_ERROR     0
#define NO_SOURCE    1
```

```c
#define NO_DEST     2
#define BAD_WRITE   3
/* ─────────────────────────────── */
/* some prototypes...*/
UBYTE OpenSourceOK(FILE *source_p, TEXT *dest_name_p);
UBYTE OpenDestOK(FILE *source_p, FILE *dest_p, TEXT
*dest_name_p);
/* ─────────────────────────────── */
UBYTE ConvertFile(TEXT *source_name_p, TEXT *dest_name_p)
{
FILE *source_p; UBYTE error_number=NO_ERROR;
   if(source_p=fopen(source_name_p,"rb"))
      error_number=OpenSourceOK(source_p, dest_name_p);
         else error_number=NO_SOURCE;
return(error_number);
}
/* ─────────────────────────────── */
UBYTE OpenSourceOK(FILE *source_p, TEXT *dest_name_p)
{

FILE *dest_p; UBYTE error_number=NO_ERROR;
   if (dest_p=fopen(dest_name_p,"wb"))
         error_number=OpenDestOK(source_p, dest_p,
dest_name_p);
           else error_number=NO_DEST;
   fclose(source_p);
return(error_number);
}
/* ─────────────────────────────── */
UBYTE OpenDestOK(FILE *source_p, FILE *dest_p, TEXT
*dest_name_p)
{
   BOOL exit_flag; int c; UBYTE error_number=NO_ERROR;
    do {
      if((c=fgetc(source_p))==EOF)
         {
          fclose(dest_p); exit_flag=TRUE;
         }
```

```
            else
            {
            /* DO SOMETHING WITH DATA BYTE */
            if((fputc(c, dest_p))==EOF)
               {
                fclose(dest_p);
                error_number=BAD_WRITE;
                remove(dest_name_p);
                 exit_flag=TRUE;
               }
            }
        }while(!exit_flag);
    return(error_number);
    }
    /* ─────────────────────────────────── */
```

Byte Conversion Code - An Example

The reason I've not dealt with any specific type of byte-by-byte conversion is simple – our generalized, and now well understood, framework can form the basis of any number of file modification utilities. Here is one such example – a straightforward black box file encryption/dechipering routine for use in other programs.

The encryption trick uses a variant of byte-orientated exclusive-ORing, an old favourite amongst programmers. The benefit of this approach is that the program which performs the encryption process can also be used to do the deciphering. Simple fixed key exclusive-ORing however is far too easy to break so, to make life a bit more interesting, I am going to use a scheme which takes into account the position of each character being encrypted. Used in conjunction with long string keys this twist, though simple to code, is surprisingly effective. (Although it isn't going to have the CIA's cipher boys quaking in their boots – with high-speed hardware this particular cipher mechanism is still going to be easily broken. Having said that you're unlikely to find anyone able to crack it using any Amiga/ST based techniques!)

The program/routine would need three parameters and as a command line utility might adopt this format:

`EncryptDecipher    <SourceFile>    <DestinationFile>    <EncryptionKey>`

A callable routine could adopt a similar parameter arrangement using this sort of function prototype:

`UBYTE EncryptDecipher(TEXT *sourcefile, TEXT *destfile, TEXT *encryptionkey)`

More Program Design Notes

To write such a program all I have done is to add a few lines of code to the parameter driven general file transfer routine which has just been looked at. There is now an extra parameter to deal with, the string used as the encryption key – I have added a suitable extra argument so that the address of the key is passed down to the routine which needs to use it.

Use of such a program? Text file encryption is one obvious possibility. Another use, which might come in handy for hard disk owners, is for encrypting potentially damaging system commands and restricting the use of certain utility programs – keep the encrypted form on the disk and temporarily decipher a copy when you want to run it. Getting right up-to-date you've no doubt heard of virus programs which can attach themselves to program code. Well, there's no way a virus could attach itself to an encrypted version of a program and get away with it... because the additional code would become meaningless after it had been deciphered! Admittedly it is a bit *over-the-top* for most purposes, but the encryption technique is another tool for fighting the virus makers so it might be worth thinking about.

Now a word about the overall program design of this encryption utility: I'm not going to repeat the program structure analysis because, other than a one line byte-modifying statement (which occurs just prior to a data byte being transferred to the destination file) the steps are the same as those outlined earlier in this appendix.

Basically we need in addition to know the length of the encryption key and, at each stage of the processing, the relative position of the data byte being dealt with. Because of this I've added two additional local variables to the OpenDestOK() routine, the routine which handles the byte transfer operations. You'll see these in the source as:

```
ULONG position;/* the 'byte number' of the character in the file */

ULONG key_length; /* length of the encryption key string */
```

Believe it or not the code for the encryption is very simple – in fact this single line of code will do the job: c=c^(*(key_p+(position%key_length))+position%256); Where does this line of code go? We already know the answer to this question from the Warnier diagram!

Here then to complete this appendix is a command line encryption utility based on the use of the 'black box' routine we devised. Remember that the function EncryptDecipher() can be taken out (along with a header containing the necessary #includes, #defines and prototypes) and used in any program which needs to use, or provide, such a facility:

```c
/* ========================================================= */
/* Example: A5-5: parameter driven encryption utility      */
/* ——————————————————————————————————————————————————————— */
/* some includes... */
#include <stdio.h>
#include <exec/types.h>
/* ——————————————————————————————————————— */
/* some defines... */
#define NO_ERROR    0
#define NO_SOURCE   1
#define NO_DEST     2
#define BAD_WRITE   3
/* ——————————————————————————————————————— */
/* some prototypes...*/
UBYTE OpenSourceOK(FILE *source_p, TEXT *dest_name_p, TEXT *key_p);
UBYTE OpenDestOK(FILE *source_p, FILE *dest_p, TEXT *dest_name_p, TEXT *key_p);
UBYTE EncryptDecipher(TEXT *source_name_p, TEXT *dest_name_p, TEXT *key_p);
/* ——————————————————————————————————————— */
/* some globals (just for the text messages of this example)... */
TEXT *message[] = {
    "function complete\n",
    "cannot open source file\n",
    "cannot open destination file\n",
    "write error - removing destination file\n"
};
/* ——————————————————————————————————————— */
main(int argc, char *argv[])
{
TEXT *source_name_p, *dest_name_p, *key_p; UBYTE error_code;
source_name_p=argv[1]; dest_name_p=argv[2]; key_p=argv[3];
error_code=EncryptDecipher(source_name_p, dest_name_p, key_p);
printf(message[error_code]);
}
```

```
/* ———————————————————————— */
UBYTE EncryptDecipher(TEXT *source_name_p, TEXT
*dest_name_p, TEXT *key_p)
{
FILE *source_p; UBYTE error_number=NO_ERROR;
   if(source_p=fopen(source_name_p,"rb"))
      error_number=OpenSourceOK(source_p, dest_name_p,
key_p);
         else error_number=NO_SOURCE;
return(error_number);
}
/* ———————————————————————— */
UBYTE OpenSourceOK(FILE *source_p, TEXT *dest_name_p, TEXT
*key_p)
{
FILE *dest_p; UBYTE error_number=NO_ERROR;
   if (dest_p=fopen(dest_name_p,"wb"))
      error_number=OpenDestOK(source_p, dest_p,
dest_name_p, key_p);
         else error_number=NO_DEST;
   fclose(source_p);
return(error_number);
}
/* ———————————————————————— */
UBYTE OpenDestOK(FILE *source_p, FILE *dest_p, TEXT
*dest_name_p, TEXT *key_p)
{
   BOOL exit_flag; int c;
   UBYTE error_number=NO_ERROR;
   ULONG position=0;   /* the 'byte number' of the charac-
ter in the file */
   ULONG key_length; /* length of the encryption key
string */
key_length=strlen(key_p);
   do {
      if((c=fgetc(source_p))==EOF)
         {
          fclose(dest_p); exit_flag=TRUE;
         }
```

```
            else
            {
            c=c^(*(key_p+(position%key_length))+posi-
    tion%256);
            position++;
            if((fputc(c, dest_p))==EOF)
               {
                fclose(dest_p);
                error_number=BAD_WRITE;
                remove(dest_name_p);
                exit_flag=TRUE;
               }
            }
      }while(!exit_flag);
   return(error_number);
   }
   /* ─────────────────────────────── */
```

Keeping It In Perspective

Well, that shows you how the Warnier techniques work. I don't use them all the time and if I know from experience exactly how a problem should be tackled then I, like other coders, will sketch out a C-ish solution directly. In more complex cases where I really needed to think about what was being done however I've found these techniques absolutely invaluable. I'd never force any coder to use these methods but will tell you now that I firmly believe that they are incredibly useful once you've had some experience in using them!

Glossary:

active screen

On the Amiga this is the screen currently displaying the active window.

active window

The window currently receiving input from a user. On the Amiga only one window can be active at any one time.

address

A number which identifies a storage location in memory.

addressing mode

a term related to the way in which a microprocessor locates the operand that an instruction is to work on. See chapters 2 and 17 for details of 68000 addressing modes.

alert

A special red/black Amiga display used for emergency messages.

algorithm

A series of rules (or a diagramatic equivalent) that, when followed, result in a predetermined or predictable outcome.

alias

An alternative name for a command.

ALT keys

Two special command keys situated on the bottom left and bottom right of the Amiga's main keyboard.

alternation

A set of two or more alternative actions with only one of those actions being performed.

ALU
Arithmetic Logic Unit

angle brackets
These characters, < and >, are frequently used to identify command line parameters. For example... dir <filename> implies that 'filename' is a parameter which you, the user, should supply.

ANSI C
A official standard for the C language that by early 1990 had been adopted by almost all major C compiler writers.

ANSI C compiler
A compiler that conforms to the ANSI C standard.

applications gadget
A custom Amiga gadget used within an applications program.

arithmetic logic unit
Part of a microprocessor which performs arithmetic and logical operations.

arguments
The values supplied when a function is used. These values are also often called parameters.

array
A data structure that allows an information set to be indexed by a subscripted variable.

array bounds
The smallest and largest acceptable index for an array.

ASCII
American Standard Code for Information Interchange consists of a set of 96 displayable and 32 non displayed characters based on a seven bit code.

asynchronous
Some operation which is executed/performed without reference to an overall timing source. Asynchronous operations can therefore occur at irregular timing intervals.

automatic variable
Another name for a local variable.

backdrop window
An Amiga intuition window which always stays at the back of the screen display and cannot be depth rearranged.

background program
A program, task, or process, which is running somewhere in

memory but not interacting directly via a terminal.

back-up

To make a duplicate of a program or data disk. Back-up copies are usually made for either safety or security purposes.

baud rate

A measurement of the rate of data transmission through a serial port. Thebaud rate divided by ten is a rough measure of the number of characters being transmitted per second.

BCD

Binary Coded Decimal.

binary

A number system using base 2 for its operations.

binary search

A method of searching an ordered table or file by successively dividing the search area in half.

bit

An abreviation of "binary digit".

bitmap

An array of bits which form a system's display memory. Modifying the data in the bitmap alters the picture on the display. The Amiga uses a bitmap display consisting of a number of two dimensional 'bitplanes'.

blanking interval

The period of time when a video beam is outside of the screen display area. It's a good time for a program to do things which might visually jar the display – the idea is to ensure that all of the necessary changes have been made before the video beam comes back into the visual area.

Boolean algebra

The mathematics of a class of logical operations closely related to set theory mathematics.

boot

To start up a computer system.

borderless window

A window without any visible edge lines.

BPS

Bits per second.

branch

A type of processor instruction which causes control to pass from one section of a program to another. The branch is achieved by altering the contents of the processor's program control register (this is the register which tells the processor where it should get its next instruction from). On the 68000 the term branch is reserved for instructions which use relative addressing.

buffer

An area of memory used to hold data temporarily whilst being collected or transmitted.

bug

A fault within a program that has not yet been found. Also see "Debug".

C

One of the best high-level programming languages that has ever been developed.

call

To activate a program, function or procedure.

chain

See linked list.

character string

A sequence of printable characters.

checkmark

A small image, usually a tick, which indicates that a menu item has been selected by a user.

checksum

A number which is used to ensure that a block of data is correct and has not been inadvertently changed. Checksums are used to verify proper transmission and reception of data, to guard against deliberate alteration of sensitive file records etc.

child process

A process which has been brought into life by a program rather than directly by a user.

clear

Change the value of a binary bit from 1 to zero.

CLI

Command line interface.

click

A rapid press and release of a mouse button.

clipping
Preventing the parts of an image which lie outside of a specified drawing area from being displayed.

close gadget
A gadget in the top left corner of an Amiga window which allows a user to remove the window from the display.

colour indirection
Powerful pixel colouring technique whereby the binary number formed by the appropriate image bits determines which colour register will be used.

colour register
The Amiga has 32 hardware colour registers which means it has the ability to select from a palette of up to 4096 colours.

command file
An ordinary (usually ASCII) textfile containing executeable system commands.

comment
A remark, social or otherwise, written within a program.

commenting out
In the assembly language world this term implies that part of the source code of a program has been eliminated not by removing it but by adding * or ; characters at the beginning of each line of a code section (thus rendering it inoperative because those lines are then treated as comments by the assembler). It is a trick frequently used by programmers during program development.

composite video
A video signal which includes both picture and sync information. Can be transmitted using single co-ax cable.

complement
"Binary complement", the process of turning all 1's to 0's and all 0's to 1's.

concatenate
Join together. Strings, files etc., may be concatenated!

constant
Any value which does not change.

contiguous
Adjacent, lying next to each other etc. A contiguous block of memory is a block whose addresses are numerically adjacent and contain no gaps.

control character
A character that signifies the start or finish of some process.

Copper
An abreviation for the Amiga's Co-processor chip.

Co-processor
Brilliant and powerful Amiga chip which handles much of the display work. This chip has its own instruction set which allows it to modify display characteristics without requiring 68000 processor intervention. Advanced Amiga programmers write their own Copper lists (Co-processor programs) for doing strange and wonderful graphics tricks.

CPU
Central Processing Unit.

crash
A term used when a computer program terminates unexpectedly or when the system hardware or software malfunctions. Usually reserved for serious problems that have no way of escape other than restarting the system.

CRT
Cathode Ray Tube

data set
A collection of data items.

debug
To eliminate errors within a program.

debugger
A program designed to help programmers find errors (bugs) in their programs. Nowadays some highly sophisticated interactive debuggers are available which can link into the original source code as a program is executing.

decimal constant
A constant written as a base 10 number.

default value
A value which will be supplied automatically if no other is given.

delimiting characters
Characters placed at the beginning or end of a character string.

depth arrangement gadget
An Amiga system gadget which allows a user to depth arrange (bring to front or send to back) a window in relation to other windows currently displayed.

Glossary

destination file
A file being written to.

digital-to-analogue converter
A hardware device which will convert a binary number into an analogue (continuously variable) level signal.

DMA
Direct Memory Access

direct memory access
A method of data transfer whereby intelligent hardware devices can read and write to memory without the main microprocessor being involved.

disable
To prevent something from being used.

display memory
The RAM area that contains data used to produce the screen image.

display mode
A particular type of screen display... low resolution, high resolution, non-interlacedd etc.

double-click
Pressing and releasing a mouse button twice in quick succession.

double-menu requester
An Amiga requester which can be opened by a double-click of a mouse button.

drag
Shifting the position of a screen object by selecting it and, whilst holding the mouse button down, moving (dragging) it to another location.

dual playfield
An Amiga display mode which allows two separate playfields to be displayed and controlled simultaneously.

editor
See text editor.

enable
To make something available for use.

encrypt
To convert a file (or other information set) into a form which cannot easily be understood. Data is usually encrypted for security purposes.

EOF
End of File

Exec
The Amiga's low level system software which controls tasks, task switching, interrupt scheduling, message passing, I/O and many other underlying system functions.

extended selection
A method of selecting more than one option from a menu.

FIFO
First In First Out

file
A set of data items held on diskette, tape or other medium.

filename
A name given to a file for identification puroses.

fill
To colour or draw a pattern into an enclosed area.

flag
A single bit within a microprocessor register or memory location which has been chosen to represent some TRUE/FALSE, YES/NO, type situation.

floating Point
A means of representing numbers in the binary equivalent of "scientific notation",i.e., by specifying an exponent and a mantissa.

gadget
An Amiga icon type object. Amiga gadgets can represent on/off switches, one and two dimensional proportional sliders, can collect text string and number messages. Some standard graphic forms are available but most Amiga programmers delight in creating their own graphics gadget masterpieces.

Genlock
Hardware device which allows the capture and playback of video tape frames.

ghosting
Overlaying an image with a layer of dots making it slightly indistinct. Ghosting of gadgets and menu items is used to tell a user that certain options are not available.

Gimmezerozero window
An Amiga window which has a separate bitmap for the border graphics.

glitch
A transient, usually unreproduceable, problem usually associated with some hardware malfunction.

hard copy
A printed listing of some computer output as opposed to the output displayed on a VDU screen.

hashing
or "Key to address transformation" is a collective term used to describe the techniques for calculating the address of a data item (or data item set) by using a mathematical function of the search key.

header file
Another term for a C include file.

hexadecimal
A base 16 numbering system using the digits 0 - 9 and the letters A - F.

hexadecimal constant
A base 16 constant which in assembler is written with the prefix $ followed by the hexadecimal digits themselves.

iconic
A "picture" representation, c.f. icons

IDCMP
Intuition Direct Communications Message Port. Arguably the most important means of two way, program <-> Intuition, communication.

I/O
input/output.

interrupt
An externally instigated request that, if accepted, causes the processor to save its current status and perform some required function. When the function has been completed the status of the processor is restored and control handed back to the interrupted program.

IntuiMessage
Messages created for applications programs by Intuition.

Intuition
Users regard Intuition as the Amiga's high level graphics interface, ie the overall Workbench orientated WIMP arrangement. Programmers take a much lower level view regarding Intuition as a mass of system routines and object definitions which can be used to simplify their programming tasks. The Intuition approach allows programmers to easily create programs which use windows,

gadgets, menus etc.

jump

A type of processor instruction which causes control to pass from one section of a program to another. The jump is achieved by altering the contents of the processor's program control register (this is the register which tells the processor where it should get its next instruction from). The 68000 implements ordinary jumps, subroutine style jumps and branches (the later term is reserved for instructions which use relative addressing).

keymap

A translation table which describes the conversion of Amiga keyboard key presses into specific numerical codes.

label

Rectangular shaped paper, often sticky, used for placing identification markings on objects.

label

An identification name used within the source code to refer to a particular section of coding.

linked list

A set of data items linked together by using pointers. Sometimes called "chains".

long word

On the Amiga this implies a 32 bit binary number.

low-level language

A computer language whose primitive operations are closely related to the processor on which the language runs. Assembly languages are low-level.

memory map

A diagram showing the allocation of the various parts of memory chosen for a particular system or program.

menu bar

A strip in an Amiga screen title bar which, when the right mouse button is depressed, displays the menu list categories.

menu button

The Amiga's right-hand mouse button.

message port

A fundamental software structure used by Exec's communication mechanism.

mutual exclusion

Gadgets and menu items are mutually exclusive if the selection of one item automatically prohibits the selection of any alternative items.

NTSC
The National Television Standards Committee standard for composite video. Used mainly in North America.

null-terminated string
A string of bytes which are terminated by a zero value.

octal
A base 8 numbering system.

operand
The value upon which an instruction or statement will operate.

operating system
A collection of routines that perform the I/O and other hardware dependent chores that are needed for a computer to function.

PAL
Phase Alternate Lines. A composite video standard used widely in the UK and western Europe.

parallel port
Hardware device which, on the Amiga, is used for transmitting data eight bits at a time. Used mainly for printer connection.parameter

Any value which must be explicitly passed to a subroutine, function, procedure or program in order for it to be properly executed.

pen
Common term for a variable which contains a colour register number.

peripheral
Any external or remote device connected to a computer system, eg a printer.

pixel
The smallest addressable part of a screen display.

playfield
Another name for a screen background.

pointer
An address, record number or other indicator that specifies the next item of a data set taken in a specified logical order. With 68000 assembly language pointers are normally taken to mean addresses.

Preferences
An Amiga system program which allows a user to set a large number of user-definable I/O characteristics.

primitives
Another name for Amiga library functions and system routines.

proportional gadget
A standard Intuition gadget that allows one and two dimensional movement to be detected. The user is able to move a knob or slider around by dragging it using the mouse. As the slider moves Intuition transmits appropriate position values to the program.

refresh
To re-draw part (or all) of a graphics display.

render
Draw an image into a display area.

repetition
Repeating a set of actions a given number of times.

requester
An Intuition window which appears asking a user to provide some information.

RAM
Random Access Memory.

ROM
Read Only Memory.

scroll
To make a graphics display move upwards/downwards (vertical scrolling) or sideways (horizontal scrolling).

select box
The area of a gadget or menu within which Intuition can recognize a left-click select operation.

select button
The Amiga's left-hand mouse button.

sequence
Operations following each other in time.

set
A collection of items.

set
The act of turning a binary 0 into a binary 1 value.

Shell
An improved CLI interface which offers a number of useful new facilities including line editing and re-use of previously typed commands.

Glossary

sizing gadget

An Amiga system gadget which allows a user to drag-alter the size of an Intuition window.

software

Any program or routine for a computer.

source code

The text version of a program, ie the program actually writen in the first place.

source file

A file from which data is being read.

sprite

A small graphical image. The term was originally applied to images whose movements were controlled directly by hardware. The Amiga supports both simple hardware sprites, virtual sprites, and a number of more sophisticated animation objects.

submenu

A secondary menu which appears once a user has selected a specific menu item.

SuperBitMap window

An Intuition window which has its own bitmap rather than using the underlying screen display's bitmap.

synchronous

Operations which are performed with reference to a controlling overall timing source.

syntax

The formal grammatical structure of a language.

terminal handler

A process which looks after terminal/keyboard input/output operations.

text editor

A program that enables text to be written, manipulated, stored etc. Word processor programs are sophisticated text editors.

title bar

An optional strip at the top of a window or screen which may contain either a name, some system gadgets, or both.

toggle select

Boolean gadgets (on/off state gadgets) can be programmed so that they switch from one state to another each time they are selected by a user. Such gadgets are called toggle select gadgets.

tool

An Amiga WorkBench name for an application program.

trackerball

An input device which is like an upside down mouse. Instead of moving the whole device around, as one does with a mouse, the user moves a ball using fingers/thumb or palm of the hand. This movement is then translated into screen pointer movement. Trackerballs, like the more common mouse device, usually provide button controls as well.

two's complement

A numerical representation in which positive numbers are represented as ordinary signed binary but negative numbers are represented by complementing the number and adding one.

UART

Universal Asynchronous Receiver/Transmitter device. A hardware device which controls the serial port link.

VDU

Visual display unit

Warnier diagram

A design diagram that uses sets of hierarchical curly brackets to indicate the logical structure of a problem, program or system.

wild card symbols

Symbols which may be used to represent *any* character in a pattern.

word

In the world of the 68000 programmer, and on the Amiga, a word is taken to mean a 16 bit binary number.

Workbench

The Amiga's inbuilt high-level interface applications program which allows users to interact with AmigaDOS, run applications programs etc, without getting involved with CLI/Shell commands.

Mastering Amiga Guides

Titles Currently Available

Brief details of the titles currently available along with review segments are given below. New publications and their contents are subject to change without notice. If you would like a free copy of our catalogue and to be placed on our mailing list then phone or write to the address below.

**Bruce Smith Books,
PO Box 382,
St. Albans, Herts, AL2 3JD
Telephone: (01923) 894355
Fax: (01923) 894366**

Note that we offer a 24-hour telephone answer system so that you can place your order direct by 'phone at a time to suit yourself.

Note that we do not charge for P&P in the UK and endeavour to dispatch all books within 24-hours.

Buying at your Bookshop

All our books can be obtained via your local bookshops – this includes WH Smiths which will be keeping a stock of some of our titles, just enquire at their counter. If you wish to order via your local High Street bookshop you will need to supply the book name, author, publisher, price and ISBN number.

Overseas Orders

Please add £3 per book (Europe) or £6 per book (outside Europe) to cover postage and packing. Pay by sterling cheque or by Access, Visa or Mastercard. Post, Fax or Phone your order to us.

Dealer Enquiries

Our distributor is Computer Bookshops Ltd who keep a good stock of all our titles. Call their Customer Services Department for best terms on 021-706-1188.

Compatibility

We endeavour to ensure that all general Mastering Amiga books are fully compatible with all Amiga models and all releases of AmigaDOS and Workbench.

Mastering AmigaDOS 3 Volume One – Tutorial by Mark Smiddy

ISBN: 1-873308-20-5, Price £21.95, 384 pages.

The place to begin if you want to learn about and effectively use AmigaDOS. Covering both AmigaDOS 2 and 3, the tutorial guide assumes no previous knowledge of AmigaDOS. From formatting a disk to pipes and multitasking, even multi-user, this volume will turn the novice into an expert with its practical approach and many fascinating examples. The disk which accompanies the book contains all the examples and many other useful AmigaDOS tools.

Mastering AmigaDOS 3 Volume Two – Reference by Mark Smiddy

ISBN: 1-873308-18-3, Price £21.95, 416 pages.

Following on from the best selling Mastering AmigaDOS 2 volumes, Mastering Amiga DOS 3, Volume Two is a complete A to Z reference to DOS commands covering versions 2.04, 2.1 and 3. The action of each command is explained and examples to try are provided. Chapters on AmigaDOS error codes, viruses, the Interchange File Format (IFF), the Mountlist and the new hypertext system, AmigaGuide, complete this valuable guide.

Mastering Amiga Scripts

ISBN: 1-873308-36-1, Price 319.95, 319 pages.

Mastering AmigaDOS Scripts contains over one hundred ready-to-run script programs. There are scripts programs for AmigaDOS versions 3.x, 2.x and 1.x so this book is applicable to all Amigas, including the Amiga A1200, A600, A500 Plus, A500, A4000, A3000 and A2000 microcomputers.

The script programs are fully documented line by line so that you can learn form them, pickng up the new techniques and programming twists which AmigaDOS guru Mark Smiddy has devised. Beginners will find the scripts easy to load and run, providing handy off-the-shelf utilities and full programs such as database and diary.

Workbench 3 A to Z Insider Guide by Bruce Smith

ISBN: 1-873308-28-0, Price £14.95, 256 pages.

Every aspect of the Amiga Workbench is documented with screen shots and examples of usage. Once you've become familiar with Workbench techniques, this alphabetical reference proves invaluable when you need to find a file, remember a menu operation or...how do you run that Commodity? Owners of A500 Plus and A2000/3000 upgrading to Workbench 3 will find this an essential add-on to their manuals.

Amiga A1200 Insider Guide by Bruce Smith

ISBN: 1-873308-15-9, price £14.95, 256 pages.

Assuming no prior knowledge, it shows you how to get the very best from your A1200 in a friendly manner and using its unique Insider Guide steps. Configuring your system for printer, keyboard, Workbench colours, use of Commodities and much much more has made this the best-selling book for the A1200.

As well as easy to read explanations of how to get to grips with the Amiga, the book features 55 of the unique Insider Guides, each of which displays graphically a set of step by step instructions. Each Insider Guide concentrates on a especially important or common task which the user has to carry out on the Amiga. By following an Insider Guide the user learns how to control the Amiga by example. Beginners to the A1200 will particularly appreciate this approach to a complex computer.

Amiga A1200 Next Steps by Peter Fitzpatrick

ISBN: 1-873308-24-8, Price £14.95, 256 pages.

For those who have mastered the very basics of the A1200 this book is the ideal companion to our Amiga A1200 Insider Guide. Leaving the basics of the Workbench and AmigaDOS behind this book takes you the next step and shows you how to get the very most out of your A1200, using both the software supplied and other material readily available.

For example, learn how to use MultiView to write your own adventure game and edit a picture! Create your own fully recoverable Ram disk, get better results when you print out, recover deleted files. We even show you how to add your own hard disk and copy software onto it! This is only the tip of the iceberg. Amiga A1200 Next Steps is worth its weight in gold!

Amiga Assembler Insider Guide by Paul Overaa

ISBN: 1-873308-27-2, Price £14.95, 256 pages.

The Amiga Assembler Insider Guide has been written for the new user who wishes to learn to write programs in the native code of the Amiga computer – assembly language. The approach taken to this often daunting subject is designed to achieve practical results with short examples which demonstrate different programming skills. Each program in the book can be assembled and run in under one minute so the beginner need have no fear of long impenetrable listings. This is programming for the novice, made all the easier though the mini Insider Guides which summarise important operations and fundamental concepts.

The book is compatible with all the main assemblers on the market. A support disk is available from the publisher which contains the A68K assembler, all the listings in the book, additional utilities and examples (cost £2.00 P&P). With the Amiga Assembler Insider Guide learning assembler on the Amiga has never been easier.

Amiga Disks and Drives by Paul Overaa

ISBN: 1-873308-34-5, Price £14.95, 256 pages. FREE Utilities disk.

Just what do you do when all your valuable data is locked in your computer? How do you copy files and install software? What do you do when you can't find a file on the Workbench screen? This book has all the answers!

Paul Overaa teaches you how to use and care for all types of disk drives in order to minimise the risk of problems, to get a better understanding of how they work and what you can do if things go wrong. Packed with practical topics, it's step by step guides are invaluable to novice and advanced users alike. Applicable to all Amigas.

Amiga A1200 Beginners Pack

ISBN: 1-873308-30-2, Price £39.95 plus £3 p&p, one-hour Workbench basics video and two books (A1200 Insider Guide and Amiga Next Steps) plus 4 disk of essential software.

Combining the Amiga A1200 Video, the Amiga Next Steps Insider Guide and the Amiga A1200 Insider Guide this bumper pack is the perfect gift for somebody you know taking their first tentative steps along the wonderful road of Amiga computing.

The disks of software contain the most sought after programs every beginner should have, including a database, a wordprocessor, a clip art selection, the OctaMed music sampler, a virus checker, a file recovery package and a disk compression utility.

If you already have one part of the pack then telephone us for an upgrade price.

Amiga Workbench 3.1 Booster Pack

ISBN: 1-873308-41-8, Price £39.95 plus £3 p&p, one and a half hour Workbench video, two books (Workbench 3 A to Z and Amiga Disks & Drives) a Quick Reference Card and a disk of essential software.

Already over 400,000 A1200 and CD32 owners enjoy the power and versatility of Workbench 3. Now the million plus owners of A500, A2000 and other recent machines can enjoy the same power with a simple chip upgrade.

The Amiga Workbench 3 Booster Pack provides the most comprehensive support for such new users. The Workbench 3 A to Z book and the 90 minute Amiga A1200 – A Deeper Look video provide the complete guide in both tutorial and reference material to Workbench 3. The Amiga Disks and Drives Insider Guide goes on to take the new user to intermediate levels, showing how to optimise the use of their machines in both speed, capacity and security. All this, a disk of essential software and the Quick Reference card make it an essential purchase.

If you already have one part of the pack then telephone us for an upgrade price.

Introduction to the Amiga A1200 Video by Wall Street Video/BSB

BSBVIDAMI001, Price £14.99, one-hour Workbench basics video.

New from Bruce Smith Books in association with Wall Street Video – Australia's leading Amiga training company – the perfect video introduction to using your Amiga A1200 and a perfect companion for the world's best selling A1200 book, Bruce Smith's classic Amiga A1200 Insider Guide. This one hour video provides a basic tutorial on how to set up and run your Amiga A1200 by using great animations and split screens to increase your understanding or the concepts being explained. Re-examine those tricky grey areas by instantly rewinding the video.

Applicable to both hard and floppy disk users the Amiga A1200 Video may also by used to understand the Amiga A4000 and at £14.99 represents outstanding value.

Introduction to the Amiga A1200 – A Deeper Look Video by Wall Street Video/BSB

BSBVIDAMI002, Price £14.99, 75 minutes video.

The follow-up to the best-selling Introduction to the A1200 from Australia's Wall Street Video. Applicable to any Workbench 3 Amiga, this video goes beyond the first steps of using your machine to comprehensively tackle all the features of Workbench 3.

Mastering Amiga System by Paul Overaa

ISBN: 1-873308-06-X, Price £29.95, 398 pages. FREE disk.

Serious Amiga programmers need to use the Amiga's operating system to write legal, portable and efficient programs. But it's not easy! Paul Overaa shares his experience in this introduction to system programming in the C language. The author keeps it specific and presents skeleton programs which are fully documented so that they can be followed by the newcomer to Amiga programming. The larger programs are fully-fledged examples which can serve as templates for the reader's own ideas as confidence is gained.

Mastering Amiga Printers by Robin Burton

ISBN: 1-873308-05-1, Price £19.95, 336 pages. FREE Programs disk

After reading Mastering Amiga Printers, any Amiga owner will be able to choose effectively the ideal printer for his or her requirements. The Amiga's own printer control software is pulled apart and explained from all points of view, from the Workbench to the operating system routines. Individual printer drivers are assessed and screen-dumping techniques explained.

Mastering Amiga C by Paul Overaa

ISBN: 1-873308-04-6, Price £19.95, 320 pages.

FREE Programs Disk and NorthC Public Domain compiler.

C is one of the most powerful programming languages ever created with much of the Amiga's operating system written using C. The introductory text assumes no prior knowledge of C and covers all of the major compilers, including the charityware NorthC compiler supplied with this book when ordered direct from BSB. It is ideal for anyone using their Amiga to catch up on computer studies!

Mastering Amiga ARexx by Paul Overaa

ISBN: 1-873308-13-2, Price £21.95, 336 pages. FREE disk.

Now a standard part of Commodore's software strategy and readily available to Workbench 2 and 3 users, ARexx has been much admired by the programming community and is now available to all as a third party product. This book is an ideal companion to the ARexx documentation, explaining ARexx's main features, how it controls other programs, its built-in functions and support libraries, methods for creating well structured ARexx programs and much, much more.

Amiga BASIC – A Dabhand Guide by Paul Fellows

ISBN: 1-873308-87-9, Price £17.95, 560 pages.

FREE Disk with ACE Freeware BASIC compiler.

BASIC is the computer programming language devised for beginners and now a standard on most computers. The Amiga doesn't usually come with a BASIC as standard but we provide one with the book so you have a head start. A number of commercial BASICs are available including HiSoft BASIC 2, True Basic and FBASIC. AMOS is also BASIC-like in its structures and keywords. This book is a substantial introduction to the language and is peppered with some of the cleverest routines around. Paul Fellows is a leading software author in his own right and his programming experience shines through in this easy to read guide. If you want to learn about programming in BASIC then this is the place to start.

Secrets of Frontier Elite by Tony Dillon

ISBN: 1-873308-39-6, Price £9.95, 128 pages.

If you want to become Elite, or just incredibly rich, then get this book. This is the ultimate guide to the ultimate space trading game. Learn how to move up the ranks of the military, how to choose the best ships and weapons, how to trade and mine to the top. Games editor Tony Dillon has researched the game and included many of the hints and tips which have come his way. Find out how to gain control of the secret Mirage ship and how to become Elite, by the back door.

Index

A

AbsExecBase 96
abstract data types 17, 71
AddIntServer() 52
ADT – see abstract data types
allocation control 33, 42, 85
AllocSignal() 66
amiga.lib 65, 87, 193
Aztec C conventions 206

B

BitMap structure 264
blitter minterm values 260
bootblock code 273
boot code checksums 282
boot sectors 274

C

copper programming . .114, 119
    CEND() macro 115
    child processes 77
    CINIT() macro 115
    ClipBlit() 235
    CloseDevice() 153
    CloseLibrary() 97
    CMOVE() macro 115
    co-processor 91
    coding style conventions 11
    colour - cycling 187
        flashing 58, 74, 77
        indirection 187
    copper instruction set . .92, 126
    copper list searching 265
    copper lists 91
    CreateExtIO() 153
    CreatePort() 65, 154, 197
    custom boot code 281
    CWAIT() macro 114
    CycleMessages 191

D

data types 18
DeleteExtIO() 155
DeletePort() 154
delta times 170, 171
device - commands 150
    serial 148
    timer 156, 198
    trackdisk 273, 276
devices 147, 155
DoIO() 156
DrawImage() 216
DrawTiles() -
    assembler form 222
    recursive form 246
DriveGeometry structure . . .274
dummy subroutines 297
dynamic resource handling . . . .
    . . . . .31, 71, 181, 195, 276

E

event handling 47, 182
exclusive-ORing 208, 340
Exec 51, 80, 95, 137
extern references 47
FindTask() 69
flashing colours 58, 74, 77
FlashMessages 79
floppy disk layout 273
Forbid()/Permit()
    use of 86, 100, 196
FreeSignal() 67
function - AddIntServer() 52
    AllocSignal() 66
    ClipBlit() 235
    CloseDevice() 153
    CloseLibrary() 87
    CreateExtIO() 153
    CreatePort() . . .65, 154, 197
    DeleteExtIO() 155
    DeletePort() 154
    DoIO() 156

Function – FindTask() 69
    FreeSignal() 67
    GetMsg() 81
    GetRGB4() 58
    LoadRGB4() 190, 198
    MakeScreen() 117
    OpenDevice() 152
    OpenLibrary) 97, 138
    pointers 34
    PutMsg() 81
    putreg() 54
    RemIntServer() 53
    ReplyMsg() 81
    RethinkDisplay() 117
    SetFunction() 141
    SetRGB4() 58
    Signal() 67
    Wait() 68

G
Gadtools library 44
GetMsg() 81
GetRGB4() 58
global prefixes 12, 300
global variable allocation 48

H
hardware copper lists 91

I
incremental testing 296
INTB_VERTB 53
intermediate copper lists 91
interprocess communications . .
. . . . .79, 192
Interrupt structure 53
interrupts 51
IntuiMessages 47, 182
Intuition .44, 116, 182, 188, 263
IOExtSer structure 148
IORequest structure 148
library access 138

L
Library Vector Offsets . .98, 139
LoadRGB4() 190, 198
LVO - see Library Vector Offsets

M
make files 49
MakeScreen() 117
masks 68
Message structure 78
Meta events 170, 171
Midi 143
Midi channel message types 176
Midi file chunk analysis 176
MidiPlayer command 168
MidiPlayer program 167
MidiPlayX 154, 157
MidiWriteX 146
mixed coding 203
mosaic effects 251
move (copper ins) 93
MPX files 145
MsgPort structure 78
multiple message ports 82
mutually exclusive operations . .
. 310

N
Node structure 53, 78

O
OpenDevice() 152
OpenLibrary() 97, 138
OpenWindowTagList() 46
OpenWindowTags() 47

P
pointer suffixes 12, 300
poll loops 14
printf() debugging 299
project management 47
PutMsg() 81
putreg() 54

Q
queueing by reference 79

R
recursion 241
Release 2 changes 45
RemIntServer() 53

replacement system function
  example 141
ReplyMsg() 81
resource handling . . . 31, 42, 71,
  . . . . 181, 195, 276
RethinkDisplay() 117
run time libraries 95
running status 171

S

SAS/Lattice C conventions . . 205
scrolling 263
serial device 148
serial device flags 149
SetFunction() 141
SetRB4() 58
shading effects 119
signal bits 68
Signal() 67
signals 65
skip (copper ins) 92
smake SAS utility 49
stack ADT access routines . . . . .
  . . . . 22, 36
stacks 19
Standard Midi files 169
string reversal 29
structure - BitMap 264
  DriveGeometry 274
  Interrupt 53
  IOExtSer 148
  IORequest 148
  Message 78
  MsgPort 78
  Node 53,78
  ViewPort 116
syntax errors 296
SysBase 96
sysex events 170

T

tag identity values 46
tag lists 45
TagItem structure 45
TD_GEOMETRY 274
tile effects 213
timer device 156, 198

trackdisk device - reading from
  280
    writing to 280
trackdisk device 273, 276

U

UNIT_MICROHZ 156
user copper lists 91, 116

V

vanilla C 37
variable name conventions
  . . . . 12, 300
vertical blank interrupt 52
ViewPort structure 116
viruses 137

W

wait (copper ins) 93
Wait() 68
Warnier diagram conventions
  309
Warnier diagrams 307

X

XDEF/XREF 205